Christian Unity

Christian Unity

An Exposition of Ephesians 4:1 to 16
D. M. LLOYD-JONES

BAKER BOOK HOUSE
Grand Rapids, Michigan 49506

ISBN: 0-8010-5607-1

PHOTOLITHOPRINTED BY CUSHING - MALLOY, INC.
ANN ARBOR, MICHIGAN, UNITED STATES OF AMERICA

Preface

It is certain that no subject has been more frequently dealt with in sermons, books, lectures, pamphlets and articles during the present century, than the question of 'Christian Unity'. This has been especially true since the First Congress of the World Council of Churches in Amsterdam in 1948.

It is equally true to say that no subject has caused so much confusion in the minds and hearts of members of churches.

Were it merely a matter of organisation, it would not be so serious; but as the exposition of this key passage in Ephesians 4:1–16 shows, it involves vital doctrines. The trouble generally arises because the advocates of what is known as the ecumenical movement are content to make vague general statements – often sentimental – or to emphasise one part of a statement instead of the whole. For instance, in verse 15, love is emphasised exclusively at the expense of truth.

We all tend to be the creatures of prejudices, and it therefore behoves us to examine ourselves and our views in the light of this crucial passage. That there have been sinful divisions in the past is painfully obvious; but the answer is not to be found in an amalgamation of organisations based on minimal truth. The greatest tragedy in the world today is not, as is so frequently asserted, a divided church, but the fact that the majority seem to place unity above truth, and that many who are genuinely interested in truth are governed in their practice by traditions.

I can but pray that this study will be blessed by God to help many perplexed and confused Christians.

[5]

As ever, I express my deep gratitude to Mrs Elizabeth Burney, Mr S. M. Houghton and my wife for their help in making its publication possible.

D. M. Lloyd-Jones

London
June 1980

Contents

Ephesians 4:1–16

CHRISTIAN UNITY

Ephesians 4:1–16

1 *I therefore, the prisoner of the Lord, beseech you that ye walk worthy of the vocation wherewith ye are called,*

2 *With all lowliness and meekness, with longsuffering, forbearing one another in love;*

3 *Endeavouring to keep the unity of the Spirit in the bond of peace.*

4 *There is one body, and one Spirit, even as ye are called in one hope of your calling;*

5 *One Lord, one faith, one baptism,*

6 *One God and Father of all, who is above all, and through all, and in you all.*

7 *But unto every one of us is given grace according to the measure of the gift of Christ.*

8 *Wherefore he saith, When he ascended up on high, he led captivity captive, and gave gifts unto men.*

9 *(Now that he ascended, what is it but that he also descended first into the lower parts of the earth?*

10 *He that descended is the same also that ascended up far above all heavens, that he might fill all things.)*

11 *And he gave some, apostles; and some, prophets; and some, evangelists; and some, pastors and teachers;*

12 *For the perfecting of the saints, for the work of the ministry, for the edifying of the body of Christ:*

13 *Till we all come in the unity of the faith, and of the knowledge of the Son of God, unto a perfect man, unto the measure of the stature of the fulness of Christ:*

14 *That we henceforth be no more children, tossed to and fro, and carried about with every wind of doctrine, by the sleight of men, and cunning craftiness, whereby they lie in wait to deceive;*

15 *But speaking the truth in love, may grow up into him in all things, which is the head, even Christ:*

16 *From whom the whole body fitly joined together and compacted by that which every joint supplieth, according to the effectual working in the measure of every part, maketh increase of the body unto the edifying of itself in love.*

I
'Therefore'

'I therefore, the prisoner of the Lord, beseech you that ye walk worthy of the vocation wherewith ye are called, with all lowliness and meekness, with long-suffering, forbearing one another in love; endeavouring to keep the unity of the Spirit in the bond of peace'.

Ephesians 4:1-3

These words introduce not only a new chapter but also a new and major division of this Epistle to the Ephesians. Like most New Testament Epistles, this Epistle can be divided into two portions; and here we have the beginning of its second half. For our convenience the Epistle was divided into six chapters, and its teaching can be divided into two portions of three chapters each.

The first section, consisting of the first three chapters, has been entirely doctrinal. The Apostle has been unfolding and displaying in his own marvellous manner the great essential doctrines of the Christian faith, everything that is central and vital to an understanding of the way of salvation. There is no greater display of the doctrines of the Christian faith than that found in the first three chapters of this Epistle. But having done that, the Apostle now moves on to the practical application of his doctrine; he goes on to show how it is related to daily life and living. So we are really at a most important point in this Epistle, a point that marks a very real division.

Yet I must point out at once that, as we reach this transition, we must not make too much of it, we must not press it too hard. We shall find that, when we come to the fourth verse in this fourth chapter, the Apostle again goes back to doctrine. It is characteristic of him that he never indulges in absolute divisions; and for the simple reason that, in the last analysis, we cannot and must not separate doctrine and practice. It is always those who think they can do so who miss the glories of the Christian faith.

The Apostle Paul, when he used the word 'therefore', makes the connection between faith and practice quite clear. He has laid down the doctrine; it has now got to be applied. But the moment he begins to deal with the application he says, 'There is one body, and one Spirit, even as ye are called in one hope of your calling; one Lord, one faith, one baptism.' In other words he is back again in the realm of doctrine. But he does not stay there. The return is intended to bring out the practical application of the doctrine, and is important as showing the mechanics of his method.

*   *   *

Here, then, in chapter 4, the Apostle proceeds to make a great appeal to the Ephesian believers to put into operation the things he has been teaching them. He reminds them of the things that inevitably follow as a natural consequence from an understanding of the great doctrines of the Christian faith. At this point I am tempted to ask a question, for to do so is an essential part of preaching. How do you react as I say that we are now about to consider the practical application of Christian doctrine? In a previous volume we have been dealing with that amazing section at the end of chapter 3, where, having been strengthened with might by faith, we have been trying to comprehend with all saints what is 'the breadth, and the length, and the depth, and the height; and to know the love of Christ which passeth knowledge, that we might be filled with all the fulness of God'. And we have looked at the might and strength and power of God, who is at work in our hearts and 'is able to do exceeding abundantly above all that we ask or think. There we have been on the very summit of the 'delectable mountains'. But now we are about to consider how such wealth of experience is related to our daily life and living. So I repeat my question. Do you feel that the remaining three chapters of this Epistle are bound to be somewhat of an anticlimax? Would you have preferred our exposition of the Epistle to finish at the close of chapter 3, leaving us free to turn elsewhere in the Scriptures to great statements of doctrine and considerations of exalted moments in Christian life and experience?

This is a very practical and a very important question. I wonder whether you feel like Peter on the Mount of Transfiguration. Peter and James and John were with our Lord on the mount; and our Lord was transfigured before them. They saw this, and the glory and marvel of it, and saw Moses and Elias, and heard the voice from heaven. Peter said, 'Lord, let us make here three tabernacles, one for thee and one for Moses and one for Elias'. In effect Peter said, 'Let us stay here; it is so marvellous. I know what is happening at the foot of the mountain; I know its misery and wretchedness; can we not stay here, can we not remain here on top of the mountain?' Is that your feeling? Let me be frank and honest and admit that I had some such feeling. But, to yield to it would be grievously wrong, something against which this great Apostle warns us. He does so through the medium of this word, this most vital and essential word – 'therefore'.

We have no right to stop at the end of chapter 3. The divisions into chapters have been made for our convenience and we should be grateful for them. But there is a sense in which they can be really dangerous. The Apostle did not write under these chapter headings; he wrote one letter, and he meant us to read the letter from the beginning right through to the end. Indeed he almost commands us to do so; and our business is to follow him. 'I therefore . . .' Follow me, he says, and it is our business to go after him. As our Lord did not consent to the proposal concerning the three tabernacles on top of the Mount of Transfiguration, but went down again to the valley to meet and deal with a father and his poor boy tormented by devils, so we must go back into life and apply the great doctrines to our ordinary daily lives. The Apostle, I repeat, invites us to follow him as he leads us on into the practical application of the great doctrine that he has been opening out before us.

Paul does this through the medium of the word 'therefore', and all I propose to do at the moment is to draw out some of the things that are suggested by this word. 'I *therefore*, the prisoner of the Lord, beseech you'. 'Therefore' is a word which in a very practical way tells us how to read the Scriptures. We need to be taught how to read the Scriptures. The main principle is, as I have been indicating, that we must never pick and choose in our reading of the Scriptures. We must read all the Scriptures, every part of the Scripture. Instinctively we do not like to do so; we have our favourite passages; there are certain Psalms or portions in the New Testament Epistles, or certain pictures in the Gospels in which we delight, and which always move us when we read them. The tendency and the danger is to be ever going back to such portions. But that is the high road to the development of an unbalanced and lop-sided Christian life and experience. Our invariable rule with the Bible should be to read it from Genesis to Revelation, to read it constantly right through, not leaving out anything, but following it through, and being led by it. If we believe that it is the Word of God, that all of it is the Word of God, it follows that there is a meaning and a significance in every part, in the historical portions and the genealogies as well as the explicitly teaching portions. So we must go through and read them all, and try to grasp the meaning of all.

We can state this in a different way. There is nothing so dangerous as to extract certain verses or certain paragraphs from the Scripture, to wrest them out of their context, and just look at them in isolation in and of themselves. There is a danger of doing so in the case of the third chapter of this Epistle. But the word 'therefore' prohibits this and insists that I must apply that teaching and go on. I must not isolate that great passage, I must work it out, I must consider what leads up to it and what follows it. While there may be a certain value in hanging up texts on the walls of our homes or reading a collection of texts in a book like Daily Light, let us never forget that such practices can be dangerous, because there is a balance in Scripture, and the context of each and every verse is always important. This very section which we are examining illustrates and emphasizes the importance of what I am stressing. It is the simple truth to say that most of the heresies that have troubled the Church throughout her long history have arisen because men and women have forgotten this simple principle. They have taken a text out of its context, and have formulated a doctrine out of it. If they had but taken it in its context they would have been saved from the error they have embraced. Remember, then, that this word *therefore* reminds us of the wholeness of the Scripture, of the importance of taking it in its entirety, and of the folly of isolating texts or paragraphs from their setting in the larger whole.

The second matter is even more important, namely, that this word *therefore* is a conjunction which leads us on, and points us to the life we are to live in the light of the doctrines we have already considered. You will find – and this is a general principle – that in all the New Testament Epistles at a point corresponding to this, you generally have this word 'therefore'. They invariably start with the fundamental doctrines. Then having done so they say 'Therefore' – in the light of this, because of this it follows. As this is clearly a vital and basic matter I must analyse it further. There is always the danger – and it affects some people more than others – of forgetting that Christianity is, after all, a way of life and a way of living. Of course there are certain people who emphasize that alone, and who know nothing about doctrine and are not interested in doctrine. Such people regard Christianity as a system of morality or of ethics. But I am dealing, rather, with people who are evangelically minded, and whose danger is to stop at doctrine only.

Some people are naturally intellectual; they have been given minds by God above the average, perhaps, and they enjoy reading and studying and reasoning and handling great truths and doctrines. Their particular danger is to spend all their time with doctrine and to stop at doctrine. They read the doctrinal portions of these Epistles and then, having come to the end of such a chapter as Ephesians 3, they tend to say, 'Of course the rest is practical application which is obvious; I know about that.' And so they do not read any further; they stop with the doctrines. They read books about doctrine and theology. That is excellent, of course, and very desirable. But it may be the very snare of the devil. There have been churches and denominations and groups in the past history of the church that have spent all their time in discussing, and arguing about, and emphasizing certain doctrines, but have forgotten the unconverted that are round and about them. They have failed to turn the doctrines into practice, they have been so absorbed by their interest in doctrines that they have even quarrelled with one another and have thus denied the very doctrines they believe. Doctrine comes first, but we must not stop at doctrine.

There is another group whose danger is to stop with the experience only. They read, for example, the closing verses of the third chapter of Ephesians, describing the wondrous possibility of knowing the love of Christ in an experimental manner and having our hearts moved and ravished by the manifestations of His love, and of being filled with all the fulness of God, and they feel that nothing else matters, that nothing else counts. There are people who figure in the history of the Church who have spent the whole of their lives in seeking experiences. This was, in a sense, the danger of the monks and the hermits; and there have been many evangelical monks and hermits! There have been people who were mystically inclined, who have virtually gone out of the world, as it were, and have been seeking these experiences and manifestations of the love of God; and they have been so concerned about such matters that they have done nothing else. The man who is interested in doctrine only, and the man who is interested in the mystical type of experience only, are alike neglecting this important word 'therefore'. This word safeguards us against all these possible dangers.

We find this same truth in another statement made by Paul in his letter to Titus. He is writing about the Lord Jesus Christ and His death upon the Cross, and says, 'Who gave himself for us'. But he does not go on to say that the Lord's purpose was that we might have some strange, ecstatic experience, but 'that he might redeem us from all iniquity, and separate' (or purify) unto himself a peculiar people, zealous of good works' (2:14). Indeed our Lord Himself had already said this in the words, 'If ye know these things, happy are ye if ye do them' (John 13:17). To know doctrine is a very responsible matter; to have high and unusual experiences carries with it a very dread responsibility. If we really do know these things, then more is expected of us. From the man who has, much is expected; to whom much has been given, much is also expected. So if we really have been grasping the great doctrines of the first three chapters of this Epistle let us remember this word *therefore*. We are not to call a halt; we are to go on to the practical life and living, to the ordinary day-to-day application of basic Christian doctrine. It is a glorious experience to be on top of that mountain; but we must go down to the valleys, to all the problems of daily life and living. Around us is this godless world which cannot know about Christ unless you and I tell them about Christ, either by preaching or by mixing with them in our work and employment and the ordinary avocations in life. We must show what we know, and what we have, and above all show Him in whom we have believed.

The word *therefore*, in the third place, reminds us that the life which we are to live is a life which always results from the application of doctrine. This is a matter which must be emphasized. 'Therefore' not only tells me that I have got to engage in practical life and living, it also tells me that the character and the nature of that life which I am to live is one that is determined by the doctrine, and results from the application of the doctrine. We can never attach too much significance to the order in which the Apostle states these things. Doctrine must always come first; and we must never reverse this order. It is, I repeat, the invariable practice in the New Testament itself to speak of doctrine before the application of doctrine. We must not act until we are clear about our doctrine. This is, beyond all question, the most vital principle of all in connection with the New Testament doctrine of sanctification. So we are entitled to say that this word *therefore* introduces us to the doctrine of sanctification. The first three chapters of our Epistle with all their astonishing teaching have not considered the doctrine of sanctification as such. This is true even of the end of chapter 3. It is the 'therefore' of chapter 4, verse 1, that introduces us to the doctrine of sanctification. The doctrine of the sealing of the Spirit, and the experience of it, is not sanctification. To know the love of Christ is not sanctification. To be filled with all the fulness of God is not sanctification. What then is the relationship between these things? It is that those are things that promote sanctification, that encourage sanctification, and give us motives for sanctification; but they are not sanctification itself.

* * *

Here then are the principles which I would emphasize at this point. In the light of this word *therefore* we must say that sanctification is not a gift to be received; it is rather something that has to be worked out in the light of the doctrine. It is an imperative, it is a command. In the same way it is clear that sanctification is not an experience, for the Apostle uses the form of an exhortation. It is most important that we should understand the relationship of these things to one another. All the great experiences to which the

Apostle has been referring, and about which he has been teaching, are simply designed to encourage us to 'work out' our sanctification, our salvation, 'with fear and trembling'. The doctrines and the experiences provide us with the motive for sanctification. They are intended and designed to create a desire within us for sanctification. They are designed to show us the possibility of sanctification by reminding us of the power that works in us in order that we may work it out. The Apostle has told us about 'him that is able to do exceeding abundantly above all that we ask or think, according to the power that worketh in us'. Having reminded us of this, he says in effect, 'In the light of this truth, I beseech you, work it out, put it into practice, put it into operation.'

To make this vital matter yet clearer I use again the illustration I used when discoursing on 'the sealing of the Spirit' in chapter 1. The relationship between experience and doctrine on the one hand, and sanctification on the other, can be stated thus. The moment we are born again our sanctification begins. The moment we receive the seed of life, new life, it begins to operate within us. We cannot take Christ in parts. He is made unto us 'wisdom, and righteousness, and sanctification, and redemption' (1 Cor. 1:30). We cannot take Him as 'justification' only and then later decide to take Him as 'sanctification'. He is a whole Christ, and He is indivisible, so the moment the life of God enters into us the process of sanctification begins.

Here, then, is my illustration. Think of a farmer or a gardener sowing seed into the ground where various machines may roll over it. There it is; it is buried, but that is not the end of the story. It is not 'dead and buried'. There is life in that seed, and it begins to sprout and to germinate and to grow. But for a while you still see nothing. But after a while a little green shoot appears above the surface. You can scarcely see it but it is there and it is alive, and you know that it is developing. But then there may come a patch of cold dry weather, with no sunshine. Nothing seems to be happening, there is no evidence of growth. But suddenly there is a change in the weather; there are some wonderful showers, and some warm glowing sunshine. And immediately you can almost see those little shoots growing, and springing up. What has happened? The life was not in the rain; it was not in the sunshine; it was in the seed itself and in the little shoots. The value of the sunshine and the rain is that they provide a stimulus to the growth. They encourage it and promote it. The life was already there in the seed. Precisely the same is true of the experience we have in the Christian life and of our understanding of doctrine. The experiences promote sanctification. When I am near to the Lord and conscious of His Presence, I do not want sin. When I feel His love sin is abhorrent and hateful to me. Really to grasp doctrine has the same effect. The experiences and the knowledge stimulate and promote and encourage; but sanctification itself is not an experience. It is the result of the life that I have received and the knowledge I have; it is something which, in the light of all this, I must myself now begin to put into practice. 'Work out your own salvation with fear and trembling, for (because of the fact that) it is God that worketh in you, both to will and to do of his good pleasure' (Phil. 2:12 and 13).

The Apostle says that he is beseeching them, he is urging them, in order to stimulate them. He does not merely tell them that all they have to do now, in the light of the great doctrines, is just to 'look to the Lord'. He could have ended his Epistle quickly at this point if he had believed such teaching concerning sanctification. There would have been no need for three further long chapters. He would simply have to write, 'Well now, in the light of all this, all you have to do is to look to the Lord and to let Him live His life in you; it is quite simple, you just do nothing, you look to the Lord and He will live His own life in you.'

But that is not what the Apostle says; instead, we read, 'Therefore I beseech you that ye walk worthy . . .' The teaching which assures us that we have nothing to do but to receive sanctification as a gift, that is to say, to allow Christ to live His life in us, by-passes the Scripture, eliminates whole sections of the Scripture. In the three chapters from this point to the end of the Epistle you find that the Apostle enters into details. He says such things as, 'Let him that stole steal no more'; he urges us to avoid 'foolish talking and jesting'. He goes into details, he exhorts the Ephesians, he reprimands them, he commands them, he appeals to them, he argues with them, he issues his great imperatives. He does so because that is the New Testament teaching of sanctification. It is the outworking, the outliving, by the power that God gives us and that is already in us, of the doctrine we have believed and the experiences we have enjoyed from His gracious hands. It is amazing that anyone could ever go astray concerning this; for our Lord Himself states the truth clearly in the seventeenth chapter of John, where He prays, 'Sanctify them through Thy truth; Thy word is truth'. It is through the Word that we are sanctified. It is 'therefore', in the light of the doctrine, that we are to live the sanctified life.

*   *   *

The way of sanctification is, first and foremost, a full realization of the biblical doctrines. We must grasp the way of salvation as outlined in them. We must see the things to which we have been called, the glorious possibilities that have been opened for us; and the more we see and understand and grasp them, the more we shall be ready, and indeed anxious, to work them out in practice. We shall see the inevitability of these things; we shall see their logical character and their logical order. Failure to understand the meaning of this word 'therefore', and its real message, leads to an entirely false way of looking at the Scriptures. There are many whose ministry is divided up in an unscriptural manner. They preach an evangelistic message, 'Come to Jesus', 'Come to Christ', 'Be saved', 'Accept salvation' – that is one message. Then they have another message which is quite distinct and separate. It is simply a constantly repeated appeal to 'surrender' or 'be willing to be made willing to surrender'. That is all that is necessary, they say; sanctification will take place because Christ will live His life in us. This is often accompanied by what is called 'Bible reading', which is a kind of running commentary on the Scripture without a clear exposition of the great doctrines and a showing of their intimate relationship to the life we are to lead. Such teaching is due to the fact that such teachers have never understood the meaning of this word 'therefore'. But in Scripture doctrine and practice are indivisibly joined together. We must never part them asunder. We must always preach them and apply them. We must not stop at the end of chapter 3, says Paul. His 'therefore' bids us go on lest we imperil our lives and our souls. We must not stop at doctrine, we must not stop at experience. We must not separate justification and sanctification except in thought. Salvation is one whole, and the 'therefore' is the link that always holds the parts together. We must never do violence to Scripture in the interests of theories or methods or particular experiences. May God give us grace to understand the meaning of this mighty word 'therefore'! Our sanctification is the inevitable result of the doctrine and the experience, because of the life of God in our souls. The process starts at once, when we are born again, and our business is to put the whole of our energy and activity into it, to work it out 'with fear and trembling'.

The Apostle also gives us the reasons why this should be so. We have been called to this, that is why all that has happened to us has happened. Read again the first three chapters of this Epistle – 'Blessed be the God and Father of our Lord Jesus Christ, who hath blessed us with all spiritual blessings in heavenly places in Christ'. Do you believe this? If you do, the 'therefore' is bound to come into your mind at once. Everything within you will make you long to be worthy of it and rise to it. Or take the tenth verse of the first chapter: 'That in the dispensation of the fulness of times he [God] might gather together in one all things in Christ, both which are in heaven, and which are on earth; even in him'. Do you believe that it is God's purpose in Christ to re-unite all things in Him? If you do, you will say, 'I must do nothing to oppose that purpose, but I must do everything to help it and to conform to it. Do you believe what God tells us in the fourteenth verse of that same chapter, where He says that the Holy Spirit is also 'the earnest of our inheritance until the redemption of the purchased possession'? Do you believe that God has made you an heir and a joint-heir with Christ, and that you are going on to receive that glorious inheritance? If you do, then you will agree with the logic of the apostle John as well as with that of the apostle Paul, and you will say, 'He that hath this hope in him purifieth himself, even as he is pure'.

It is to the extent that we grasp the truth of the doctrine that the desire to be holy is created within us. If I really believe that while I was 'dead in trespasses and sins' God quickened me, sent His Son into the world to die for me and for my sins that I might be saved from hell, and might be saved for heaven – if I really believe that, I must say, 'Love so amazing, so divine, demands my soul, my life, my all'. It is logic, and it *demands* my soul, my life, my all. I cannot resist such logic – I must! And so we work through all the great doctrines which the Apostle has been laying before us in the first three chapters, and we remember that we are 'no longer strangers and foreigners, but fellow citizens with the saints, and of the household of God'. If I believe that truth as I live my life in this world, I realize that I have no right to live to myself. 'Therefore'! It is undeniable logic, an inevitable deduction. It is because I believe the doctrine that I want to be holy and I want to be more and more sanctified. 'Be ye holy for I am holy,' says the Lord (1 Peter 1:16).

Thus we see the importance of this word *therefore* and the importance of not picking and choosing portions of Scripture, not consulting our feelings only, but being led by the Word of God, that we may ever be 'to the praise of the glory of His grace'.

2

Worthy of our Calling

'I therefore, the prisoner of the Lord, beseech you that ye walk worthy of the vocation wherewith ye are called, with all lowliness and meekness, with long-suffering, forbearing one another in love; endeavouring to keep the unity of the Spirit in the bond of peace'.

Ephesians 4:1–3

Having seen how a true understanding of Christian doctrine and experience leads to a desire to live a holy life, we now come to consider the character of the life which we are to live. The Apostle first of all gives us a general description of it, and then proceeds to deal with it in its particular aspects and in detail. The general character of the life is that it is to be 'worthy of the vocation wherewith we are called'. Then having laid down the general character he mentions one particular aspect of the life, namely, that we are 'to endeavour to keep the unity of the Spirit in the bond of peace'. And this we are to do 'with all lowliness and meekness' and so on. Thus he continues with argument after argument until the end of verse 16. After that he turns to more direct and practical arguments with the words, 'This I say therefore, and testify in the Lord, that ye henceforth walk not as other Gentiles walk'. Such is the general analysis of the Apostle's method; general description first, then particular. I must emphasize that this is the Apostle's invariable practice; he never goes on to particulars without first laying down general principles. It seems to me that many people get into trouble in their Christian lives because they rush to particulars. 'What about this or that?' they ask. The answer to such questions is to go back and to find a general principle. The details can never be properly understood except in the light of the whole. The whole is greater than the

[23]

parts, and controls our understanding of them. The particular problems that arise in the Christian life must never be considered in isolation; to do so is to court error and heresy and much trouble in practice. The Apostle therefore always starts with the general; and it is only after he has made that clear that he comes down to the realm of the particular and the detail.

*   *   *

We start therefore with the general description Paul gives of the character of the Christian life, 'I therefore, the prisoner of the Lord, beseech you that ye walk worthy of the vocation wherewith ye are called'. If we but knew what these words mean most of our problems would be immediately solved. Another better translation expresses it thus, 'That ye walk worthy of the calling with which ye are called'. 'Vocation' in a sense means 'calling', but by now it has developed a slightly different meaning which may lead us astray.

Every word here is of great importance and significance, so we must look at them one by one. The first word is 'worthy'. The learned authorities tell us that it has two basic ideas in it, both of them important. The first idea is that of equal weight or balancing. Think of two things which are of the same weight, so that when you put them on opposite sides of the scale there is no tilting to one side or the other, but they balance perfectly. That is the original derivation of the word translated here by 'worthy'. So what the Apostle is saying is that he is beseeching them and exhorting them always to give equal weight in their lives to doctrine and practice. They must not put all the weight on doctrine and none on practice; nor all the weight on practice and just a little, if any at all, on doctrine. To do so produces imbalance and lopsidedness. The Ephesians must take great pains to see that the scales are perfectly balanced. However packed your head may be with knowledge, if you are failing in your life you will be a hindrance to the spreading of the Kingdom, you will bring the cause of God and His Christ into disrepute. But it is equally true to say that if your conception of the Christian life is that it means no more than that you live a good life, that you should be moral, and that doctrine is of no importance, again you will be a hindrance to the cause. There must be true balance, we must be 'worthy of the vocation wherewith we are called'.

The Bible frequently uses this argument. It is found for instance in the sixth chapter of the Epistle to the Hebrews where we read, 'But, beloved, we are persuaded better things of you, and things that accompany salvation, though we thus speak. For God is not unrighteous to forget your work and labour of love which ye have showed toward his name, in that ye have ministered to the saints, and do minister. And we desire that every one of you do show the same diligence to the full assurance of hope unto the end' (vv. 9–11). The author of the Epistle commends them for having shown marvellous diligence on the practical side of their lives, but then urges them to show the same diligence in the matter of grasping the doctrines of the faith and especially that of the full assurance of hope to the end. Those Hebrew Christians were in trouble because they had failed to maintain the balance between doctrine and practice; they were not being 'worthy' of their calling.

The other idea contained in this word is of something that is 'becoming'. It is interesting to observe how the translators of this Authorised or King James Version translated the same word in the Greek original in different ways at different points. They might very well have translated as follows, 'I therefore, the prisoner of the Lord, beseech you that you walk in a manner which is "becoming of" the calling wherewith you are called', because when they translate the same Apostle, in the first chapter of his Epistle to the Philippians, where he again writes about himself in prison and his suffering they have, 'Only let your conversation be as it *becometh* the gospel of Christ' (v. 27). It is exactly the same idea. The idea conveyed is of matching, it is of putting on a piece of clothing that is consistent with another, something that is suited to and matches something else.

Paul means, negatively, that we must always avoid a clash of colour or appearance. There must never be a clash between our doctrine and our practice. This is something which is recognized in the matter of dress; there must never be a clash of colours that is not becoming. There are certain colours that do not match, which do not go together; and when you see a person with such clashing, contrasting colours you say that that person is lacking in taste. We can extend the idea and say that the same clothing is not always becoming at every age. There is nothing quite so ridiculous as to see an elderly person dressing as if he or she were young, and vice versa. There are certain things that are not becoming. This is the idea that the Apostle conveys here; there must never be an element of incongruity or of sharp contrasts in our lives.

I am aware of the modern art that delights in that kind of thing. The same is found in much so-called modern music which despises melody and seems to delight in cacophony and clashes and discords. But that is perversion, and not art. True art always has beauty, because it always has as its centre the idea of balance and of congruity. There is no true beauty apart from that. This has been recognized throughout the ages; so let us beware of these modern perversions. Now the Apostle is using this kind of picture: 'Let your walk' he says, 'be as becometh the calling wherewith you are called'.

We can take the idea yet further by noting the word which the Apostle used in writing to Titus where he talks about 'adorning the doctrine' (Titus 2:10). The idea is that the doctrine is, as it were, the foundation or basic garment and that the life is a kind of adornment which is added on to it. His exhortation is that we must always be careful that our decorations, our adornments, are suited to, and are congruous with, and match, this foundation garment which we have already put on. The doctrine is the foundation; the life is the adorning. The purpose of the adorning is to make the doctrine attractive, to cause people to admire it, to look at it and to desire to have it. The Apostle here, as everywhere else, does much more than issue a general appeal to Christian people to live a good life and to be philanthropic. The appeal is always in terms of the doctrine; the life must always issue from it, must always match it. You and I are to live the kind of life that will adorn the doctrine.

*   *   *

The Apostle proceeds at once to tell us what the doctrine is. It is 'the vocation', 'the calling wherewith we are called'. We are to be worthy of the calling wherewith we have been called. Here again we are dealing with a phrase that is very typical and characteristic of the New Testament, and as it is so constantly repeated it is important that we should grasp the terms without any question or misunderstanding. The doctrine it conveys is that we are to live this kind of life for the reason that we are 'the called'. This is one of the characteristic terms by which the New Testament generally describes Christians. Christian people are 'the called of Jesus Christ'. A church, the Church, is nothing but a gathering of 'the called'. The very term in Greek for Church is *ecclesia*, which means 'the called out ones'. The Apostle has referred to that in the previous chapter: 'Now unto him that is able to do exceeding abundantly above all that we ask or think, according to the power that worketh in us, unto him be glory in the church' – amongst 'the called ones' or 'the called out ones'. Christians are those who have been called out of the world, 'out of darkness, into his marvellous light' (1 Peter 2:9). The Christian must never be thought of as someone who has decided to take up a certain type of life. The Christian life must never be thought of in terms of something that we have decided to take up. It is the exact opposite, it is something into which we have been 'called'. That is why it is unfortunate that this has been translated in the A.V. as 'vocation'. We even misuse the word 'vocation' and talk about a man taking up a vocation. But one does not take up a true vocation; it is something to which you have been called. That is why we must hold on to the word 'calling'.

So the Apostle's teaching is that the way in which we are to live the Christian life is first of all to remember always that we have been called to it, called from darkness, called to light. The Apostle has been emphasizing this idea from the beginning of the Epistle. In the first chapter he has said, 'Blessed be the God and Father of our Lord Jesus Christ, who hath blessed us with all spiritual blessings in heavenly places in Christ: according as he hath chosen us in him before the foundation of the world, that we should be holy and without blame before him in love: having predestinated us unto the adoption of children by Jesus Christ to himself, according to the good pleasure of his will' (vv. 3–5). He has reminded his readers of it in the second chapter: 'You hath he quickened, who were dead in trespasses and sins' (v. 1) and so on. But now once more he returns to it and emphasizes it anew and afresh. I am concerned to emphasize that this is the greatest motive of all to sanctification. The chief reason why we are to live a holy and a sanctified life is that we are the 'called ones'. Certainly it is right not to sin and right to live the Christian life, and these things are good in and of themselves, but primarily we are to live a holy life because we have been 'called' to this.

*   *   *

We must therefore look at this whole idea of the calling as taught in the Bible. It teaches that there are two types of call. The first is a general call which is made to everyone. 'God commandeth all men everywhere to repent' (Acts 17:30). There is a universal call which goes out from the Church to the whole world to repent and to believe the Gospel. That message is addressed to every person. But that is not the only meaning, and we find that it is used in another way which is much more particular, for in addition to the general call there is what has been called the 'effectual' call. Not all who hear the general call respond to it. Two groups are found among those who have received the general call. In the one group, all remain unbelievers, but in the other group are those to whom the call has come effectually. These are the true Christians.

Let me consider some examples and illustrations of this. In the First Epistle to the Corinthians the Apostle Paul says that the 'preaching of the Cross is to them that perish foolishness; but unto us who are saved it is the power of God' (1:18). There are two groups of people – those to whom the preaching of the Cross is foolishness, and those to whom it is the wisdom of God. That is a fundamental distinction. There are the 'perishing', and there are the 'saved'. Then Paul continues: 'The Jews require a sign, and the Greeks seek after wisdom: but we preach Christ crucified, unto the Jews a stumblingblock, and unto the Greeks foolishness; but unto them which are *called,* both Jews and Greeks, Christ the power of God, and the wisdom of God' (vv. 22–24). The contrast is between the perishing and the saved: those to whom the Cross is a stumblingblock and foolishness, and those to whom it is the power and the wisdom of God. The Christians are saved; the believers are always described as the 'called ones', that is those who have been separated from all others, and have been moved into a new position.

Another matter of importance is that we must observe the point at which the calling comes in this question of salvation. We must understand that 'calling' comes before justification. The Apostle states the matter clearly in the Epistle to the Romans: 'Moreover whom he did predestinate, them he also called: and whom he called, them he also justified: and whom he justified, them he also glorified' (8:30). 'Predestination', 'calling', 'justification', and ultimately 'glorification'! This means that salvation is the result of the mighty action of the Spirit of God in the soul whereby He introduces a new principle of life and of action that enables us to believe. We are 'called' to believe. Our Lord Jesus Christ Himself expresses this clearly in John's Gospel: 'No man can come to me except the Father which hath sent me *draw* him' (6:44). It is the call which draws him. There is power in the 'call' which draws him, he cannot come without it.

Furthermore, consider the account given of the first convert to the Gospel in Europe as found in the Acts of the Apostles. Paul preaches to the little prayer meeting of women outside the city walls of Philippi on a Sabbath, and we read that 'we sat down, and spake unto the women which resorted thither. And a certain woman named Lydia, a seller of purple, of the city of Thyatira, which worshipped God, heard us, whose heart the Lord opened, that she attended unto the things which were spoken of Paul' (16: 13,14). The 'call' is described there as the opening of the heart, which makes a person attend and believe. Without that opening of the heart the Word has no effect. The Apostle has already said this clearly at the beginning of chapter 2 of this Ephesian Epistle when he wrote: 'You hath he quickened, who were dead in trespasses and sins' (v. 1). He repeats it in verse 5; 'Even when we were dead in sins, hath quickened us . . .' A dead person cannot quicken himself; God alone can quicken. And by an effectual call He does so.

A wonderful illustration of all this is found in John's Gospel in the case of Lazarus. Lazarus had died, and had been dead for four days; his body was in a grave and putrefaction had already started. Our Lord arrives on the scene and commands the mourners to 'take away the stone'. Then He spoke, saying, 'Lazarus, come forth', and he came forth from the tomb. The power was in the call. The power was in the word spoken. That is what Paul means here, by 'the calling wherewith you are called'. The word had come effectually, with power, to these

Ephesian Christians; the Holy Spirit was in it; the preaching had been 'in demonstration of the Spirit and of power'. When the word comes in the power of the Spirit it calls our souls from spiritual death and the grave into life and into newness of living. The Apostle states the fact again in the Epistle to the Romans: 'God, who quickeneth the dead, and calleth those things which be not as though they were' (4:17). Abraham and Sarah, though they were over ninety years of age, were enabled to have a son. This was impossible naturally, but not with God. When God calls savingly He gives the power and makes the call effectual. It becomes certain; it must happen, and it does happen. We who are Christians are the 'called' out of the death and grave of sin. When we were yet dead in trespasses and sins, the mighty word came and 'called' us, and enabled us to hear. It quickened us and put life into us. Quickening is the giving of life.

The Apostle Peter says the same thing in his First Epistle, when he writes about being 'Born again, not of corruptible seed, but of incorruptible, by the word of God, which liveth and abideth for ever' (1:23). The word of the Gospel has life in it, and when it comes in the power of the Spirit, and the seed is implanted, our response is made. Furthermore the Apostle Peter uses the same argument as the Apostle Paul uses here. 'But as he which hath called you is holy, so be ye holy in all manner of conversation'. Again he argues in the second chapter, saying, 'Ye are a chosen generation, a royal priesthood, an holy nation, a peculiar people; that ye should shew forth the praises of him who hath called you out of darkness into his marvellous light' (2:9).

That is precisely what the Apostle Paul is arguing here, that we have been called in order that we may show forth these things. Be worthy, he says, of the vocation, the calling, by which you have been called. We do so by applying the doctrine and knowledge which we have. We have to live as those who realize that we have been called by God into this heavenly calling. We can only do so as we know the doctrine. So we must remind ourselves of some of the things which must always be in our minds governing our conduct and behaviour. We have been called to this great and marvellous high calling and our lives must match the calling and be in accord with it.

But what are the things which we must always remember? The

first is, 'Blessed be the God and Father of our Lord Jesus Christ, who hath blessed us with all spiritual blessings in heavenly places in Christ'. That is stated in the third verse of this Epistle to the Ephesians. In itself it answers every argument and every excuse we may put forward. There is no point in talking about our difficulties, or the problems of life in this complicated modern world of the twentieth century. What matters and counts is that we have been blessed with 'all spiritual blessings in heavenly places in Christ Jesus'! There is nothing beyond that; everything we need is at our disposal. It is all in Christ; we are in Him and He is in us. We must always remember this fact, and live in a manner that illustrates it.

The Apostle goes on to remind us also in the next verse, 'According as he hath chosen us in him before the foundation of the world, that we should be holy and without blame before him in love' (v. 4). God has called us not merely that we might not go to hell, and not only that we might know that our sins are forgiven; He has chosen us 'to be holy', and to be 'blameless before him in love'. We have no right to argue or to question or to query. That is the life to which He has called us.

The Apostle reminds us next that God has 'predestinated us unto the adoption of children by Jesus Christ' (v. 5), to which he adds in chapter 2 that 'we are fellow citizens with the saints and of the household of God' (v. 19). We have been called into the family of God; we are God's children. And we are to live in a manner that will reflect credit and glory upon the family and upon our Father. The Britisher in any foreign country should always be conscious of the fact that the honour of his country is in a sense in his hands. The honour of the family is in the hands of the child of the family when he goes to a party; and if the child does not behave as he should, the hosts will not blame the child but the parents; and rightly so. The honour of the family is in the hands of the child, and you and I are children of God. So as I walk the streets of life I must always remember that I am a child and a member of God's family: 'Having predestinated us unto the adoption of children by Jesus Christ'. And because I am a child, I am an heir, so the Apostle reminds these Ephesian Christians that they have the Holy Spirit, 'which is the earnest of our inheritance until the redemption of the purchased possession'

(v. 14). I must think not only of what I am now, but also of what I am going to be. I am not only a child of God, I am an heir and a joint-heir with Christ. We read of people being groomed for certain things, and taught manners and conduct and deportment and behaviour before being presented at Court or before taking part in some great occasion. So we are to live as always remembering that there is a day coming in our lives when we shall be presented to God. 'Now unto him', says Jude, 'who is able to keep you from falling, and to present you faultless before the presence of his glory with exceeding joy . . .' (v. 24). We are to live as realizing that we are going on to glory. And having been presented we shall be given our reward, and enter into our inheritance. It is coming – 'the purchased possession'. We only receive the firstfruits and have foretastes of it in this world; but we are hereafter to receive it in fulness.

Not only so; the Apostle has been reminding us already, at the end of the first chapter, that as members of the Church we are members of the body of Christ – 'the church which is his body, the fulness of him that filleth all in all'. We are joined to Christ as members of a body belong to the head. We are 'of his flesh and of his bones', as Paul will tell us in chapter 5. In chapter 2 he reminds us that not only have we been quickened with Christ, but also that we have been raised from death with Christ. Indeed we are at this moment 'seated with Christ in the heavenly places'. We must live, I say, as realizing that we are seated in the heavenly places even at this very moment. And then we must always remember that Christ dwells in our hearts by faith, and that there is something of the fulness of God in us. That is the way to sanctification, to holiness. That is the way to live – to realize that these things are true.

*   *   *

Finally, we must never forget the way in which the calling has taken place. What is it that has made it possible for me to come from death to life, from the grave of sin to newness of life, and to be seated in the heavenly places with Christ? The answer is that it is entirely due to the free grace of God. 'By grace . . . through faith; and that not of yourselves, it is the gift of God' (chap. 2:8) 'We are his workmanship' (chap. 2:10). While we were dead and desperate and hopeless and the creatures of lusts, He quickened us, in spite of it. And above all let us constantly remind ourselves of what made it possible for God to do this. Our salvation is 'by the blood of Christ'. 'Ye who sometimes were far off are made nigh by the blood of Christ' (chap. 2:13).

The Apostle Peter states it thus: 'You have not been redeemed with gold and silver from your vain conversation, but by the precious blood of Christ, as of a lamb without blemish and without spot' (1 Peter 1:18). So when sin comes and tempts you, or when you are doubtful as to whether you can go on with the Christian life, or feel that it is hard and makes excessive demands, remember the price that was paid for your deliverance, your ransom. Christ gave His life unto death that we might be rescued and that we might become holy.

Then remember always the power that is given to us, 'the exceeding greatness of his power to us-ward that believe' (chap. 1 v. 19). Let us remember also that we must be 'strengthened with might by his Spirit in the inner man' (chap. 3 v. 16), and that God 'is able to do exceeding abundantly above all that we ask or think, according to the power that worketh in us' (chap. 3 v. 20).

Finally note that the Apostle makes this appeal as 'the prisoner of the Lord'. Thereby I believe that he is saying in effect, You are to live as I am trying to live, and as I am living. I am living the life of a prisoner; I am actually in prison at the moment. And I am in prison because I do not decide what I do; I am the servant of Jesus Christ, I am His bondslave. It is because I am loyal to Him and preaching His Gospel that I am in prison; but that does not worry me; I am in His charge, I am not in charge of myself. He has called me, and I am His bondslave, His servant, His prisoner, and you are to live as the prisoners of Jesus Christ. 'Ye are not your own; ye are bought with a price' (1 Cor 6:19–20). We have no right to live as we choose and as we please. We were the prisoners of Satan; we are now the prisoners of Jesus Christ. We should have no desire save to please Him. 'Let nothing please or pain me, apart, O Lord, from Thee' should ever be the expression of our constant desire. If we but saw and grasped the meaning of our calling, in all its parts, there would be no problem about Christian living. We would 'count it our supreme delight to hear His dictates and obey', with Philip Doddridge and the saints of all the centuries.

[33]

3
Keeping the Unity of the Spirit

'With all lowliness and meekness, with longsuffering,
forbearing one another in love; endeavouring to keep
the unity of the Spirit in the bond of peace.'

Ephesians 4:2–3

In these two verses which are intimately connected with the first
verse of the chapter, the Apostle, having described the general
character and nature of the Christian life into which we have been
called by God through His grace, now turns to the particular
applications. The general character of the life is that it is to be
'worthy of the calling to which we have been called'. That must
ever be central and uppermost in our minds. We have been called
to a particular kind of life. When we were dead in trespasses and
sins we were called and quickened and brought into it. Or, as the
Apostle has earlier expressed it, 'We are his workmanship, created
in Christ Jesus unto good works, which God hath before ordained
that we should walk in them' (2:10).

The fact that the Christian life is described as a 'walk' is significant. 'Walk' suggests activity, movement, and progress. We are
to 'walk' worthy of our vocation. We do not stay where we were
or as we are; we do not say 'Ah, now I am saved, my sins are
forgiven, all is well', and spend the rest of our lives talking about
our conversion, always looking back and remaining in that
position. The Christian life is one of progress, of ever going
forward; there are always fresh things to be discovered and fresh
experiences to be enjoyed.

*   *   *

The first particular matter which the Apostle mentions is that we
are to 'endeavour to keep the unity of the Spirit in the bond of

[34]

peace'. Why did the Apostle choose this as the first particular? The answer is to be found in the first three chapters of this Epistle where Paul has been emphasizing this great principle of unity. He has said plainly and specifically in the tenth verse of the first chapter that this was the primary objective which God had in mind when He purposed, before the foundation of the world, and before time, to send His only begotten Son into this world. It was 'that in the dispensation of the fulness of times he might gather together in one [or that He might re-unite in one] all things in Christ, both which are in heaven and which are on earth, even in him'. This is the primary objective in God's plan of salvation. Sin is a disruptive force. Sin always divides, it always separates, it splinters. It divides a man within and against himself. It has produced the constant fight and struggle which we are all aware of in our lives. There is the constant problem of good and bad, right and wrong; shall I? shall I not? Sin also produces division between man and man; it leads to enmity and war and strife. The world has been shattered by sin.

So the central object of salvation, in a sense, is to re-unite, to bring together again, to restore the unity that obtained before sin and the Fall produced this terrible havoc. The Apostle has worked this out, saying in chapter 1 verses 11–13, 'In whom also we [the Jews] have obtained an inheritance', and then 'In whom ye [Gentiles] also trusted, after that ye heard the word of truth, the gospel of your salvation'. Then Paul works it out in greater detail in the second chapter, showing how 'the middle wall of partition' has been broken down and how 'of twain one new man', one new body, has been made. This unity in Christ of Jew and Gentile, he says in chapter 3, is the mystery which has now been revealed (vv. 5ff). So it is inevitable that when he comes to the particulars of the Christian walk and life, the preservation of this unity must be mentioned first. This is God's grand design; it is what displays God's glory above everything else. So the peculiar mark of the Christian calling is that it preserves this 'unity of the Spirit in the bond of peace'. This is the first step in the working out of the 'therefore' in the first verse of the fourth chapter. It is the first thing we must remember as we strive to 'walk worthy of the calling wherewith we are called'.

The Apostle shows the importance which he attaches to this

question of unity by the fact that he continues to deal with it until the end of the sixteenth verse in this chapter. In verse 17 he begins to deal with the conduct and behaviour of believers in detailed practice; but this matter of unity is the first thing.

*　　*　　*

Let us now observe how he deals with it by analysing the statement. In verses 2 and 3 he makes a general appeal with respect to this unity. Then, in verses 4 to 16, he supplies them with reasons and arguments for keeping unity. First of all he makes an appeal to them; and then in order to help any who might be doubtful about this, or not clear in their minds as to why they should strive in this respect, he introduces the doctrine concerning the whole nature and being and character of the Church.

For the moment we are concerned with the general appeal – 'With all lowliness and meekness, with longsuffering, forbearing one another in love; endeavouring to keep the unity of the Spirit in the bond of peace'. All who are abreast with modern trends in the Christian Church will agree that there is no subject which is being talked about so much, and written about so much, at this present time as this question of unity. It is the age of œcumenicity, with endless talk and writing about unity, union and re-union. How important it is therefore that we should consider what the Apostle has to say concerning this theme. There is much loose talk with regard to it; but our concern should always be scriptural; we must get to know exactly what the New Testament teaches about this matter.

The first thing, therefore, which we must look at is the character, or the nature, of the unity. We start by observing that the Apostle is not merely appealing for some general spirit of friendship, brotherliness, or camaraderie. Neither is he appealing only for some common aim or a series of common aims as against something which is a common enemy. These negatives are important because so much of the modern talk about unity is entirely in such terms. It is all very vague and nebulous. Frequently the call to unity is stated in terms of the fact that the world of today is sadly divided. As on the one hand there are atheistic powers, Communism and Humanism, so on the other hand, we are told, it is the business of all who in any way believe in God to come together and to act together. We must not be too particular in regard to what we believe, but we must have the spirit of fellowship and of friendship and of working together against the common enemy.

Clearly we must examine this attitude, and must keep this modern idea of unity in our minds as we follow the Apostle's teaching in this chapter. We must stress at once one thing which is of the utmost importance. Whatever be the unity of which the Apostle speaks, it is a unity that results directly from all he has been saying in the first three chapters of the Epistle. You must not start in chapter 4 of the Epistle to the Ephesians. To do so is to violate the context and to ignore the word 'Therefore'. In other words you cannot have Christian unity unless it is based upon the great doctrines outlined in chapters 1 to 3. 'Therefore'! So if anyone comes to you and says, 'It does not much matter what you believe; if we call ourselves Christians, or if we believe in God in any sense, come, let us all work together', you should say in reply, 'But, my dear Sir, what about chapters 1 to 3 of the Epistle to the Ephesians? I know of no unity except that which is the outcome of, and the offspring of, all the great doctrines which the Apostle lays down in those chapters'. Whatever this unity may be, we are compelled to say that it must be theological, it must be doctrinal, it must be based upon an understanding of the truth.

Let us next observe that the word 'Spirit' has a capital 'S' – 'Endeavouring to keep the unity of the Spirit'. This refers to The Holy Spirit. Paul is not writing about the manifestation of some human spirit of friendship, he is not thinking in terms of the so-called public school spirit, or the cricket team spirit, or that of the football team. It is a capital S, it is The Holy Spirit. In verse 4 he repeats the same emphasis, 'There is one body, and one Spirit', the Holy Spirit. Everywhere in this context the word 'Spirit' must be interpreted as referring to the Holy Spirit Himself. It is because this fact is so constantly forgotten that most of the modern talk about unity seems to me to be entirely un-scriptural. It is entirely human, it is something that belongs to man; it is not the unity that is produced by the Spirit Himself. Let us proceed to look at this in the form of a number of statements.

The unity about which the Apostle is concerned here is produced and created by the Holy Spirit Himself. He alone can produce this unity; and it is He alone who does produce this unity. This is obviously a matter of fundamental importance. The Apostle makes it quite clear that this is a unity which you and I can never produce. He does not even ask us to do so, he does not call upon us to do so, he does not exhort us to do so. What he asks us to do is to be careful not to break the unity that is already there, and which has been produced and created by the Holy Spirit Himself. We are to maintain it, not create it. It is the unity of the Spirit. It is His work, it is something that He does in us.

Because that is true the following deductions are also true. The unity about which the Apostle is concerned is a living and a vital unity. It is not a mechanical unity. There is all the difference in the world between a coalition or amalgamation and a true unity. Amalgamations and coalitions consist of a number of disparate units coming together for a given purpose; but the unity of the Spirit starts within and works outwardly. It is comparable to the unity found in a flower, or a tree, or in animal bodies. It is something essentially organic and vital, not something artificially produced. It is something which is inevitable because of its very nature. It is not an external, but an internal unity.

Furthermore, this unity can only be understood as the work of the Holy Spirit is understood. If we lack a right understanding of the doctrine of the Holy Spirit we cannot understand this unity. If we call the Holy Spirit 'it', or regard Him as merely a power, and do not realize that He is the Third Person in the blessed Holy Trinity, we cannot understand this unity, and it will be non-existent. Nor can this unity ever be felt and experienced or put into practice unless the Holy Spirit is in us and has done His gracious work within us. This explains why it is sometimes so difficult to discuss this subject with certain people. They do not agree about the doctrine of the Holy Spirit, they do not agree about regeneration and re-birth. Their idea of Christianity is that it simply means doing good and being moral and religious, or taking an interest in a particular denomination and its activities. No profitable conversation or discussion is possible with such people as their whole conception of the Spirit is different. No unity is possible between such people and those who take the scriptural view of the work of the Spirit. If the Holy Spirit is not in us we cannot experience this unity; it can only be experienced by those in whom He dwells and whom He has enlightened. But if the Holy Spirit is in that other person and also in me, at once we are conscious of a bond of unity because the same Spirit is in us both, and we recognize it in one another. These surely are quite basic and fundamental considerations.

*   *   *

A vivid illustration of the unity brought about by the Holy Spirit has already been given in the second chapter. These Ephesian Gentiles who once were 'far off', 'aliens from the commonwealth of Israel', have now been brought into God's covenant with the Jews. He has acted in them, He has acted in the Jew, and so they are one. And therefore to talk glibly and lightly about forgetting our differences and getting together and finding a common basis or a common denominator is to talk about something which is entirely different from what Paul teaches here. The setting aside of differences may be accomplished in politics or in industry or in many other realms. But when you start with the Holy Spirit and His Person and His activity you cannot speak in that manner. If He is not in me I can have no spiritual fellowship with a man in whom He dwells. If He is not in him, but in me, there is no fellowship. If He is in both of us there is true fellowship; and this is the only basis of fellowship. It is where He reigns, and where the fellowship of the Holy Spirit is experienced, that this unity exists. Hence the benediction at the end of the Second Epistle to the Corinthians: 'The grace of the Lord Jesus Christ, and the love of God, and the fellowship of the Holy Spirit be with you all' (13:14). Where the Spirit reigns there is unity.

We shall see when we come to consider verses 4–6 how the Apostle works all this out in detail. For the moment we can sum it up by saying that the unity produced by the Spirit is primarily spiritual, unseen and internal. Of course it expresses itself also visibly and externally, for as Christians we worship together, we belong to churches together and come into contact with one another constantly. But the thing itself is internal. Let us note again the importance of the order. We do not start with that which is external and then hope to arrive at the internal. We start with the internal and then proceed to express it externally.

We must bear this in mind constantly as we read modern books about œcumenicity or listen to sermons and appeals. Their great argument and appeal is that as hitherto divided and separate people we must begin to act together, to work together, to pray together, and then we shall begin to feel the spirit of unity. But that is a denial of the Apostle's teaching. In every manifestation of life the internal principle comes first, and then the outward manifestation. It was so in creation; it is the same in reproduction. Two very small cells contain the life out of which a complete body will develop. A body does not consist of a collection of parts and portions loosely and haphazardly joined together. Every individual part or member develops out of the central life. And it is precisely the same in this great and vital matter of spiritual unity. The unity of the Spirit cannot primarily be seen; indeed it is something which can scarcely be defined. When it is present we recognize it, we feel it when we come into contact with another in whom the Spirit dwells. Our souls are invisible; and yet the soul is the most important thing in man. Furthermore, we do approach the soul and spirit through the body; it is the soul and spirit that manifest themselves through the body. So it is with this principle of unity.

*   *   *

Having thus considered the nature, the character of the unity, let us now look at our duty with respect to it. The particular words which the Apostle uses explain it perfectly. The first word is 'endeavour'. We tend to think of this word endeavour as 'making an attempt at'; but that is not the root meaning of the word. It really means 'to be diligent' and derives from a word which suggests speed. We are to hurry to do something, to show great concern about, expressing solicitude – 'endeavouring to keep'. Above everything else, says the Apostle, as Christians in this calling to which you have been called, hasten to do this, be diligent with respect to it, never forget it, let this be the chief thing in your life; above all else show great concern and solicitude with respect to this unity that exists among you.

The next word is 'to keep' – 'endeavouring *to keep* the unity of the Spirit'. 'To keep' means 'to guard', 'to hold fast', 'to preserve'. The Apostle does not ask us to make a unity or to create a unity.

It exists because we are Christians, he says, and we are to guard it. We cannot be Christians without the work of the Holy Spirit; we cannot be Christians unless the Spirit resides in us. And He is in all true Christians. The unity is there, and what we have to do is to guard it, to keep it, to preserve it. Our first and chief concern as Christians should be to guard and to preserve this precious, wondrous unity of the Spirit. God's grand design, the thing which God is doing through the Church, and by means of which, we have been told in chapter 3, verse 10, even the principalities and powers in the heavenly places are going to be astonished and amazed when they see it, is to produce and maintain this unity between the redeemed, whether Jew or Gentile. If we believe in God, we must ever feel that our first duty is to guard this unity, to preserve it at all costs, to strain every nerve and be diligent in endeavouring to keep it and manifest it.

The manner in which we are to do so is stated by the Apostle in plain words. They can be grouped together thus. The first two words describe us and our own internal disposition. The following words describe our relationship to others. The first expression is 'with all lowliness'. 'Lowliness' is humility, and especially humility of mind. This particular emphasis is found in all the lexicons. It means modesty. It is the opposite of self-esteem, self-assertion, and pride. Humility is one of the chief of all the Christian virtues; it is the hallmark of the child of God. Humility means having a poor opinion of yourself, and of your powers and faculties. To use the word of our Lord in the Sermon on the Mount, it means to be 'poor in spirit'. It is the opposite of what is found in the so-called man of the world; it is the opposite of the worldly spirit which urges man to trust in himself, and to believe in himself. It is the opposite of all aggressiveness and self-advertisement and ambition and all the brazenness of life at this present time. There is nothing sadder about this present age than the appalling absence of humility; and when this same lack is found in the Church of God, it is the greatest tragedy of all. As Chrysostom said long ago, 'Nothing will so avail to divide the Church as love of power'.

Next to 'lowliness' the Apostle places 'meekness', which invariably accompanies it. 'Meekness' means an inner mildness and gentleness. Yet it is compatible with great strength. Moses was

[41]

the meekest of all men, and yet he was a strong man. In his inner being he was a very mild man, a gentle man. And our Lord Himself was meek. 'Meekness' really means readiness to suffer wrong, if need be, the committing of everything to God. The Apostle Paul himself was a very meek man. At the same time he could say some very strong things; he could be firm and powerful; there is something magisterial about his statements. Yet as we read his epistles we find this element of humility and of meekness everywhere. He has already manifested this meekness in the third chapter where he writes, 'Unto me, who am less than the least of all saints' – though he was the greatest of all – 'is this grace given, that I should preach among the Gentiles the unsearchable riches of Christ'. Humility and meekness are the first essentials in guarding the unity of the Spirit in the bonds of peace. These are the virtues found in our Lord himself. He says, 'Come unto me, all ye that labour and are heavy laden, and I will give you rest. Take my yoke upon you, and learn of me; for I am meek and lowly in heart: and ye shall find rest unto your souls' (Matthew 11:28–30). Matthew, in the twelfth chapter of his Gospel, quoting from Isaiah, describes our Lord thus: 'He shall not strive, nor cry aloud, neither shall any man hear his voice in the streets. A bruised reed shall he not break, and the smoking flax shall he not quench, till he send forth judgment unto victory' (vv. 19–20). Such was His character as we find it portrayed in the Gospel portraits of our blessed Lord. And we belong to Him, and are members of His body. So the Apostle in writing to the Corinthians makes use of this argument: 'Now I, Paul, myself beseech you by the meekness and gentleness of Christ . . .' (2 Cor 10:1). Writing in his Second Epistle to Timothy and giving him advice, Paul says, 'But foolish and unlearned questions avoid, knowing that they do gender strifes. And the servant of the Lord must not strive; but be gentle unto all men, apt to teach, patient, in meekness instructing those that oppose themselves; if God peradventure will give them repentance to the acknowledging of the truth' (2:23–24). That is how you are to behave, says the Apostle to Timothy in effect; there will be people who will not agree with you; do not be annoyed by them and become angry. You must not strive with them; but rather try to get them to see the truth; put it before them in a way which will appeal to them, try to win them to it, wean them from error and win them to the truth.

* * *

The Apostle Peter gives a similar exhortation in a very striking manner. In his first Epistle he says, 'Yea, all of you be subject one to another, and be clothed with humility: for God resisteth the proud, and giveth grace to the humble' (v. 5). Note the interesting expression, 'be clothed with humility'. The word that is translated 'clothed' means 'putting on the apron of humility'. Surely when Peter wrote these words he had in his mind the scene of which we read in the thirteenth chapter of John's Gospel. We are shown the very Son of God here on earth; and this is what we are told about Him: He knew whence he had come and whither He was going. He knew that He had come from God and that He was going to God. But He took a towel and He put it on Himself as an apron, and He stooped down and washed the feet of His disciples. Then He said to them, If I who am your Lord and Master do that to you, do ye the same to one another. 'If I have washed your feet, wash one another's feet'. 'Be clothed with humility'. 'Put on humility as an apron'. Gird yourself with the towel of humility; stoop right down, and wash the feet of others. This is the secret of preserving the unity of the Spirit in the bond of peace.

But Paul adds the word 'all' – 'with *all* humility and meekness'. Why does he add the word 'all'? It means 'with every possible' humility and meekness, 'with every kind of', 'in all situations', 'at all times'. We are not to put on this apron on Sundays only, and then forget it during the remainder of the week. Always keep it on, always be clothed with humility, wherever you are, whatever you are doing, whoever the person is, whatever the time – 'all humility and meekness'. Never be without it.

This is to be our fundamental disposition and character. Are we humble? 'Let no man think of himself above that which he ought to think' says the Apostle. 'Let him that thinketh he standeth take heed, lest he fall'. It is our wrong conceits of ourselves that cause division. One is proud of his birth, another of his family; one is proud of his money, another of his nationality, his status, his business acumen. Another is proud of his brains, his understanding – perhaps of doctrine – and he is so proud of it that he is causing division and thereby denying his doctrine!

[43]

Humility! Humbleness of mind! Said Oliver Cromwell to certain Scottish presbyters, 'I beseech you, in the bowels of Christ, consider it possible you may be mistaken'. That is humility. And meekness goes with it; and we are to show it everywhere.

That being our fundamental disposition, we are to manifest it in our dealings with others. 'Longsuffering' – which simply means suffering long. It means holding yourself in control for a long time and not giving way to passion. You may be confronting a person who is irritating by his conduct – by what he says or by what he does. Well, says the Apostle, just hold out, do not give way to that desire to demolish him or to smash him or to humiliate him. Hold on, be 'longsuffering', do not give way to passion. In the Bible longsuffering is attributed to God Himself. If God were not longsuffering not one of us would be still alive, not one of us would be a Christian. If God were not longsuffering there would be no Christianity at all. Longsuffering is His attitude to us: so let it be our attitude towards one another. We have to suffer ourselves, and others have to suffer us. Let all suffer long!

Then we come to 'forbearing'. All these words are related. To 'forbear' means 'to hold yourself up against'. A person tempts you to engage in a wrong attitude or action. Hold yourself up against the temptation. Put up with it; bear it; endure it; suffer it. All these things are difficult, are they not? Yes, but we are called to such a glorious life that it is of necessity difficult. Thank God it is! Others may not understand things as we do, or they may not be doing things in the way that we would like them to be done. Do not retaliate at once; as one who is concerned about the preservation of the unity of the Spirit in the bond of peace, bear with them and try to understand them. A person may be irritable because he has been having a very trying time, or he may not be well physically. Perhaps he has not had advantages and opportunities in life, perhaps his brain power is not what it ought to be, perhaps he has not had your opportunity of hearing these particular truths expounded. Make every excuse you can for this other person, whether it applies to his conduct or his doctrine or anything else. Try above everything else to win him to your position if you are convinced that you are right. Do not merely try to score over him, do not strike him, do not dismiss him, do not be contemptuous of him, do not be impatient with him. We

[44]

must be patient with one another, we must be forbearing, we must be longsuffering.

But notice the Apostle's further addition! '. . . with all lowliness and meekness, with longsuffering, forbearing one another *in love*'. If you love people you will be longsuffering and forbearing toward them because you will have their interests at heart. You will not be so much concerned to show that you are right and they are wrong. You will be anxious that they should be right as well as yourself. You love them and are interested in them, and concerned about them; and because of that you are patient with them. If you love a child you will be patient with him. He may ask you the same question a thousand times but you will still go on answering patiently. You do something and the child says, 'Do it again', and you do it again, and again; and you go on until you are almost exhausted. You even enjoy doing so, though you are almost collapsing physically. It is because you love the little child. He does not know, he does not understand; and it would be very wrong to expect him to understand at that age. You have to come down to his level, to put on the apron, to get on your knees, to be one with him. And if you love him you do so readily and gladly.

*   *   *

What the Apostle is really saying is that, as we manifest these characteristics, we are preserving the unity. This is so because we are peaceable, we are peace-loving, and we are people who are easy to live with; we are peacemakers. This unity of the Spirit is kept together, is bound or banded together, by peace, 'by the bond [or the band] which is peace'. And as we are peaceable and peace-loving and peace-making we preserve peace and we preserve the unity.

In all this the Apostle Paul has been repeating the Beatitudes that our Lord Jesus Christ uttered at the beginning of the Sermon on the Mount. This is what He said concerning the people He had come into the world to produce: 'Blessed are the poor in spirit', 'blessed are they that mourn', 'blessed are the meek', 'blessed are they that do hunger and thirst after righteousness', 'blessed are the peacemakers'. These are the characteristics of the Christian. This is the calling to which we have been called. If we fail here, success anywhere else is useless. If my way of asserting that which is right means that I break the peace, I am not right, I have failed to keep the balance of truth, or there is something lacking in my character. The end of all doctrine is to preserve this unity of the Spirit in the bond of peace. The end of all conduct is to be the same. This is the teaching of the Beatitudes, and also of 1 Corinthians 13. Indeed it is 'the fruit of the Spirit', which is 'love, joy, peace, longsuffering, gentleness, goodness, meekness, faith, temperance' (Galatians 5:22–23). Indeed, the Apostle is really saying, Do not quench the Spirit, do not grieve the Spirit, but allow the Spirit to produce His own glorious fruit in you and amongst you. And as you do so the unity of the Spirit Himself will be preserved among you by the wonderful bond and band of peace.

'With all humility and meekness, with longsuffering, forbearing one another in love'.

4
The Body of Christ

'There is one body, and one Spirit, even as ye are
called in one hope of your calling: one Lord, one
faith, one baptism, one God and Father of all, who is
above all, and through all, and in you all'.

Ephesians 4: 4–6

In these words the Apostle Paul goes on to give us an abundant
reason, an overwhelming reason, why we should 'with all lowliness and meekness and longsuffering, forbearing one another in
love, endeavour [be urgent] to keep the unity of the Spirit in the
bond of peace'. Indeed in these three verses he introduces one of
his great statements with regard to the doctrine of the Christian
Church. This will be his subject until the end of verse 16.

As we begin to consider it let us observe the amount of space
which is given in the New Testament to the doctrine of the
Church. In a sense it is the great theme of all the epistles. It is true
that the Apostle was constantly concerned, as were the other
writers, with particular difficulties and problems in the lives of
members of the Church; but he always deals with them in terms
of his doctrine of the Church. This is a most important and vital
principle. As we read these epistles let us note how invariably
every appeal that is made to us is never made directly; it is always
made in terms of membership of the Church and of our relationship to the Church. We are all parts and portions and members of
the Church, so if we do not understand the New Testament
doctrine of the Church there is a sense in which all its appeals and
exhortations and indicatives will be quite meaningless to us.

Most of our troubles arise chiefly from the fact that we per-
sistently start with ourselves; we are too subjective. This is one
of the main results of sin. Sin puts man himself in the centre. It
makes me feel that I alone am important, and that what I feel and
what is happening to me is what really matters. We spend our

time in thinking about ourselves and our personal interests. The New Testament teaching takes us right out of that by giving us a wonderful picture of the Church, and of ourselves as but units and members in this great mystical body of Christ. The moment we begin to see things in that way we are delivered out of this miserable, morbid subjectivity. The way to cure ourselves of most of our ills and problems is to lift ourselves right out of this subjectivity and to see ourselves as the New Testament describes us, and especially in the words, 'ye are the body of Christ, and members in particular' (1 Cor 12:27). Indeed this is what the Apostle has been doing from the beginning of this Epistle. Individual Jews and Gentiles in the grand purpose of God and by His grace have been called and saved and brought together. And here it is now stated in terms of the Church. What we have to do therefore is to see ourselves as members of the Church. As we do so we shall be delivered from most of our troubles and trials. This being true of all our problems, it is particularly true of the question of unity – 'the unity of the Spirit in the bond of peace'.

*   *   *

There are clear indications in the New Testament that there were already troubles concerning a true understanding of the nature of the Church. Take, for instance, the church at Corinth. Paul's reason for writing his First Epistle to the Corinthians was that there were divisions, sects, schisms in that church. And what he says to them in effect is that all their troubles stem from their failure to understand clearly the nature of the Christian Church. They were thinking of themselves still in an atomistic manner, as individuals, and had formed themselves into little groups of individuals. If they had seen the idea of the Church as a whole, as a united body, this would be quite unthinkable. So there, as here, he gives them an exposition of the doctrine of the Church.

In these three verses he does so in a very interesting manner. He plays on the word 'one' – '*one* body, and *one* Spirit, even as ye are called in *one* hope of your calling; *one* Lord, *one* faith, *one* baptism, *one* God and Father of all, who is above all, and through all, and in you all'. He repeats the word *one,* and thereby establishes this principle of the essential unity of the Church.

This statement is interesting from many standpoints, including

[48]

what we may call the mechanics of interpretation, for the word *one* occurs seven times. There is surely a suggestion here of the number of Divinity, the number of God, of perfection, but I do not wish to stress the point. It may well be that Paul deliberately did this in order that we may see that the unity of the Church is a manifestation of the perfection of the Godhead. Another interesting matter is the way in which he groups them. Three are found in the fourth verse, three in the fifth verse, and the seventh in the sixth verse. The last, observe, is a collection, a summary, of all unities in itself. The Apostle also repeats the word *all* – 'One God and Father of *all*, who is above *all* and through *all* and in you *all*'. This again emphasizes the same notion and idea of unity.

Another most important point is that each of the three groups is arranged around one of the Persons in the blessed Holy Trinity. The first three belong to the Holy Spirit. The second three belong to the Lord Jesus Christ, the Son. And finally we have God the Father Himself. To see the significance of this is the only way in which we can grasp this doctrine of unity and see its importance in our practical daily life and living. The moment we see it we are taken right out of our petty, morbid self-concern and are made to stand face to face with the blessed Holy Trinity, the Three in One, the One in Three. The Church is a reflection and a manifestation of the blessed Holy Trinity.

Such is the way in which the Apostle handles the doctrine of church unity. He does not leave it as a personal appeal to us to be kind and longsuffering and good. These graces are essential but the fundamental principle is that we should see ourselves as members of the Church, and see the Church as a reflection on earth of the oneness of the Triune God – Three in One, One in Three, Holy Spirit, Son, Father. Surely it must be evident that the real trouble with modern Christians is that they neglect doctrine! We talk about being practical, but we cannot be practical unless we know how to be practical, and why we should be so. Before we can respond to direct personal appeals we have got to see what we are, where we are, and where God has placed us. We have been 'called'.

One final point in this matter of interpretation; note the order which the Apostle employs. He starts with the Holy Spirit, he then goes on to the Son, and he ends with God the Father. Why this order? Why not God the Father, God the Son, God the Holy Spirit? Why does Paul reverse the order? There is but one answer to that question, namely, that he is primarily concerned to be practical. He starts with the Church as she is, consisting of people who are members of her. The Church is a fellowship of the Spirit, a community of the Spirit. He starts with us exactly where we are and as we were. Then he takes us to a higher point – the Church as a body, the Head of which is Christ. Finally, the head of Christ is God the Father. So he moves from where we are indwelt by the Spirit, through the one and only Mediator, to God the Father. His method is practical and experimental; he is not interested in dry-as-dust doctrine, something remote and far away; he is meeting us where we are. He shows us that we are where we are and what we are because of the work of the Spirit; but the Spirit would never have come, would never have been sent and given, were it not for the Son and what He has done. And the Son would never have come were it not that 'God so loved the world that he gave his only-begotten Son'. This is all intensely practical. As Christians we are not left to ourselves. The Holy Spirit is in us, and He will lead us to the Son. He will teach us how to pray, for 'we know not what to pray for as we ought, but the Spirit maketh intercession for us with groanings which cannot be uttered' (Rom 8: 26–27). And He will bring us to the Son; and as our Mediator and great High Priest the Son will introduce us to the Father.

The Apostle is concerned to show us that there is no need to argue about this question of 'the unity of the Spirit in the bond of peace'. The unity is already there, it is inevitable. The translation in the Authorised Version brings this truth out clearly by saying, 'There is one body'. The words 'There is' are supplied; they are not in the original. The translators very rightly supplied them. In other words they remind us that the Apostle is not appealing to us to form the unity; what he is telling us is that this unity is already there, and that all he is asking of us is not to break it – 'endeavouring to keep it', to guard it, to safeguard it. He is not making some great appeal to us to come together. He is urging us to be careful not to break the unity in any way or to be the cause of any kind of rupture or of schism.

*   *   *

Let us then look at this unity as it is to be seen in connection with the Holy Spirit and His work. That is the theme of the fourth verse. With his desire to be practical the first thing the Apostle does is to remind us of what we are as members of the Church. In doing so he uses this analogy of the body – 'one body'. Any careful examination of Paul's epistles will lead us to the conclusion that this was his favourite illustration when he was dealing with the doctrine of the Church. He has other illustrations as can be seen in early chapters of this Epistle. In the second chapter he compares the Church to a great empire – 'fellow citizens with the saints'. He also says that Christians are 'members of the household of God', in other words the Church is like a family. Not only so, the Church is like a building, 'You have been builded together on the foundation of the apostles and prophets'. Later, in chapter 5, we shall find him comparing the Church to a bride saying that the Church is the bride of Christ, and that the relationship between the Lord Himself and the Church is the relationship between a husband and wife. But he seems to use this particular illustration of the body more frequently than any other. And particularly in connection with the matter of unity, this appears to give a picture more clearly than any other.

He has already used this illustration twice in this Epistle. He does so at the end of chapter 1 where he writes, 'and hath put all things under his feet, and gave him to be the head over all things to the church, which is his *body*, the fulness of him that filleth all in all'. He has repeated it in the second chapter in the words, 'and that he might reconcile both unto God in one *body* by the cross, having slain the enmity thereby' (v. 16), and in his statement about making of twain one new man he is really using the same illustration (v. 15). In those instances he has merely mentioned it in passing, but here he expounds it. I have often compared Paul's method to that of a musical composer, who in the overture suggests his themes, and no more than suggests them. But then in the body of the work he takes up the suggestions and deals with them and works them out in greater detail.

*   *   *

What does the Apostle mean by referring to the Church as 'one body'? This is a most important question, and especially at the

[51]

present time with all the interest in church unity and ecumenicity. It is surely obvious that the Apostle must of necessity be referring to the mystical, unseen and spiritual Church. It cannot mean the visible and the external church for the good reason that the visible and external church consists of many bodies, a multiplicity of bodies. The Apostle was therefore not thinking of that. He is thinking of the essential Church, the mystical Church which is invisible, the mystical body of Christ. The failure to grasp this very important New Testament principle has led to many tragedies in the history of the Church. Because she fails to understand this, the Roman Catholic Church says that she is the only true church and that all other visible churches are not churches at all. And there have been others who have made the same claim, completely failing to understand the mystical, internal, invisible character of the true and the essential church. The Apostle is therefore asserting that there is only one true Church. There cannot be many because the Church is the body of Christ, and a man cannot have many bodies; there is only one. There is one perfect mystical Church, unseen and spiritual. There is only one body. This Church consists of people of all types and kinds and colours, from many continents and climes. But these diversities make no difference to this invisible, mystical Church. There are people in this Church from all nations under heaven, from all tribes and peoples throughout the earth.

In the same manner time makes no difference to this fact. The early Christians are in this body. The martyrs of the Reformation are in this body. The Puritans, the Covenanters, the first Methodists, they are all in this body; and you and I are in this body if we are truly in Christ. The Church spans the centuries. Natural abilities play no part in this matter. It matters not what you may be, whether you are ignorant or knowledgeable, clever or lacking in faculties, great or small, wealthy or poor. All these things are utter irrelevancies; this body is one. It is the Church of all the ages – the fulness of God's people. It is the only body, it is the unseen, mystical Church. The one thing that ultimately matters for each one of us is that we belong to this body. We can be members of a visible 'church' and, alas, not be members of this mystical unseen Church. The New Testament itself teaches so. Membership of a visible 'church' may be as useless as circumcision was in the days of the early Church. The one thing that matters is that we are found in this mystical, unseen, spiritual Church which alone is the body of Christ.

*   *   *

There are certain things that we must understand about this 'mystical, unseen Church', and clearly Paul felt that this picture, this analogy of the body, conveys them well. The best way for us to grasp this teaching is to consider what the Apostle says in the twelfth chapter of his First Epistle to the Corinthians, where he deals with it in a most exhaustive manner. The first thing that emerges is the organic character of the unity that is in the Church. The Church is a new creation, and in bringing her into being God has done something as entirely new as was the creation of the universe. He did not simply take a Jew and a Gentile and bring them together somehow in a kind of coalition, and make them sit down together round a table and agree to be friendly. No! The Church is a new creation. She is not a collection of parts. The old has been destroyed, there is no longer Jew and Gentile. That distinction is done away with in this body. There has been a destruction before there has been a new creation. We have been delivered from the things which separated us before God 'created of twain one new man'.

This can be seen plainly in the analogy of the body. The body consists of ten fingers, ten toes, two hands, two feet, two legs, two arms, and so on. But the body is not a collection of these parts; and not one of them has been created independently or separately and then put together. That is not how the body develops and comes into being. As we have said earlier, it all starts from one cell which begins to develop and to grow and shoots off little buds. One of these buds will eventually be the right forearm and arm and hand; another goes off to form the same on the left. Then the bud that forms the trunk comes down, and the legs come off the trunk. It all comes out of the original primitive cell. The parts have never had an independent being, they are all offshoots, outgrowths of this central primitive cell. That is why there is an essential unity in the body.

The illustration shows that which is true of us as members of the true Christian Church. It is at this point that the visible churches, which are essential, may well mislead us. What happens in them is that there is a church roll, and when a person joins a church his name is added to those already in membership. It has to be done that way, but it tends to give us a false notion of the nature of the mystical Church. We are not added to Christ in that sense. The true church is a new creation, and all who belong to her are born of the Spirit, born of Christ, 'partakers of the divine nature'. Once we see the truth in such terms, the inevitability of the unity is obvious.

The second element which the Apostle emphasizes is the diversity in the unity. This scarcely needs any exposition because it is so obvious. To state the matter negatively, what we see in the Church is unity, not uniformity. In his use of the analogy in 1 Corinthians chapter 12 the Apostle uses sarcasm and ridicule. He had received letters from those who belonged to the household of Chloe and from others, telling him that one member was saying 'I am of Paul', another 'I am of Apollos', another 'I am of Cephas'. They were divided into factions and were wrangling and arguing. The Apostle's way of dealing with that is to tell them that they had clearly forgotten that the Church is the body of Christ. That, he says, is as if the eye says to the hand, 'I have no need of thee', and the foot says the same to the ear. He ridicules all that, and proceeds to teach the principle that in the Church, as in the human body, there is diversity in unity.

Both these truths must be emphasized. Any teaching that represents the members of the Church as manifesting a dull uniformity is unscriptural. There is variety in the essential unity. Look at a finger and contrast it with an eye. At first there does not seem to be anything in common. The finger seems very ordinary. But then consider the eye. I sometimes think that there is no instrument in the world that is comparable to the eye. Think of its delicacy, its subtlety, the refinement, the balance, the tenderness – what an instrument! At first sight it appears as if there can be no relationship at all between an eye and a finger, or a foot, or other parts of the body which are still less comely. And yet the truth is that though they are all so different, look so different, and subserve different functions, they are all one in this essential sense that they all belong together and are all essential parts of the body. The body is not complete without every one of them being there. Diverse, yet one!

Then take the analogy in terms of the interdependence of any one part upon the others. Not one of them has any real sense or meaning or existence on its own in and of itself. As the Apostle puts it, if the whole of the body were a hand it would not be a body. If the whole were a foot it would not be a body. What makes the body a body is that all these various parts are one in this organic whole, in this essential unity; and they are all absolutely interdependent on one another. The eye cannot say to the hand, I have no need of you. If you have no hands you will find yourself very crippled and rather helpless. The eye cannot work the whole body. There is no independence in the body. Each part derives its meaning, its essence, from its relationship to the rest. That is the truth about the body; and it is equally true, says the Apostle, about the Church. Each organ needs the others, and each one benefits by the functions of the others.

Then look at his argument about the less comely parts. He says that if you have a right conception of the body you will not despise any part of your body. No part is unimportant. Every part counts. Every single member of the Church is important. People sometimes say of themselves in the church, 'I am not a very important member'; to which the reply is that there is no such thing as an unimportant member. What they mean, of course, is that they do not have some very obvious striking or unusual gifts that others have. They may mean that they cannot speak or preach or pray in public eloquently. But they are despising the gift that they have got. 'On the less comely members we bestow the more abundant honour', says Paul. In the life of the church every member is essential to the harmonious working of the whole. I have sometimes stated it thus, that the mere fact that you are a member of a church and sit in a seat, is a great thing in and of itself. It helps the preacher because it is disheartening to a preacher to have empty seats in front of him. In the church, persons and actions all matter; and therefore anything we do to cut across this idea of the interdependence is not only being false to the doctrine, it is introducing an artificial division, it is being guilty of schism in some shape or form.

*   *   *

Another principle that is evident is that all the parts of the body work together to the same grand end and have the same objective. Each part of the body has its own function, but it plays its part in the whole. A man thinks with his brain and acts with his will. But he must have some instrument through which to carry out his purpose. If I want to shut a book I do so with my hands; I think it, I will it, but I put it into practice with my hands. If I am without hands and without arms I cannot shut the book. So all the parts subserve one great function, and they all work to the same great end and objective. The Church is the body of Christ, and we are members in particular. The Apostle has already told the Ephesians that it is through the Church that God is going to reveal certain things, 'to the intent that now unto the principalities and powers in heavenly places might be known by the Church the manifold wisdom of God' (3:10). The principalities and powers are looking down from heaven; and it is through the Church, through you and through me, every one of us, all of us together, that these principalities and powers are really beginning to understand the manifold wisdom of God. It is to that we are called.

*   *   *

But let us not forget one other matter mentioned by the Apostle in 1 Corinthians 12. Because of this essential unity, if one member suffers all the members suffer with it. You cannot say 'My little finger only is ill'. No! If the little finger is ill you are ill. If there is pain there, you are feeling pain. You cannot divorce yourself from your little finger. Because of the unity of the body the same blood flows in all its parts. This vital power animates the whole. Hence, if one member suffers, all the members suffer with it; and if one member is honoured, all the members glory with it. If we truly understood this doctrine of the Church, any idea of competition, rivalry, self-seeking, self-importance would be utterly impossible, indeed would be ludicrous. And as and when we are guilty of such things we are simply proclaiming that we have never understood the doctrine of the Church. The way to avoid that error is to be clear about the doctrine. Do not rush to the practicalities; get hold of the doctrine first.

What a privilege we have and enjoy! You and I are members of the body of Christ. That is our relationship to Him. He is the

Head; and we are the several members. There is nothing beyond this, no greater privilege. The Psalmist in Psalm 84 says, 'I had rather be a doorkeeper in the house of my God, than to dwell in the tents of wickedness'. That was wonderful – to be a door keeper in the palace of the King, as it were. But this New Testament blessing goes infinitely beyond that! We are in Christ, we belong to Him. As Christians we are parts of His spiritual, mystical body. 'Now ye are the body of Christ, and members in particular'. If we realize that, we shall inevitably 'endeavour to keep the unity of the Spirit in the bond of peace'.

5
'One Spirit'

'There is one body, and one Spirit, even as ye are
called in one hope of your calling; one Lord, one
faith, one baptism, one God and Father of all, who is
above all, and through all, and in you all.'

Ephesians 4:4–6

We turn now to the second term which the Apostle uses. A
number of questions arise at this point, the first being, if the
Church is the body of Christ, and if the Church is like a body,
where has it come from, why has it been formed and come into
being, what constitutes its life? What is it that enables the body
to function? What is it that makes the body a living, vital organism? The Apostle answers these questions at once, by saying that
it is the Holy Spirit – 'one body and one Spirit', with a capital S.
In other words the Church is the result of the activity of the Holy
Spirit Himself. It is He who operates in the Church, in the produc-
tion of the Church and in the maintenance and the well-being and
the life of the Church. The Apostle is concerned to show how
inevitable this doctrine of the unity of the Church is, because of
the fact that the Holy Spirit is in the very centre of the body and
permeates the life and being of the entire organism.

The Apostle says 'one Spirit'. There is only one Holy Spirit;
and He is indivisible. This is really the basis of everything the
Apostle has to say here. There is only one Holy Spirit, who is a
Person, and therefore indivisible. There are many evil spirits. In
the sixth chapter of this Epistle the Apostle reminds us that 'We
wrestle not against flesh and blood, but against principalities,
against powers, against the rulers of the darkness of this world,
against spiritual wickedness in high places' (v. 12). There is a
plurality of evil spirits. There are thousands, perhaps millions, of
evil spirits. But there is only one Holy Spirit. There is not a

multiplicity of Holy Spirits corresponding to the multiplicity of
evil spirits. It seems to me that this truth is frequently forgotten.
Still more important is the fact that He is called the *Holy* Spirit.
This is to differentiate Him once and for ever from all these other
spirits.

This same truth is found in the Gospels. Take, for instance, the
case of the poor man of Gadara whom our Lord healed. Recall
the answer which the man gave to our Lord, 'My name is Legion,
for we are many' (Mark 5:9). It was not merely one evil spirit that
was in that poor man, there was a legion of evil spirits in him. We
recall also the illustration our Lord used in his teaching, that if an
evil spirit is cast out by some merely human power he will come
back and bring seven more with him even worse than himself
(Matt. 12:43-45). There are many evil spirits. The biblical teaching
is that there is a great kingdom of evil headed up by the Devil
(Satan), 'the prince of the power of the air'; but he has his
emissaries, his underlings whom he employs – 'principalities,
powers, rulers of the darkness of this world, spiritual wickedness
in high places'. There is a great mass of such powers, a host of
them. But there is only one Holy Spirit, this one blessed Person,
the Third Person in the blessed Holy Trinity. It is He who functions in the Church and creates the unity of the Church. And this
unity is indivisible because the Person of the Spirit is obviously
indivisible. We must always bear in mind also the fact that the
Spirit in the Church is not an influence. We must never speak of
Him as 'it', as we often tend to do. The Holy Spirit is a Person. He
is as much a Person as the Father. He is as much a Person as the
Son. 'When *he* shall come', says our Lord, *He* will do certain
things.

*   *   *

We can deduce certain other truths from this which will also help
to bring out and emphasize the indivisibility, and therefore the
unity of the Church. Because it is the Holy Spirit Himself, and
because the work is His work, we are entitled to say that He
always does the same work; and it is because He does the same
work in us all that there is this essential unity in the Church. We
must not misunderstand at this point. There are minor and
superficial differences in the manifestations of His work, but it is

all essentially one. It has often been pointed out that there are no two flowers which are absolutely identical. They belong to the same family, the same group, the same species; but there are no two that are perfectly identical. You may have two buttercups, for instance. They are both buttercups but there is always some minute difference. The same is true of the members of a family, even in the case of what we call 'identical twins'. But they are never actually identical; they may appear to be almost so, and yet there is always some difference. The same applies in the Christian life. Because the work is that of the Holy Spirit it is always the same work; but Christian people are not like postage stamps. This is of the greatest importance because it provides us with one of the best ways of differentiating between the work of the Holy Spirit and man's work. Man goes in for mass-production, and works in a mechanical manner, with the result that there is a sameness in what he does and produces. Psychological methods also produce the same kind of person, the same type. This sameness is one of the ways in which the spurious and the false and the counterfeit always tend to reveal themselves. But when the Holy Spirit does God's work within us, it is in all cases essentially the same work, but it is always a living vital work, not mechanical and not identical in detail.

In his teaching at the end of the second chapter the Apostle has already touched on this matter. Comparing the Church to a building, he wrote: 'In whom all the building, fitly framed together, groweth unto an holy temple in the Lord' (v. 21). The Apostle was probably thinking of the account of the building of the temple in the Old Testament. We are told that the stones were prepared before they were brought and put into the building. This work was done far away in a quarry so that there should be no noise of hammers heard as the actual building was being erected. But there was this preliminary work of preparation. The stones as found in the quarry were not to be used; they had to be trimmed and shaped in order that they might fit into their appropriate positions in the walls and thus together become part of the building. In the same way a work of preparation is absolutely essential in us before we can be parts of the Church. Much has to be done to the natural man before he can become a member of the body of Christ, or a stone in this glorious edifice which is the temple of God. Failure to realize this and to remember it accounts for most of the problems in the life of the Christian Church today, as it has always done throughout the centuries.

The visible Church, alas, is composed of many who have never undergone this work of regeneration; and that is why, as we have already said, they may belong to the visible, but not to the invisible Church. There are many and varied ways in which people become members of the visible church. It is sometimes a pure accident of nationality. If you are born in a so-called Christian country, at least if you were so born until comparatively recently, the probability was that you would be brought up in a religious atmosphere. In countries in the world called pagan this would not be true. In other instances it is often a pure accident of belonging to a certain family or to a certain tradition. These are the factors that so frequently operate. Many of us have known what it is to be made a member of a church, not because the Holy Spirit had done anything in us, or to us, but simply because of one of these accidents. When I was personally received as a full member of the Christian church in which I was brought up, I was asked one question only. I was asked to name the brook which our Lord and the disciples had to cross while going from the Upper Room to the place of trial. I could not remember the answer to that question; nevertheless I was received into the full membership of the church. That literally is what happened to me at the age of fourteen. And similar things have happened to many others. Perhaps at a given age the minister or the clergyman had a conversation with your parents, suggesting that it was time for you as an adolescent to become a full member of the church. You may in addition have attended an instruction or preparation class, or confirmation class. You had no living experience; you did not really know what it was about fundamentally; it was 'the thing to do'. That is what so often happens in the visible church; but it does not happen in the invisible Church. You can become a member of the visible church in that way; you will never become a member of the body of Christ in that way. Before we can become members of the body of Christ the Holy Spirit has to do a work of definite preparation. As you are by nature you cannot be bound to the Lord in all His glory and His purity, because by nature you are 'a child of wrath, even as others', 'dead in trespasses and sins'.

The Apostle Paul himself makes this terribly plain and clear in his First Epistle to the Corinthians, where he writes in chapter 6, 'Know ye not that the unrighteous shall not inherit the kingdom of God? Be not deceived: neither fornicators, nor idolaters, nor adulterers, nor effeminate, nor abusers of themselves with mankind, nor thieves, nor covetous, nor drunkards, nor revilers, nor extortioners, shall inherit the kingdom of God. And such were some of you' (vv. 9–11). But they were now in the kingdom. How had it happened? The answer is – 'but ye are washed, but ye are sanctified, but ye are justified in the name of the Lord Jesus, and by the Spirit of our God' (v. 11). Without this work of the Holy Spirit upon us and in us, we are not and cannot be members of the body of Christ. Without it, also, there can be no unity. Individual churches and groups of churches are divided because other elements – the national element, and many other elements – are accounted more important. It is all so unscriptural and unspiritual. The churches, speaking generally, are based upon and governed by man-made traditions. Most of the divisions persist because people have not realized that apart from the work of the Holy Spirit there is no true church, no body of Christ, whatever may be the case externally and in appearance.

*　　*　　*

As we turn, then, to this work which the Holy Spirit does, let us examine ourselves in order to make sure that this preliminary work which is essential before anyone can be a member of the body of Christ, has been done in us. The first work which He always does is conviction of sin. By nature we were satisfied with ourselves, content to go on, imagining that all is well, that we are good people, or perhaps knowing that we are bad people, but still knowing no conviction of sin. But when the Holy Spirit begins to work He convicts us of sin. Our Lord said: 'When He is come, He will convict the world of sin, and of righteousness, and of judgment' (John 16:8). In doing so He causes us to realize something of the truth concerning the holiness of God. We may have talked about God for years; we may have 'said our prayers' to Him, but we have never thought much about Him, and we know nothing about Him truly until the Holy Spirit begins to deal with us.

These two things happen together. I am made to see myself. I begin to understand that the trouble with me is not so much that I do things I should not do, but that I should ever desire to do them. I become aware of the fact that there is something within me that is vile and rotten and wrong, a perverted and a twisted nature; and I begin to realize that I do not know God, that I am really at enmity against God, that there is a hatred of God in the depths of my heart. I was happy to talk about God as He did not interfere in my life, and I could turn to Him when in need and pray to Him for help. But I did not want God to dominate my life, I did not want to be guided by God. The Holy Spirit awakens us to a realization of all this. He also leads us to a conviction of our lost condition, of our emptiness, and our woe. When this happens there is one inevitable result, namely, that we are humbled, we are brought low; we are made to see ourselves as we really are. Our pride is ridiculed and we begin to say with Isaac Watts –

> *'Forbid it, Lord, that I should boast,*
> *Save in the death of Christ my God:*
> *All the vain things that charm me most,*
> *I sacrifice them to His blood'.*

Furthermore,

> *'[I] pour contempt on all my pride'.*

There is nothing left in which we can make our boast, or which makes us think we are better than others. We see the truth about ourselves; and we know that the same is true of others. The Apostle Paul, while Saul of Tarsus and before the Holy Spirit did His work in him, was a great boaster – 'A Hebrew of the Hebrews, of the tribe of Benjamin, circumcised the eighth day', a man who sat at the feet of Gamaliel, the best of scholars, exceeding all others in zeal and energy and the service of God. But later he came to say, 'But what things were gain to me, those I counted loss for Christ'. His privileges and his works had become 'dung' and 'loss'. In writing later to Timothy he said, 'It is a faithful saying, and worthy of all acceptation, that Christ Jesus came into the world to save sinners, of whom I am chief' (1 Timothy 1:15). He had lost his pride, his boasting, his everything; he is nothing;

in his view there was no greater sinner in the universe. Charles
Wesley expresses the same truth in the words –

> *Just and holy is Thy Name,*
> *I am all unrighteousness;*
> *False and full of sin I am,*
> *Thou art full of truth and grace.*

In these happenings we see the work of the Holy Spirit. If every
member of the visible church felt and spoke in such a manner,
there would be no trouble in the church. The work of the Holy
Spirit guarantees unity. If we were all humbled, lying in dust and
ashes and shame and sorrow, and aware of the vileness that is in
ourselves, there would of necessity be unity. The Holy Spirit
produces a unity in failure, a unity in sin, a unity in shame, a unity
in utter helplessness and hopelessness. It is because the members
of the church are not convicted of sin that there is no unity. They
are still holding on to things of which they can boast, things in
which they can glory. Our first great need is to be brought down,
to be humbled and humiliated, to see our nothingness; and this is
the first work of the Holy Spirit in us.

The next step is 'quickening' and 'regeneration'. There is no
absolute order about these matters; but we must have them in
some kind of order in our minds. They seem to happen much at
the same time. This quickening, or regeneration, is the giving to
us of a new principle of life. One cannot be a Christian without
being born again. Our Lord stated this truth once and for ever
to Nicodemus (John 3:1-8). You cannot be a member of the body
of Christ unless you have something of His life in you. You can
join the church or be a member of a society, but you cannot
belong to Christ unless His life is in you. The terms used to
describe this are regeneration, new creation, being born again.
When we are made Christians the Holy Spirit does not merely
improve us a little, He not only gets rid of a few spots and stains
here and there. He does very much more than trim us a little and
as it were put a new coat of paint and a little varnish on us. No!
we have to be re-made from the very foundation. 'You hath he
quickened', says the Apostle at the beginning of chapter 2 of this
Epistle. The Christian is a 'partaker of the divine nature'. He is a
'member of the household of God', of the family of God. I repeat

[64]

that this does not mean that we are identical in every single detail; but it does mean that we have this new life, and it is the same life in every one of us. We are all partakers together of the divine nature of this same essential new life. We belong to the same family, we are related to one another as brothers and sisters; the same blood, as it were, is coursing through our arteries and veins. That is the basis of Christian and Church unity. It is when that is absent that the divisions arise.

The result of this new birth is that we are enabled to exercise faith, and have a measure of understanding. 'For by grace are ye saved, through faith; and that not of yourselves: it is the gift of God' (2:8). We do not stay with this now as we shall have to deal with it later. I but note that it is the same faith in all. According to the Apostle Jude, we are all sharers in 'the common salvation'. There is only 'one Lord, one faith, one baptism'. There is only one blood that can atone for our sins, that can cover us and our sins, and put us right with God – only one! 'There is none other name under heaven given among men whereby we must be saved' (Acts 4:12). The special work of the Holy Spirit is to glorify the Lord Jesus Christ. So the position is that we have all been licking the dust together; then we have all been given this same new life. And we are now all looking together at the same blessed Person. We should have no time to look at one another, to compare and contrast ourselves with one another; we are all to look at Him and to glory in Him. As we are thus united in Him there is no room, there is no time for division. We all have the same desires. 'Blessed are they that do hunger and thirst after righteousness'. We are no longer seeking places of importance and honour and prominence. The real tragedy in the Church is that she has forgotten this doctrine of one body and the one Spirit. The work of the Spirit is forgotten; things which belong to the old natural life raise up their heads and cause schism and division and trouble.

*   *   *

The next step in the work of the Holy Spirit in us is the work of incorporating us into the body of Christ, the Church. Having prepared us He now incorporates us into the one body. He unites us to the Lord Jesus Christ Himself, and therefore we are united to one another. The Apostle Paul states this clearly in 1 Corinthians

12:13 – 'For by one Spirit are we all baptised into one body, whether we be Jews or Gentiles, whether we be bond or free; and have been all made to drink into one Spirit'. Note again the capital S. It is the Spirit who baptises us into the body of Christ. This is unconscious work as far as we are concerned in experience; but because it is a fact we gradually become conscious of it as we live together – 'We know that we have passed from death to life because we love the brethren' (1 John 3:14).

The Holy Spirit then animates the life of the whole body Himself. The Apostle expresses that truth in the First Epistle to the Corinthians: 'Know ye not that ye are the temple of God, and that the Spirit of God dwelleth in you? If any man defile the temple of God, him shall God destroy; for the temple of God is holy, which temple ye are'. (1 Cor 3:16–17). When he says, 'Know ye not that ye are the temple of God?' he is speaking of the Church collectively. In chapter 6 of that Epistle he speaks about the individual when he says, 'Know ye not that your bodies are the temple of the Holy Ghost?' – but in chapter 3 he refers to the Church. The Holy Spirit Himself is the Agent through whom, and by means of which, the organic unity of the body is preserved. He is in this matter comparable to the life of our physical bodies, or indeed to the blood in our physical bodies. He is the unifying Spirit which connects all together and makes them one; and when He is not present the body is dead. That is why we speak of a 'dead' church. But in so doing we are not speaking of the invisible Church because she is never dead, but always alive. We can go further and say that while He animates the whole body He animates each separate part also at the same time. That is seen in the contrast between 1 Corinthians 3:16–17, and 1 Corinthians 6:19–20. This is a great mystery, but it is a fact. The Holy Spirit does exactly the same work of sanctification in every single one of us. Sanctification means our being made like the Lord Jesus Christ, and therefore all who are being sanctified must have a fundamental similarity because they are all becoming more and more like Him; and ultimately, as the Apostle John says, 'When he shall appear we shall be like him' (1 John 3:2). Then we shall be perfectly sanctified; every spot and wrinkle will have gone, and we shall be like Him and like one another. The Spirit's work of sanctification is the same in all.

[66]

This in turn leads on to the fact that the Holy Spirit produces the same fruit in all of us, when He is dwelling in us. Controlling us, He produces His own fruit in us, which is always the same. It is always 'love, joy, peace, longsuffering, gentleness, goodness, faith, meekness, temperance'. Wherever the Christian may be, in England or America or China or Japan, the fruit of the Spirit is always the same; and where such fruit is present there is of necessity unity. We cannot of ourselves produce such fruit, it is He alone who can do so. We see all this very clearly in 1 Corinthians 13, the great hymn of love. If we all corresponded to that picture there would never be any divisions. None of us would be puffed up; we would all be hoping all things for one another and believing the best about one another. We would have that love that never faileth. It is as the Spirit does His work that this unity comes into being. What divides us is our natural personalities. They are sinful and they divide; they assert themselves, and there is always the element of selfishness and of self-centredness. And there is inevitably a clash of personalities. When you become a Christian you do not lose your personality in a fundamental sense, but you are no longer governed by your personality; your personality is governed by the Holy Spirit, and so through your personality the various graces, the fruit of the Spirit, begin to show themselves. We all recognize this fruit when we see it; and we love it in one another. These awkward, angular personalities of ours no longer obtrude themselves. We ourselves, our personalities, are there, but there is so much fruit that we cannot be seen. Nothing is to be seen but the graces; and so there is this blessed, wondrous unity.

Paul states this very clearly in the fifth chapter of his Epistle to the Galatians. He contrasts there what he calls 'the works of the flesh' and 'the fruit of the Spirit'. 'Now the works of the flesh are manifest, which are these – adultery, fornication, uncleanness, lasciviousness, idolatry, witchcraft, hatred, variance, emulations, wrath, strife, seditions, heresies, envyings, murders, drunkenness, revellings, and such like'. Each one of these works divides, and so the Apostle adds, 'of the which I tell you before, as I have also told you in time past, that they which do such things shall not inherit the kingdom of God'. How can they? Such things lead to division, to war; they are ugly and vile. But then he describes a

[67]

completely contrasting picture and we seem to be looking at a magnificent orchard, full of beautiful fruit. We must look at the individual specimens. 'But the fruit of the Spirit is love'. And love always unites. Then 'joy'. This also unites. Our Lord says that the woman who found her lost coin went out and said to her neighbours, 'Rejoice with me, for I have found the piece which I had lost' (Luke 15:9). The shepherd who had found his lost sheep spoke similarly. Then 'peace', the opposite of war and division. 'Longsuffering', instead of fighting and division. 'Gentleness, goodness, faithfulness, meekness, temperance'. These terms are self-explanatory, and each one promotes unity. When the Holy Spirit produces this fruit there is no room left for division or discord. He thus produces the unity; and our business is, 'with all lowliness and meekness, and with longsuffering, forbearing one another in love', to keep this 'unity of the Spirit in the bond of peace'. The Spirit is represented in the form of a dove which from the days of Noah's ark represents gentleness and peace; and this work in us always produces gentleness and peace. His work in us always produces such fruit, and so leads to unity.

Has He done His work in you? Has He done the work of preparation and the work of incorporation? Is He dwelling in you, and is He producing His glorious, gracious fruit in you?

*

6
Revival

'There is one body, and one Spirit, even as ye are called in one hope of your calling; one Lord, one faith, one baptism, one God and Father of all, who is above all, and through all, and in you all'.

Ephesians 4:4–6

We continue our study of the fourth verse: 'There is one body, and one Spirit, even as ye are called in one hope of your calling', and we do so particularly in the light of the account which we have in the second chapter of the Book of the Acts of the Apostles of what happened on the Day of Pentecost at Jerusalem. That event is basic not only in our understanding of the doctrine of the Holy Spirit but also of the question of the unity of the Christian Church. That is why Whit-Sunday, the anniversary of the Day of Pentecost, has come to be regarded as a festival of the Church which emphasizes the question of unity. That is good as long as we approach it in a scriptural, and not in a sentimental manner.

So far we have been dealing with what we may call, for lack of a better term, the ordinary or regular work of the Holy Spirit. That work can be divided into ordinary and extraordinary, into that which is usual and that which is special. This is an important distinction. In addition to His regular work in all Christians, the Holy Spirit gives particular gifts to individual members of the Church. The Apostle teaches in the twelfth chapter of his First Epistle to the Corinthians that He gives apostles, prophets, teachers; also that some Christians have gifts of miracles, some have healings, some have faith, and so on. In doing so he reminds us of the truth that it is only as we realize that the gifts are from the Spirit that we have true unity. The moment we begin to think of them as something we possess, or something of which we can boast, there is division. This was one of the main causes of division in the church at Corinth; some had very special gifts and others had ordinary gifts. Trouble arose because the men with the special gifts were despising those with the ordinary gifts; and the ordinary were envious of the special; and so the church was divided. But they were also dividing about the personalities of certain of their teachers; some said 'I am of Paul', others 'I am of Apollos', and others said they were followers of Cephas. In other words, failing to realize that every gift, including apostles and teachers, comes from the Spirit, they were attributing the gifts to persons and thus they were causing division. The antidote to that evil is to realize that there is only one Spirit, that He is the Giver of all these gifts, and that He dispenses them severally according to His own sovereign pleasure and wisdom.

The Apostle Paul, speaking of himself and his ministry, states this very plainly in his Second Epistle to the Corinthians when he says, 'We have this treasure [this power to preach and this understanding of the gospel] in earthen vessels, that the excellency of the power might be of God and not of us' (4:7). He says in effect that this is the explanation of his frequent physical weakness, of his being cast down, and of his bearing about in the body the dying of the Lord Jesus. It is clear that the Apostle Paul had a constant personal struggle with physical infirmity, with weakness, disease of his eyes, and various other troubles. In the light of this, he says, no one could attribute the character and results of his ministry to him. He suffered these things in order that it might be clear that the power that worked in him, and through him, was not his own, but the power of God through the Lord Jesus Christ, and the blessed Holy Spirit.

*   *   *

A yet more special work of the Holy Spirit is that which is manifested in what we call the ordinary operations of the Spirit that go on constantly in the Christian Church, week in, week out. People are brought under conviction, believers are made to see their inadequacy and their unworthiness, and stimulated to pray. The Holy Spirit does His work of sanctification in the Church constantly; but there is also clearly taught in the Scripture, and in history, an unusual, extraordinary, and special work of the Spirit from time to time. We can regard this as general and particular.

[70]

The general extraordinary work of the Spirit is seen in the life of the Church at large; the particular in individuals in the Church. It is the general extraordinary work of the Spirit which is called Revival. There is no subject which is of greater importance, or of greater urgency, for the consideration of the Christian Church today than this subject of Revival. If I have any understanding of the times, if I have any understanding of the biblical teaching concerning the nature of the Church, and the work of the Holy Spirit, I do not hesitate to assert that the only hope for the Church at the present time lies in Revival. I see no hope in any kind of movement or organization or any special effort planned by men. The one supreme need of the Church is Revival.

I would define a Revival as a repetition in some degree, or in some measure, of that which happened on the Day of Pentecost in Jerusalem, as recorded in the second chapter of the Book of the Acts of the Apostles. It is a pouring out, or pouring forth, of the Spirit of God upon a number of people at the same time. Sometimes it has involved one church, sometimes a district or a neighbourhood, sometimes a whole country. The effect of this in general is that the Church is raised up to a new level of experience and of understanding; and at the same time many outside the Church, and some who are only nominally in the Church, are convicted and are converted and are brought into a saving knowledge of the Lord Jesus Christ. It is important that we should be clear about this definition, because there is an unfortunate teaching today on the part of many to regard an evangelistic campaign as a revival, and to announce it as a revival. We shall see as we proceed that that is an impossible definition of revival. You cannot announce a revival, you cannot say that a revival is going to start on a particular day, as such people do. They put up posters announcing Revival Meetings. That is impossible by definition: what they mean is an evangelistic campaign, which is something entirely different from a revival. A revival may break out in an evangelistic campaign, but a revival is not an evangelistic campaign in and of itself.

We must consider this subject from many aspects. There are many Christians today who never even consider this question of revival. In fact many disapprove of it and say that it should not be preached, and that most certainly it should not be sought.

They are afraid of anything which produces enthusiasm or fervour. There are many reasons for this attitude. There is, for instance, a type of sacramental teaching which leaves no room for the doctrine of revival. It teaches that the Holy Spirit exerts His influence only through the sacraments, and that the sacraments act miraculously. You receive grace in a wafer or through the water of baptism. Grace has been mechanized and linked with things material. According to this view the Church goes on receiving grace and the influence of the Spirit through the sacraments, and can only receive them through the sacraments. Hence you will never read of revival in the so-called 'Catholic' sections of the Christian Church. They have mechanized the working of the Spirit, and they have tied it down to the sacraments; and they exclude any other possibility. They regard what happened on the Day of Pentecost as wild enthusiasm. Of course they do not say so; but that is what they are really saying in effect. Everything is under the control of the priest; the life of the Church is maintained in this quiet manner constantly, and blessing must always come about in that way.

Another school of thought is sometimes found among evangelical Christians. It teaches that the Holy Spirit was given once and for all on the Day of Pentecost. He came upon and into the Church then. It is therefore wrong, they argue, to pray for an outpouring of the Spirit. There was only one outpouring, there can never be another, and it is incorrect to pray for another. The Holy Spirit is in the Church, they teach, and all you have to do is to surrender yourself to His influence and His power. He will then fill you and all who do the same; and so the Church will be filled with the Spirit. But, they teach, you must never ask for an outpouring, you must not ask our Lord to send and shed forth again the Spirit as He did on the Day of Pentecost. This is obviously a very serious matter, for if such teaching is correct there is really no room for revival, and we should certainly not pray for revival. But it is surely quite un-scriptural.

In the Acts of the Apostles itself there is teaching which shows that it is quite wrong, for the Holy Spirit was not only shed forth, and came upon and filled the Church, on the Day of Pentecost only, but this happened subsequently. In chapter 4 of the Book of the Acts we read: 'And when they had prayed, the place was shaken where they were assembled together, and they were all filled with the Holy Ghost, and they spake the word of God with boldness' (4:31). That is surely a repetition of what happened on the Day of Pentecost. Here are these apostles and other disciples and followers who had been baptized and on whom the Holy Ghost had come on the Day of Pentecost. Two of the apostles had been in prison because of their preaching; after their release they went back to the assembled church, and they all prayed together and asked God to have mercy upon them and to vindicate them. The Holy Spirit then came upon them, and the very walls began to shake; and they were all filled again with the Spirit, and boldly testified concerning the resurrection. A similar thing happened in Samaria as recorded in chapter 8 of Acts; and again at Caesarea in the household of Cornelius. The Holy Spirit, we are told, fell upon him and the assembled company, as He had done on the Day of Pentecost at Jerusalem. Peter, who was sceptical and hesitant about admitting Gentiles into the Church, had to admit when he saw that the Spirit had been poured upon them 'even as on us at the beginning', that God had received them (Acts 10 and 11). The same is true of those disciples whom the Apostle Paul found at Ephesus, as recorded in chapter 19 of Acts.

*   *   *

In addition to that, and outside the history recorded in the Canon of the New Testament, there is the amazing history of the Christian Church herself. As we look at the subsequent history of the Church what you find is that the story of the Church has not been one of a constant level of achievement and advance and success. On the contrary we find a history of ups and downs throughout the running centuries. Indeed there is a sense in which it can almost be said that the history of the Church is the history of revivals followed by periods of deadness and then by the coming of revival again. We see the wonderful beginning in the Book of Acts and read of the mighty power and the trans-forming things that happened. But that gradually passed away and we move on to the Dark Ages, the Dark Middle Ages, that period of torpor and lethargy and of lifelessness in an evangelical sense, in the history of the Christian Church. In spite of this there had been occasional movements of the Spirit, condemned by the institutional church as heretical movements – the Montanists, the Cathari, the Waldenses and others. Then came the brilliant, blazing Protestant Reformation, which was a true 'revival', a return to the Book of Acts, a restoration of the ancient power, and all to which it led. But again that seemed to pass, until we come to the Puritan era, which in some senses was a revival. Then came the great revivals of the eighteenth century in several countries. And there were further revivals in the nineteenth century, notably from 1857 to 1859. Such has been the history of the Church. That any Christians should therefore teach that we are not to look and long for and pray for revival and expect it, and look for an out-pouring of the Spirit of God, seems to me not only to be un-scriptural but to be a denial of what is most glorious in the history of the Church.

It is in fact vital to realize that revivals are God's way of keeping His work alive. This is seen also in the Old Testament. We find the children of Israel falling into sin, forgetting God, and becoming indolent and slack; then God suddenly raises a prophet or a king and revives His work among them. This is seen in the times of King Josiah, and King Hezekiah, and at other times. These are revivals in which God manifested Himself and something of His glory. And so it has proved to be throughout the long history of the Christian Church. There have been times when true Christian-ity had almost disappeared, and certain clever sceptics and infidels were quite confident that the end had come. It is just at such times that God sends revival and the moribund Church is raised to a new period of activity and success and glory.

Looking at the matter from a different angle, we can say that there is nothing which so clearly proves the supernatural and divine character of the Church, and which so evidently shows the work of the Holy Spirit, as a revival. It is in revivals that we see clearly that it is the power of the Spirit that really matters, and alone matters, in the Church; and above all that there is nothing that so promotes unity in the Church as a mighty spiritual revival and re-awakening. As I have stressed repeatedly, the tragedy of the modern situation is that men think of unity in the Church in terms of organization, not in terms of this power of the Spirit: for it is the Spirit alone who can produce unity. Unity is always vital, energetic, organic; and it is only the Holy Spirit of God who can produce it in the church.

*   *   *

Bearing this in mind, let us see what the history of revivals teaches us. The first thing we discover when we read the history of revivals illustrates this point concerning unity perfectly. The history of all revivals is almost always identical in character. This is truly astonishing, because it is not true about the general history of mankind. There are differences in the reactions to life, and in the behaviour of men in general from age to age and from country to country. There are local customs, there are national customs; there are characteristics that belong to one century which do not belong to another, and so on. But the remarkable thing about every revival is that it seems to be like every other revival. Whether it is in the first century or the sixteenth century, the seventeenth century or the eighteenth, the nineteenth or the twentieth century, it is always the same. The history of any revival always reminds us of the second chapter of the Book of the Acts of the Apostles. There is always, as it were, a return to that initial outpouring of the Spirit. The explanation of this is that revival is essentially the work of the same Spirit. There is only one Spirit, and He always works in revival in the same fundamental manner. This applies not only to all centuries but also to all countries.

These details are of great importance, because there is nothing that is more strengthening to faith than to observe such facts. Take, for instance, the history of the Reformation of the sixteenth century. That Reformation took place at much the same time in Germany, Switzerland, France, and this country. Now is that an accident? Can that fact be explained in human terms? Revival cuts across national barriers, it demolishes all these distinctions. This is seen strikingly in the second chapter of Acts. Jews and proselytes had come together at the feast of Pentecost; they had come from various countries and had the characteristics of those countries; and yet they were all made one, as it were, by the Holy Spirit. This is always the characteristic of a revival.

Another remarkable fact is the way in which revival happens in a variety of places at the same time, as I have already remarked in regard to the sixteenth-century Reformation. The eighteenth century shows precisely the same phenomenon. In 1734 there was the beginning of a revival in America in the New England States, in a little town called Northampton where the minister was the great Jonathan Edwards. Let us not forget what conditions of travel were two hundred years ago; and also that there was no telegraphy, let alone wireless telegraphy. But at the same time a revival occurred in Wales in the year 1735. Still more interesting, it broke out in two places in Wales, through the lives of two men who had never met and who had never heard of one another at all – Daniel Rowland and Howel Harris. They met two years later, and when they did so they were astounded at the identity of the things that had happened to them. It happened in a village where Rowland was an ordained clergyman, a curate; it happened in the other place about fifty to sixty miles distant through the life of Harris who was a schoolmaster, and who was never ordained. The same thing happened to the two men at the same time; and they were led to similar things. In 1736–7 the same thing happened in the life of George Whitefield; and in 1738 in John Wesley and Charles Wesley. A little later in Scotland in the lives of godly ministers and in churches in Cambuslang and Kilsyth there was this same movement of the Spirit. It is surely remarkable and amazing that these movements of the Spirit should take place at the same time among people who had little or no contact with one another.

Likewise in the nineteenth century the same happened again. In 1857 a great revival broke out in America, then in Ulster in 1858 and in Wales and parts of England in 1859. The point I am emphasizing is that these things cannot be explained in human, naturalistic terms. It is the one Spirit operating in His Church, and He does the same thing at the same time. This has indeed been true in this present century. There was a revival in Wales in 1904 and 1905, and also in Korea at almost exactly the same time, 1905 and 1906. So it has happened throughout the ages. These undoubted facts should awaken us to see that this is how God acts, and that this is the only hope for the Church, and above all. that we must pray for this.

*　　　*　　　*

Turning to the features and characteristics of a revival we find in general what we read of at the beginning of the second chapter of Acts. 'And when the day of Pentecost was fully come, they were all with one accord in one place. And suddenly' – revivals come suddenly and often unexpectedly. The Apostles and others were waiting because the Lord had told them what would happen 'not many days hence'. They were praying together 'with one accord' because they knew something was going to happen; but they did not know when. 'And suddenly . . .' In the subsequent history of the Church we can add to the word 'suddenly' the word 'unexpectedly'. We should thank God for this, because it brings us strong consolation in an arid period such as this in which we are living.

We cannot tell when the Holy Spirit is going to visit us and to revive His work. The point I would emphasize is that He comes. It is He who comes. 'And suddenly there came a sound from heaven as of a rushing mighty wind, and it filled all the house where they were sitting; and there appeared unto them cloven tongues like as of fire'. Revival is not the result of anything that men do. It is something that men cannot do. This, too, appears regularly in the history of revivals. Often, we find that God has used one particular person more than any others in a time of revival. And often we find that the man He chooses is a man whom no man would have chosen. It is not always some great or gifted or unusual man. It is sometimes some very humble and inconspicuous man, thus demonstrating the fact that it is the Spirit's work. It cannot be explained in terms of men or their gifts or personalities. So the honour and the glory must be given to the Holy Ghost. 'Not by might, nor by power, but by my Spirit, saith the Lord'.

* * *

Nothing is more profitable than the reading of the history of revivals. You will find that sometimes revival has come after a group of people, perhaps a mere handful, who were almost breaking their hearts because of the state of religion in their district, and because of the deadness and lifelessness of their church, met together to pray God to intervene. They were almost at the point of giving in, perhaps, but still they went on with their little prayer-meeting. One day they had gone to the meeting more or less dejected and disconsolate, but there they were praying, when 'suddenly' they were all aware that something had happened; the Spirit of God had come upon them, and they were transformed. The meeting could not end, as it were. This continued the next day and for months, and people came from everywhere to see what was happening. That is how God acts in revival – suddenly, unexpectedly, it comes.

What happens is that such Christians suddenly become aware of a presence, of a power, of a glory, and are filled with a sense of marvel. The word 'marvel' is found in the second chapter of the Book of the Acts: 'They were all amazed and marvelled, saying one to another . . .' The Apostles and the others were themselves filled with a sense of wonder. What happens at such a time is that God the Holy Spirit makes His presence felt so powerfully that men and women who may have believed the gospel for years are suddenly aware with a new directness of the glory of God, and of the majesty of God, and of the greatness of God. It is no longer a matter of faith; there is a kind of directness. They feel and know that God is there, God seems to be filling the building. This is, of course, entirely beyond understanding and explanation, and even beyond expression and description. The Church does not understand it; the world understands it still less.

Its effect upon the believers is to give them a new clarity of understanding of truths they have previously believed. The Apostles began to speak, we are told, about 'the wonderful works of God'. Christian people in a time of revival have often said that they have seen things more clearly in a second than in the whole of their previous lives. There is the well-known experience of John Flavel, the Puritan, who once had an amazing experience along these lines when alone. He said that he learned more in that one experience than in the whole of his life of Bible reading and of reading books about the Bible, and prayer. There is a new sense of clarity, a luminosity with respect to it all. That is what happens, and that is how the Holy Spirit produces unity. People who have been doubtful and uncertain and hesitant, and therefore arguing with one another, are suddenly filled with the Holy Spirit and with a new understanding. They feel that they almost see the Lord Jesus Christ and they know Him as the Son of God and their Saviour with a new certainty. It happens to all who experience it, and so there is a real unity.

[78]

The tragedy is that men are trying to produce unity by telling us that it does not matter very much what we believe, that as long as we all come together and work together, and do not argue about doctrine, we shall all be one. But the unity of the Spirit comes through understanding, not through discounting understanding and saying that the knowledge of doctrine does not matter. The great characteristic of revival is that men understand the doctrine and the truth in a way they have never done before. Not only so, they begin to rejoice as they have never done before, and are filled with an assurance and a sense of certainty of their relationship to God. They are sometimes so filled with joy that others looking at them say, 'These men are filled with new wine'. But it is 'the joy of the Holy Ghost'; they are thrilled with this new sense of their relationship to God, Father, Son and Holy Spirit.

This, in turn, leads to a desire to tell others, and so they begin to speak and to tell forth these 'wonderful works of God'. The Apostles did so with a boldness and an authority they had never known before. The Peter who had denied that he knew Christ but a few weeks before, because he was afraid he was going to be put to death, spoke on the Day of Pentecost with boldness and authority. He chastised the Jews and condemned them, and held them face to face with judgment. The greatest need of the Church today is such boldness, authority and power. What can we do with a generation such as this in which we find ourselves, with its pride of knowledge and learning, its scoffing and its arrogance? Through the power of the Holy Spirit it can be shaken, convicted of sin, and renewed. Man cannot do this work, but the Spirit can, as He did on that Day of Pentecost, and as He has done from time to time since then in periods of mighty revival.

One cannot but note in the records in the Book of Acts the sense of oneness which believers had. They all kept together. At one stage they even sold their goods and lived a kind of communal life. This was because they felt that they were one, not in a mechanical sense but because nothing mattered now but this new life. They had been fused together; they all felt the Spirit overwhelming them and governing them. This sense of unity is inevitable when the Spirit is present in power.

*　　　*　　　*

Looking at the other side of the picture we see the effect this had upon others. They came running together asking, 'What is this?' And Peter preached, and they were convicted and broken down. Jews who had cried but recently about our Lord, 'Away with him, crucify him', listening to the preaching about Him cried out, 'Men and brethren, what shall we do?' This always happens in times of revival. There are certain people of whom one would be tempted to say, speaking naturally, that nothing could ever convert them, who are suddenly convicted and converted by the Holy Spirit. Thus it has happened in all revivals in the Church throughout the centuries.

Nothing so attracts people to the Church as revival. Men are trying to advertise the Church today; the Church is setting up publicity departments, and has publicity agents; and we are told we must advertise the Church to the people. But if a revival were to break out here or anywhere else, there would be no need to advertise it. People would come from everywhere, as they did on the Day of Pentecost, asking 'What is this?' When the power of the Spirit is present people come in amazement, perhaps in curiosity, and often it happens that 'fools who came to scoff remain to pray'.

What are we to do about all this? What is the way to revival? The answer is that we must realize our own impotence, we must realize that in and of ourselves we can do nothing. The power is of God, the agent is the Spirit. What we have to do 'with one accord' is to 'continue steadfastly in the apostles' doctrine and fellowship, and in breaking of bread, and in prayers'. Doctrine must come first. The Holy Spirit's chief work is to glorify the Lord Jesus Christ. So there is no value in our prayers if we do not believe in Him, in His unique deity, in His incarnation, virgin birth, miracles, atoning death, resurrection and ascension. The Spirit glorifies Him, and we must therefore believe in Him and be 'of one accord' in our doctrine.

We must also pray. We must spend our time in praying for the Spirit, as these people prayed during those ten days. And you will find in the history of the Church throughout the ages, that as God's people have prayed, and have been brought to see their own impotence and helplessness, they have gone on in the name of Christ their Saviour and Mediator and have pleaded with God to pour forth His Spirit again. And often when they thought the end had come, and there was no hope, suddenly God answered them and poured forth His Spirit upon them. If you are really burdened by the times in which we live, if you are really grieving in your heart as you see the godlessness of the world, if you have a compassion in your hearts for men and women in the bondage of sin and of Satan, your first duty is to pray for revival. When revival comes more can happen in a day than may happen in a century of the ordinary work of the Church. When He comes in power the stoutest hearts are broken, the mightiest intellects are broken down, and men and women cry out, asking for mercy and seeking to know the way of salvation. The first task, the first duty, of Christian people and of the Christian Church today is to pray 'with one accord' and plead for a repetition of Pentecost, a Holy Ghost revival, God again coming in authority and might and power into the midst of His people. The Holy Ghost is still at hand in all His power; so pray God to send Him. And when He comes we shall see things that will astound us and amaze the scoffing, unbelieving world that is outside.

7
One Hope

'There is one body, and one Spirit; even as ye are called in one hope of your calling'.

Ephesians 4:4

We come now to the third aspect which the Apostle emphasizes in connection with the work of the Spirit: 'even as ye are called in one hope of your calling'. Perhaps the best way to approach this phrase is to ask a question. And, incidentally, one of the secrets of enjoying the study of the Bible is to discover the art of asking questions. In other words, do not simply take the statements as they come; but to make sure that you understand the sequence, stop for a moment and ask a question. Here we have an instance of the value of doing so. The Apostle says, 'There is one body, and one Spirit'. We can understand that sequence, 'There is one body', and it is clear that the life of the body, the power that keeps the body alive and enables it to act, is obviously 'the one Spirit'. The Apostle goes naturally from 'one body' to 'one Spirit'. But then he says, 'even as ye are called in one hope of your calling'. The question is, Why should he add this to 'the one body' and 'one Spirit'? The Apostle did not write this haphazardly or accidentally. There is a logical sequence here and an inevitable connection.

I suggest that there are two reasons which make it inevitable that this should be the third thing he mentions. The first is to understand why the Holy Spirit has done in us who are Christians that which He has done. Why has He called us effectually, as the first verse in our chapter reminds us? While we were dead in sins we were called and quickened by the Holy Spirit: He convicted us of sin, and enabled us to see the merit of Jesus' blood. He gave us new life; He called us out of the world, and baptized us into the body of Christ. Is all this an end in itself, or is there some further purpose behind it all? The answer is that all these things have taken place merely as a preparation for something that is yet to take place. This is a step in a great process; an interim activity which is to lead to a final activity. The Church is not an end in and of itself; the Church is the body, the instrument which God is using through Christ and by the Holy Spirit to call out of mankind a new humanity, a new people for Himself, which He is finally going to perfect and cause to dwell in a renovated glorified world free from all sin. Everything is designed to lead up to that ultimate glory, the final appearance of Christ and the setting up of His eternal kingdom. Thus the sequence 'one body, one Spirit, one hope of your calling' becomes clear. The body is being prepared for the great day that is yet to come.

A second reason why the Apostle introduces this phrase at this point is that the Holy Spirit, in addition to His work of preparing us for incorporation into the body, His special work in revival, does another special work which is more personal. The Apostle has already referred to this in the first chapter where he writes, 'In whom ye also trusted, after that ye heard the word of truth, the gospel of your salvation: in whom also after that ye believed, ye were sealed with that Holy Spirit of promise, which is the earnest of our inheritance until the redemption of the purchased possession' (vv. 13–14). This refers to the work of the Spirit, as a 'seal' and as an 'earnest'. Having made us Christians, having put us into the body of Christ, He seals us, and acts as an earnest; and the whole object of the sealing and the earnest is with respect to the 'purchased possession' of which he speaks. The sealing is, as it were, the stamp placed upon us to show that we belong to God, that we are His children and that we are inheritors of the great inheritance that is coming. The earnest is a foretaste of that inheritance, or the firstfruits of it. It is an instalment which is given us here and now as a guarantee of the fact that we shall receive it fully.

The moment we think of the 'sealing' and 'earnest' aspects of the work of the Holy Spirit we are made to think of this pur-chased possession, this marvellous inheritance that God is pre-paring and holding for them that love Him. That is why Paul says here that there is 'one body, and one Spirit, even as ye are called in one hope of your calling'. That is the inevitable connection. At the same time we see the marvel and the wonder of the Scriptures, their orderly arrangement of truths. As Christians we are not to hold a number of odd unrelated ideas in our minds; there is a plan of salvation, there is a scheme of redemption, and there are steps and stages which lead from one step to the next in a logical inevitability. Here, we have an example of that truth. Any true consideration of the work of the Holy Spirit, therefore, of necessity must lead us to a consideration of the blessed, glorious hope that lies ahead of every true Christian.

*   *   *

The Apostle is repeating himself, and reminding these Ephesian Christians of what he had said in the first chapter where he tells them that he is praying for them, that God may give them 'the spirit of wisdom and revelation in the knowledge of him'. 'The eyes of their understanding being enlightened', he prays that they may know what is 'the hope of his calling'. His desire is that they might know the hope to which God has called them, that they might know and realize and appreciate and understand the grand purpose which God has at the back of this great plan of redemption. 'The hope of his calling'! They must also know 'the riches of the glory of his inheritance in the saints'; and, then, 'the exceeding greatness of his power to us-ward who believe'. In his first chapter, he is praying for it in general, but here he deals with it, and adverts to it, specifically in connection with this principle of unity. He appeals to them 'with all lowliness and meekness, with all longsuffering, and forbearing one another in love', to endeavour 'to keep the unity of the Spirit in the bond of peace', because they are 'called in one hope of their calling'. Nothing so promotes unity, and guards it and keeps it, as our realization of the blessed hope that lies ahead of us, the same glorious inheritance which we are to share.

It is largely because we fail to keep our eye on 'the hope of our calling' that there are so many divisions and distinctions and misunderstandings. We must not only dwell negatively on what we were called from; we must rather dwell on what we are called to. Our tendency is to dwell on that from which we have been called, and to look back at it, and to talk about it. That of necessity causes divisions and distinctions. The devil, our adversary, cannot prevent our becoming Christians, but he can cause much damage among us. One of his methods is to make us look back on that from which we were called, rather than forward to that to which we are called. The result of doing so is shown in the case of the early Church. Some of the believers had been Jews, some Gentiles, some Barbarians, others Scythians; some bond, some free; some male, some female. When they looked back they were reminded of those divisions and distinctions and animosities. So if these things are perpetuated in the life of the Church, of necessity distinctions and divisions arise; and this is one of the most prolific causes of division. In the same way, looking back often reminds us of the fact that the details of one conversion are different from those of another. This is often found in meetings when people relate their experiences or give their testimonies, as it is called. They start with what they once were, and immediately an element of division enters. One may have been a Jew; another a Gentile. Their status in life was different, and their behaviour may have varied from respectability to gross and flagrant sin. At once there are endless divisions.

I can illustrate this by means of an incident that I myself once witnessed. I was engaged with other people in an open-air meeting. I had not originated the meeting, but I was taking part in it with others; and I happened to be in charge on this occasion. I followed the procedure that was usually employed, and this is what happened. One man stepped forward into the ring and he gave his experience, his story, an account of his conversion. He told us that he had been a terrible man, guilty of dreadful sins, but how in spite of that the grace of God had laid hold on him and had converted him. Then another man stepped forward, an older man, a man who had been converted some ten or fifteen years before the first speaker. This is almost literally what he said: 'You have heard our brother telling you about his conversion and about the life of sin out of which he was converted. He does not know what sin is; I will tell you what sin is'. Then he began to describe his former life in lurid detail. It seemed to me that the meeting was becoming a competition in crime. The second man was not conscious of this, but what he was really doing was boasting of his sinfulness; he was drawing a distinction between his sin and the sin of the other man, in order to prove that his conversion was therefore a greater conversion than the conversion of the other. But that is all wrong and utterly unscriptural. All conversions are identical in an ultimate sense. It takes grace and the power of Almighty God to save any soul. It does not matter whether you were Jew or Gentile, male or female, Barbarian, Scythian, bond or free; what you were is irrelevant, it does not matter. But we are constantly perpetuating these differences and divisions with the result that some people are considered to be more important in the Church than others. They are still thought of in terms of what they were by nature, or of their social position, their wealth, their ability, or something else that belongs to the natural man. All this happens because we persist in forgetting that we are not to look at what we were saved from, but should look at what we are saved to.

May I round off this particular matter by repeating the famous story of what happened in the case of Philip Henry, the father of the commentator, Matthew Henry. The young Philip Henry fell in love with a young lady who belonged to a higher class of society than his own; and she fell in love with him. They wanted to get married, so she began to speak to her parents about this. They did not like the proposal. They did not know this man Philip Henry, they did not know his family. The father turned on her at last and asked, 'Where has he come from?' And the daughter, good Christian that she was, gave her immortal answer saying, 'I do not know where he has come from, but I do know where he is going'. What else really matters? As Christians we are to look at 'the hope of our calling'. These other things are the result of the Fall and sin and division. The world was never meant to be divided into Jew and Gentile, Barbarian, Scythian, bond or free, high or low, great and small. We must not look back at those things; we must look forward to 'the hope of our calling'. That hope is one, is always the same, and is for us all.

*   *   *

I would emphasize the fact that we must not only not look back and dwell upon that from which we were saved, but we must not even dwell upon our conversion experiences, that is to say, upon the actual details of the experience of conversion itself, for that

[86]

also is something which inevitably tends to divide us. There are some who have had a very dramatic conversion, involving agonies of repentance and remorse which may have lasted a long time. At last, at some most dramatic moment, they saw the light and were saved. There are others who really cannot give the exact moment, the exact time, of their conversion. It was quiet, almost unobserved. They cannot identify any particular event or moment; but what they do know is that, whereas they were once dead, they are now alive; they know that they love the Lord Jesus Christ, and desire Him above everything else, and want to be with Him and to be like Him. The two types of experience are very different. As a pastor and a minister I can testify to the harm and the damage, the divisions and the distinctions, that stress upon the form of conversion experience causes in the life of the Church.

This works in a variety of ways. Sometimes it does great harm to the man himself who has had the dramatic conversion. He becomes proud of it; he becomes a kind of show piece, he is a different Christian from others, and he tends to despise the man who is not quite sure of the way in which it happened or when it happened. On the other hand the Christian who has had a quiet experience is sometimes made to think that perhaps he is not a Christian at all because his experience does not conform to the dramatic pattern. He is given the impression in meetings where testimonies are given, that only the dramatic is true. The quiet people are never called forward to speak, and so he begins to wonder whether he really is a Christian and in the Kingdom. It is thus that wrong and sinful divisions and schisms often enter into the life of the Church.

Let me emphasize this by repeating something I once heard the famous John Macneil saying in this connection. In a sermon he was imagining a conversation between two of the blind men who were healed by our Lord and Saviour Jesus Christ – the blind man whose healing is recorded in the ninth chapter of John's Gospel and the blind man whose healing is recorded in the eighth chapter of Mark's Gospel. In the case of the man in the ninth of John our Lord spat upon some clay on the ground, and mixed it, and anointed the man's eyes with the mixture of clay and spittle, and told him to go and wash in the Pool of Siloam. In the case of the man in Mark's Gospel He did none of this; and John Macneil was imagining these two men meeting later on and having a conversation together; and he described the conversation in his own inimitable way thus: The man in the ninth of John asked the man in the eighth of Mark, 'What did you feel like when He put that mixture of clay and spittle on your eyes?' 'Clay and spittle?', said the man of Mark 8, 'I do not know anything about clay and spittle'. 'What', said the other man, 'don't you remember how He spat upon the ground and made the mixture and put it on your eyes? I am asking, What did you feel?' But, said the man of Mark 8, 'There was nothing put on my eyes'. And on and on the conversation went, the man in the ninth of John repeating his questions, and the other man displaying his ignorance. At last the man in the ninth of John said to the other, 'Look here, I do not believe you have been healed at all; you must still be blind. If He did not put the clay on your eyes, you are still blind'. 'In other words', said John Macneil, 'two religious denominations came into being at once – the Mud-ites and the Anti-mudites'.

But, alas, that illustrates what happens among us far too frequently. There is this constant tendency to look back. The one way to deal with this problem is to say with the great Apostle Paul, 'Forgetting those things which are behind, and reaching forth unto those things which are before, I press toward the mark for the prize of the high calling of God in Christ Jesus' (Phil 3:13–14). What matters is not how you came into the Kingdom; the vital question is, Are you in the Kingdom? It matters not whether your birth was a dramatic, exciting one, or whether it was quiet and almost unobservable. Thank God, it does not matter! Nowhere are we told in the Scripture that you have to be able to give the precise moment, or the precise verse that was used, or the name of a certain preacher. These things do not matter. The one thing that matters is that you should be in the Kingdom.

Unfortunately there is a great tendency today to look back. We read of special reunions being held of Christians who were saved in a particular campaign or in a given year! Thus the Church is divided in terms of certain evangelists' converts or the particular year of conversion. Thus schisms are caused in the Church. This is sinful; and the cause of the sin is that we are failing to look forward to 'the hope of our calling'. We are not forgetting the things that are behind and looking forward unto the prize of the high calling of God in Jesus Christ as we should.

*   *   *

But we must go yet further and say that we must not even dwell on what we are now. We must always be looking forward, because if we dwell on what we are now there will still be the tendency to divide and to separate. This tendency has come into the Church increasingly in the last hundred years. We divide ourselves into young people, middle-aged, old people; brotherhoods, sisterhoods, and many other groupings. We do so because we persist in looking at ourselves as we are now, instead of looking together at what we are going to be, that is, to 'the hope of our calling'. I am not suggesting that these differences have no significance at all; but I do say they must not be underlined and emphasized. We do not find such divisions in the early church; they were all one. Age differences did not count; and they should not count now. An old man may be a babe in Christ; and a young person can be spiritually mature. The one thing that matters is this unity, this one-ness; the other divisions belong to nature, to time, and to unregenerate man, rather than to the Spirit. The Apostle, although he had advanced further than most people, still says, 'Not as though I had already attained or were already perfect; but I press toward the mark for the prize of the high calling of God in Christ Jesus'. The New Testament everywhere urges us in various ways to look forward. Our Lord says, 'Let not your heart be troubled. Ye believe in God, believe also in me. In my Father's house are many mansions. If it were not so I would have told you' (John 14:1–3). The Apostle Paul in writing to the Romans says, 'For I reckon that the sufferings of this present time are not worthy to be compared with the glory which shall be revealed in us' (Romans 8:18). In his Second Epistle to the Corinthians he says, 'Our light affliction, which is but for a moment, worketh for us a far more exceeding and eternal weight of glory: while we look not at the things which are seen but at the things which are not seen, for the things which are seen are temporal, but the things which are not seen are eternal' (4:17–18). He continues in chapter 5: 'For we know that if our earthly house of this tabernacle were dissolved, we have a building of God, an house not

[89]

made with hands, eternal in the heavens' (v. 1). He writes to Titus thus: 'looking for that blessed hope, and the glorious appearing of the great God and our Saviour Jesus Christ' (2:13). This is the great characteristic of the New Testament teaching. The Apostle John writes in the same manner: 'Beloved, now are we the sons of God, and it doth not yet appear what we shall be: but we know that, when he shall appear, we shall be like him; for we shall see him as he is' (1 John 3:2).

The fact is that we in our folly are constantly looking at the present. We are interested in hydrogen bombs and atomic bombs, and what may be happening in South Africa and the Middle East here and now, and so become divided. One is in favour of fighting, one is against fighting; one takes a certain political view and another takes the opposite; some are socialists, others are conservatives, and so the Church is divided. This is because we look too much at the present and do not look at 'the hope of our calling'. It is not that, as citizens of earthly States, we are not to have views on these matters or take part in applying them: but that they are not to influence us in the Church; still less is the Church herself to be engaged in such matters. By and large we have forgotten that we are strangers and pilgrims in this world.

The fact is that the New Testament does not offer us very much in this world. The Lord Jesus Christ said, 'In the world you shall have tribulation; but be of good cheer, I have overcome the world' (John 16:33). The Apostle Paul re-echoes that by saying: 'In this tabernacle we groan, being burdened, earnestly desiring to be clothed upon with our house which is from heaven' (2 Cor 5:2). 'Now we see through a glass darkly; but then face to face' (1 Cor 13:12). How important it is, therefore, that we should look at this 'calling wherewith we are called' – 'the hope of our calling'! Let us not look back, let us not spend our time in looking at the present and comparing and contrasting ourselves with one another, but let us look forward to 'the hope of our calling'. There is only one hope; there is the same hope for all; and we are all going together to the same glory. There will be no divisions and distinctions there.

*　　*　　*

We are going forward to a life which is entirely free from sin. It is sin that always divides and separates. The object of the coming of our Lord Jesus Christ is that the works of Satan and of sin should be abolished and destroyed (1 John 3:8) and that everything should be re-united again in Him (Ephesians 1:10). And thank God this is coming! There is a day coming when we shall all be faultless and blameless, without spot or wrinkle or any such thing. What a wonderful prospect! Now we have spots and wrinkles. Some have many and some have few. We are all so different, and we look at one another, and there is division. But a day is coming when there will be neither spot nor wrinkle nor any such thing, and we shall all be perfect. There will be no sin in us and there will be no temptation outside us. Not only will sin be taken out of us, it will be taken out of the entire universe. There will be 'new heavens and a new earth, wherein dwelleth righteousness' (2 Peter 3:13). And we shall be with the Lord. We shall see Him as He is, and we shall enjoy Him together. When we stand in His presence, and see Him as He is, we shall not be interested in anything else. We shall be 'lost in wonder, love and praise'. There will be no divisions and distinctions. No one will be interested to know whether you were once a Jew or a Gentile, or a Barbarian, or a Scythian, bond or free, whether you were born into a great family or whether you were born in a slum. Thank God, all that will have gone; we shall all be looking at Him, and nothing else will be remembered. 'The unity of the Spirit in the bond of peace'.

Furthermore, as I have been reminding you, we shall not only all see Him together, but, still more remarkable, we shall be like Him. I believe that our identities will be preserved, but we shall all be like Him. The Apostle Paul says to the Philippian believers that we should be looking for our Saviour to come back because He has the power to 'change our vile body [this body of our humiliation] that it may be fashioned like unto his glorious body, according to the working whereby he is able even to subdue all things unto himself'. In this life some of us are lame, others can walk in a sprightly manner; some of us may have beauty, others of us are ugly; some of us have ability, others of us may lack it. That will not count there; we shall all be like Him. Even our bodies shall be like 'the body of his glorification'. There will be neither jealousy nor envying, neither despising nor condemning.

May God forgive us for ever being guilty of such things in the realm of the Church, in the body of Christ!

Indeed, in the new heavens and the new earth which He will bring in, we shall not only all be with Him, we shall be reigning with Him, 'kings and priests unto God' for ever and ever. That is to be our destiny, all of us who are Christians. Our expectation is one and the same. Even here and now we are having the same foretaste of glory, partaking of the same first-fruits. How then can there be divisions and distinctions in the Church? The way to Church unity, the way to safeguard the unity of the Spirit in the bond of peace, is to do what Paul says to the Colossians: 'Set your affection on things above, not on things on the earth' (Col 3:2). Set it there as one sets a compass or a camera. Set your affection there and keep it there; keep constantly gazing at Him. Look at the things which are above, not at things which are on the earth, and join in singing a hymn translated into English by S. Baring-Gould which says:—

> One the light of God's own presence
> O'er His ransomed people shed,
> Chasing far the gloom and terror,
>   Brightening all the path we tread;
>
> One the object of our journey,
>   One the faith which never tires,
> One the earnest looking forward,
>   One the hope our God inspires;
>
> One the strain that lips of thousands
>   Lift as from the heart of one;
> One the conflict, one the peril,
>   One the march in God begun;
>
> One the gladness of rejoicing
>   On the far eternal shore,
> Where the one almighty Father
>   Reigns in love for evermore.
>
> Onward, therefore, pilgrim brothers,
>   Onward with the cross our aid!
> Bear its shame, and fight its battle,
>   Till we rest beneath its shade.

[92]

Soon shall come the great awaking,
Soon the rending of the tomb;
Then the scattering of all shadows,
And the end of toil and gloom.

8
One Lord

'One Lord, one faith, one baptism'.

Ephesians 4:5

This vital statement must be considered as a part of the complete statement from verse 4 to verse 6: 'There is one body, and one Spirit, even as ye are called in one hope of your calling; one Lord, one faith, one baptism, one God and Father of all, who is above all, and through all, and in you all'. In it the Apostle continues with the theme of unity about which he is so greatly concerned. This unity must characterize the life of the Church, he says, because the Church is ultimately the work of the blessed Holy Trinity. In verse 4 we have looked at it in terms of the work of the Spirit, 'one body, and one Spirit, even as ye are called in one hope of your calling'. Now Paul proceeds to describe it in terms of the work of the Son; and also in terms of the work of the Father.

In this fifth verse we have come to the second of the three divisions into which the Apostle divides his teaching, namely, the unity of the Church in view of the doctrine of the second Person in the blessed Holy Trinity, the Son of God, our Lord and Saviour Jesus Christ. I remind you again of the order in which the Apostle places these things, the sequence which he employs. Having started with the work of the Spirit because that is the practical approach, he now proceeds to consider the part played by the Son because the central work of the Holy Spirit is to glorify the Son, as our Lord Himself said, 'He shall not speak of himself – he shall glorify me' (John 16:13–14). This does not mean that He will not speak about Himself, but that He will be given what to speak, namely, teaching which will glorify the Son. The Father sent the Son and the Son glorified the Father; then the Father and the Son sent the Spirit, and the Spirit glorifies, in particular, the Son. The Apostle Paul teaches us that, 'No man can say that Jesus is the Lord but by the Holy Ghost' (1 Cor 12:3). The Holy Ghost leads us to our Lord; it is He alone who enables us to see Him and to know Him. 'The princes of this world', the Apostle tells those same Corinthians, 'did not know him, for had they known him they would not have crucified the Lord of glory. But God hath revealed these things unto us by his Spirit, for the Spirit searcheth all things, yea, the deep things of God' (1 Cor 2:8–10).

A further reason why the Apostle now proceeds to speak about the Son is that having considered the Church as the body – 'one body' – one inevitably asks, Who is the head of the body? for a body does not function without a head. The answer is the Lord Jesus Christ Himself. The Apostle has already reminded us of this in the first chapter where, talking about Him, he says, '[God] hath put all things under his feet, and gave him to be the head over all things to the church, which is his body, the fulness of him that filleth all in all' (vv. 22–23). We find the same truth stated by the Apostle frequently in his various epistles. It is important to observe this doctrinal approach. These things are not put down accidentally, there is a definite system here. The Holy Spirit illumines the mind, and here we see an illuminated spiritual mind working out the truth.

The Apostle is still concerned to emphasize the unity of the Church. The doctrine of the Person of the Son is put before us in order that it may lead us to maintain 'the unity of the Spirit in the bond of peace'. The Apostle introduces this great doctrine in but two words, 'one Lord'. Generally he does not state it quite as simply as that. In 1 Corinthians 8, verse 6 he has 'one Lord Jesus Christ'. Surely he uses this brief form here in order to emphasize his point about the unity. The Lord Jesus Christ in and of Himself leads to unity and always produces unity; so one of the best ways in which we can see and understand this biblical doctrine of the unity of the Church, and preserve it, is to keep our eyes steadfastly on the doctrine of the Person of the Son of God. Such is the argument, and we now proceed to consider how it works.

*   *   *

First of all there is the uniqueness of our Lord's Person. 'One Lord' means that there is only one who can really and truly be described as 'the Lord'. We should always keep our eye on this title as we read the New Testament. 'It is the Lord', said the Apostle John to the Apostle Peter when they saw Him standing on the sea-shore after a vain night's fishing (John 21:7). There has never been anyone like Him; there never will be. There had never been anyone like Him in the world before He came, there will never be another like Him until He comes again. He stands entirely alone in all the glory of His absolute uniqueness. Our business as Christians is to be ever looking at Him and considering Him – Jesus of Nazareth. As you look at Him you seem to be looking only at a man. And He was a man. He belonged to time, He was in time, He was in the world. And yet, in a sense, to speak thus is already wrong. Our statements about Him must never be made separately and alone. When you look at Him you are not only looking at a man, you are looking at the same time at God the eternal Son, you are looking at 'the Lord of glory'. We must always think and speak of Him in the same manner as the Scriptures do. Take, for instance, the statement at the beginning of the Epistle to the Hebrews: 'God, who at sundry times and in divers manners spake in time past to the fathers by the prophets, hath in these last days spoken unto us by his Son, whom he hath appointed heir of all things, by whom also he made the worlds'. It continues: 'Who being the brightness of his glory, and the express image of his person'. Such is the One at whom we are looking, the brightness of the glory of God, and the 'express image', the full 'effulgence', of God's essential glory.

The Bible's claim, and it must ever be ours, is that the incarnation of the Son of God is a unique event in history. It had never happened before; it will never happen again. Once and for ever! This is the staggering truth, baffling to the understanding, which we believe. It is the essence of our faith. Paul writes concerning Him: 'Who being in the form of God, thought it not robbery to be equal with God [did not count his equality with God as something to be clutched at, and to be held on to], but made Himself of no reputation and took upon him the form of a servant' (Phil 2:6-10). 'The Word was made flesh and dwelt among us', says the Apostle John in his Gospel (1:14). This is the unique

[96]

event of all history, 'one Lord'. The only one! The Apostle tells
the Corinthians in his First Epistle to them that this is a great
mystery, a mystery hidden from the foundation of the world but
then revealed (2:7). What makes us Christian is that we have been
given a measure of understanding of this 'hidden mystery', the
incarnation of the Son of God. 'One Lord' – the only One at
whom you can look and say, the man-God, the 'theanthropos'
God-man – two natures in one Person.

*   *   *

What are the implications, or what are we to deduce from this
emphasis on the 'one Lord'? The Apostle is using the expression
in the interests of his appeal to maintain 'the unity of the Spirit in
the bond of peace'. It works out in the following manner. Christ,
and He alone, is Christianity. 'Christianity is Christ'. It is not a
collection of ideas; it is not a collection of thoughts or philosophies; it is not a mere matter of teaching. Primarily Christianity
is the Lord Himself and our relationship to Him. Teachings and
thoughts and philosophies vary, and they therefore tend to
divide. But here it is a question of personal relationship, the
knowledge of a Person, and of being in a given relationship to
this Person. The argument is, that as the Person is one, so the
relationship must be one. There is only one Lord, therefore there
is this essential unity in all who belong to Him and in all who are
truly related to Him. The great danger threatening the life of the
Church is ever that of forgetting the Person of the Lord Jesus
Christ, of concealing Him and hiding Him behind various things.
There are certain essential doctrines, but we must never allow
even these to come between us and Him. They are simply derived
from Him and are meant to lead us back to Him. Much of the
trouble in the Church throughout the centuries has been due to
the fact that people have forgotten the Lord Himself. We are
such frail creatures, and so fallible, that we tend to go to extremes
in one direction or another. But all of us are guilty in respect of
the fact that the Person Himself is lost sight of, and that other
things are given prominence and come between us and Him, who
is 'one Lord'.

A second deduction which we must draw is that because there
is only one Lord He cannot be divided. This is the argument which

this Apostle Paul uses in writing to the Corinthians in the first chapter of his first Epistle. I am being informed, he says in effect, that there are divisions among you at Corinth. I am told that one says, 'I am of Paul', and another says, 'I am of Apollos', and another says, 'I am of Cephas'. He then asks his question, 'Is Christ divided?' He is asking them whether they realize the consequence of forming parties, and of thus aligning themselves behind certain men and certain names. He tells them that they are trying to divide Christ, and that this cannot be done, because He is One. There is only one Lord, and He is indivisible.

This is the high doctrine of the two natures in one Person. The two natures are so joined together in Him that they cannot be divided. As we read the history of the Church and note the various heresies that have arisen we find that it has generally been due to the fact that Christian people have forgotten 'one Lord'. In a sense they have been making a multiplicity of Lords. Quite early in the Christian Church there were those who taught that the two natures in the one Person were fused into one and were no longer distinguishable. There were some, however, who went to the other extreme and who said there were two Persons – God and Man; not two natures in one Person, but two Persons, Christ as God, Christ as man. These heresies are still taught in the modern church. Sincere men in their desire to emphasize the two aspects of our Lord's Person go too far. They preach of Jesus Christ as God and Jesus Christ as man in isolation from each other. We must never do that. Jesus Christ is always the God-Man: so we must be very careful and wary about saying that He did certain things as God, and other things as a man. No! He is the God-Man, indivisible. Christ cannot be divided in any sense. Thank God for this. He is always the same, He always will be the same. 'Jesus Christ, the same yesterday, and today, and for ever' (Hebrews 13:8). A hymn by Horatius Bonar reminds us that there is 'no night' in Him, and 'no change' in Him. This is true, whatever may happen in the world. This is the greatest comfort of the saint. Jesus Christ is one, the Lord is one, there is only One, and He is always, ever, eternally the same.

Let us always draw these deductions. Christianity is Christ, this One Lord. He makes it. Without Him there is no Christianity. He is essential to it. In this respect it is unlike all other teachings.

Other teachings can be divorced from their propagators, for example, Buddhism from Buddha; it would not make any vital difference. But in Christianity our Lord is everything. It all results from this amazing, unique fact of the Incarnation and of what He has done.

Another inevitable deduction is that we cannot believe in parts of Him. We either believe in Him or else we do not believe in Him. We cannot divide Him in that respect either. Once more the Apostle expresses this very explicitly in the first chapter of the First Epistle to the Corinthians which is the best commentary on this matter: 'But of him are ye in Christ Jesus, who of God is made unto us wisdom, and righteousness, and sanctification, and redemption' (v. 30). He – Christ the Lord, the one indivisible Lord – is 'made' all that to us. Therefore to believe on the Lord Jesus Christ is to believe in the whole of Him and to believe everything that is in Him. We cannot say – we must not say – that we have believed in Him for 'righteousness' but not yet for 'sanctification', not yet for 'redemption', or that at one point we have only taken Him for our justification, and that later it is possible for us to take Him for our sanctification. That would be to divide Christ. We take the whole of Christ; there is no alternative.

This doctrine leads to a most important question. Is it right to form movements round different aspects of His work, and to separate them and to divide them from the whole? Is it right to have a movement which teaches justification only, another which emphasizes sanctification only, another His Second Coming only? We do not 'take' His teaching only; it is by Him that we are saved, and He is one, and He is indivisible. Christ cannot be divided – 'one Lord'. We must be very careful to start with this great doctrine of the one Lord, and to remember also that He is made the same to all believers. He is not one thing to one, and another thing to another. There are not many Christs, there is only one; and if I believe in Him I am in the same position as all others who believe in Him. 'One Lord', therefore one Church.

*   *   *

The second great principle which we must emphasize is the uniqueness of His work. This follows, of course, from the uniqueness of His Person. And we must look at it; and we should be looking at it constantly. We can never take these truths for granted, we can never assume that we know them. We must always remind ourselves of them, because if we do not, says the Apostle, there will soon be a division, there will be some sort of schism. The point we are emphasizing now is that there is only one Saviour. That there are not many Saviours, but only one Saviour is the great theme of the New Testament. This is what makes Christianity a unique faith. The world believes in many saviours, in many deliverers. It has its lists of saviours which it is always repeating. It talks about Moses and Jeremiah and Isaiah and John the Baptist, and Jesus, and perhaps one of the Apostles, Peter or Paul, and then adds some great men who have figured in the history of the world. Some lists add Confucius and the Buddha and perhaps Socrates and Plato. But the New Testament denounces such an idea and says that our Lord Jesus Christ is unique, that He is the one and only Saviour. To deny this is to deny the central and most essential truth of the Christian faith.

I would emphasize this truth by asserting that there is an aspect of intolerance in the Christian faith: and I go further and assert that if we have not seen the intolerant aspect of the faith we have probably never seen it truly. There are many statements in Scripture to substantiate this assertion that to place anyone by the side of Jesus Christ, or to talk of salvation apart from Him, or without Him at the centre, is a betrayal and a denial of the truth. The Apostle Peter, addressing the Sanhedrin at Jerusalem, said, 'There is none other name under heaven given among men whereby we must be saved' (Acts 4:12). The authorities were trying to prohibit Peter and the other Apostles from preaching in the name of Christ and working miracles in His name. Peter, 'filled with the Spirit', made that reply. An alternative translation runs, 'there is no second name'. His is the only name. 'One Lord'. Peter says that there must be no addition to Him, that we must not place another name by the side of His name. He is alone and all-sufficient. He must be alone. There is no other who has come down from heaven to earth. There is no other who is both God and man. His uniqueness must be preserved. He does not need an assistant, He has done everything. He cried on the Cross, 'It is finished'. He left nothing for us to add, nothing for anyone to make up. 'He trod the winepress alone'. No one else could do so; but He has done it.

Or take what the Apostle Paul says in his First Epistle to the Corinthians. There were people in the Church at Corinth who were not clear about all this. They had been converted, but still they tended to believe that though they had come to believe in the one God, there were other gods, the gods in whom they used to believe, the gods whom they had formerly worshipped, and to whom they used to take their sacrifices in the pagan temples. They were not yet clear about this; some of them were 'weaker brethren'. So Paul says to them, 'Though there be that are called gods, whether in heaven or earth (as there be gods many, and lords many), but to us there is but one God, the Father, of whom are all things, and we in him; and one Lord Jesus Christ, by whom are all things, and we by him' (1 Cor 8:5–6). People talk about gods, but there are no gods; there is only one God. These supposed gods are figments of men's imaginations; they are but projections of men's ideas; they have no being, no existence. There is only one God. And there is only one Lord Jesus Christ. There could be no other, there is no other. Again, in writing to Timothy, Paul says, 'There is one God, and one [and only one] Mediator between God and men, the man Christ Jesus' (1 Tim 2:5). One, and one only! There is no one who can come between God and man except this Person. To use the language of Job of old, there is no 'daysman' who can bring us together, apart from Christ. God is in heaven in His holiness and we are on earth in our sin. How can we pray to God, how can we go to God, how can we listen to God and enjoy access to God? There is only one way. We need a Mediator between us, says the Apostle, 'One God, the one Mediator between God and men, the man Christ Jesus' – the One who 'was made the ransom'.

It is only as we grasp the uniqueness of this one Person that we really begin to understand the true nature of the Church. If one man believes that he can go to God direct as he is, and another knows that he cannot, except by the blood of Christ, there is division. If we say that we can find God apart from and without Christ and Him crucified, we are not in the Church. Whatever we may be, and however good our life may seem to be, it is not good enough. There is only one Mediator; there is only one Saviour;

there was only One 'good enough to pay the price of sin'. There is only One who could take unto Him all human nature, and bear the burden and the load of our guilt of sin, and deal with it once and for ever – One only! One Lord, one Saviour! No other! There never will be another and there is no need of another. Any teacher or teaching that disputes this is what the New Testament calls anti-Christ; and there are many such. But the Apostle Paul says, 'I determined not to know anything among you save Jesus Christ, and him crucified' (1 Cor 2:2). He knew much about philosophy and the ideas of the Greeks, and he knew the ideas of the Jews; but he sets both of them aside. The Incarnation is unique and the death of Christ is unique. Why talk about anything else when God has done this once and for all? Why did God ever send His Son into the world if we can get to God without Him?

Yet again, the Apostle says of Christ, 'In him dwelleth all the fulness of the Godhead bodily' (Col 2:9). And again, 'In him are hid all the treasures of wisdom and knowledge' (Col 2:3). Why do men look anywhere else? All that we need to know about God and salvation is in Christ, and only in Christ. Furthermore, says Paul to the Colossians, 'Beware lest men spoil you through philosophy and vain deceit' (2:8). If we do not hold the Head, which is Christ and Christ alone, we are yet in our sins, and do not know God, and are not related to Him. He is One in His Person, and One in His work as Saviour, the only Saviour, the only Mediator between God and man. At one and the same time Christianity is intolerant and unifying. It must be intolerant – 'Though we or an angel from heaven preach any other gospel to you than that which we have preached unto you, let him be accursed', says Paul (Gal 1:8). If an angel from heaven, he says, comes and preaches to you and he denies what I have told you about this blessed Person, let him be accursed. He was intolerant. And we must be intolerant. We must not put anyone near Him, He is alone; and we must never say that God can be known without Him. We must be utterly intolerant at this point. And because all true Christians are intolerant at this point, and are all in Him, they are all united, welded into one. Intolerance, and absolute unity! Is not this the New Testament Gospel? We must preserve both. We must say at one and the same time, that there cannot be such a thing as a World Congress of Faiths and also that all true Christians are one in Christ Jesus. It is precisely because we are all one in Christ that you cannot have a World Congress of Faiths. Such an idea is a farce; indeed it is a denial of Christ. Christianity cannot participate in such a Congress. It cannot enter into any proposal or conference that says that Christianity is marvellous, but, after all, God gave insights to the Buddha, to Confucius, Mahomet and others and we can learn something from them. The Christian does not need to learn from such quarters, because 'all the treasures of wisdom and knowledge are in Christ'. He does not need them, is not interested in them, because he has it all in Himself. Even to give a glance at any other is a denial of Him. Intolerant, and yet unifying!

* * *

Finally, as the Lord is unique in His Person, and unique in His work, He is also unique in His relationship to us. Here again we see how the unity exists inevitably. In life we are all involved in various personal relationships. For instance, a student is in a relationship to his teacher or tutor; but there is no-one to whom we are related as we are to Christ. Our relationship to Him lies essentially in the fact that He owns us. He owns us because He has bought us. Recall how the Apostle Paul, in his farewell speech to the elders of the church at Ephesus, as recorded in Acts, chapter 20, expresses the matter thus: 'Feed the church of God which he hath purchased with his own blood' (v. 28). To the Corinthians he said, 'Ye are not your own, for ye are bought with a price' (1 Cor 6:19-20). Such is the relationship of Christ to the Christian; and it is absolutely unique. He is the One who has purchased us. When we were dead under the law, and slaves of Satan, He bought us out, He ransomed us, He redeemed us, He has paid the necessary price. 'There was no other good enough to pay the price of sin. He only could unlock the gate of heaven and let us in'. As our Lord, He is our Owner; because He has purchased us we belong to Him. That is the relationship.

This, in turn, leads to the fact that He is the Master of us all. He said to the disciples in that Upper Room on the occasion when He washed their feet and then dried them with the towel, 'Ye call me Master and Lord, and ye say well, for so I am' (John 13:13). And this is the unique relationship which subsists between us and

Him. There is only one Lord, there is only one Owner, there is only One who died for me and purchased me. There is none other. And this is true of every one of us as Christians. The implications are obvious. We no longer belong to ourselves. We are no longer our own masters. We have no right to believe what we like, we have no right to do what we like. We are not our own. This is the precise argument used by Paul in writing to the Corinthians. He tells them that in committing sin they did not realize what they were doing: 'Know ye not that your bodies are the temples of the Holy Ghost which dwelleth in you, which ye have of God, and ye are not your own? For ye are bought with a price' (1 Cor 6:19–20). If we all realized this truth there would be perfect unity.

We are not our own masters; and it is equally true to say that no-one else is our master. Also we are not the masters of anyone else. No-one is to lord it over us; and we are not to lord it over anyone else. Our Lord Himself has stated this quite plainly in Matthew's Gospel: 'But be not ye called Rabbi: for one is your Master, even Christ; and all ye are brethren. And call no man your father upon the earth; for one is your Father, which is in heaven. Neither be ye called masters: for one is your Master, even Christ. But he that is greatest among you shall be your servant. And whosoever shall exalt himself shall be abased; and he that shall humble himself shall be exalted' (23:8–12). One Lord! Because He is the one Lord we are all on a level. Not one of us is a master. He is the Master, and we are all in the same position; and should serve one another. He stated this again very plainly on that feet-washing occasion. He said, 'Ye call me Master and Lord, and ye say well, for so I am; if I then, your Lord and Master, have washed your feet, ye also ought to wash one another's feet' (John 13:13–14). This follows by inevitable logic. Whoever you are, He says, I am the Master, and ye are but the servants; and if I the Master have done this, you must all do it. Paul says, 'Let him that glorieth, glory in the Lord' and 'Ye are bought with a price. Be ye not the servants of men'. And again, in the sixth chapter of this Epistle to the Ephesians he says, in his particular injunctions, 'And, ye masters, do the same things to them [your servants], forbearing threatening: knowing that your Master also is in heaven; and there is no respect of persons with him' (v. 9). This is the doctrine of Christ as our Lord, as the One who owns us, as the One who has authority over us. Again, we find Paul saying exactly the same thing in the Epistle to the Colossians, 'Servants, obey in all things your masters according to the flesh; not with eyeservice, as men-pleasers; but in singleness of heart, fearing God: and whatsoever ye do, do it heartily, as to the Lord, and not unto men, knowing that of the Lord ye shall receive the reward of the inheritance: for ye serve the Lord Christ'. Further, 'Masters, give unto your servants that which is just and equal; knowing that ye also have a Master in heaven' (3:22–24 and 4:1). The doctrine of the one Lord leads inevitably to the doctrine of the one Church and to 'the unity of the Spirit in the bond of peace'. We are all joined to Him, the same Person; and He is in us all, and is our 'all in all'.

The love we are to seek to know, says Paul, is 'the love of Christ·that passeth knowledge' (Eph 3:19). But above all, the Apostle uses this argument in his great exposition of the Incarnation in the second chapter of the Epistle to the Philippians which we have already quoted. He describes the self-humiliation of our Lord in order that he may say, 'Let this mind be in you also', the mind that was in Christ, and which led Him to do so much for us. And again, 'Let nothing be done through strife or vainglory; but in lowliness of mind let each esteem other better than themselves', and 'look not every man on his own things, but every man also on the things of others' (Phil 2:3–5). Surely all must agree that if only we were all clear about our relationship to Him, and in our doctrine of the Second Person in the blessed Holy Trinity, most of our problems would be solved immediately. If we but knew Him in such a manner as to be able to say with Paul, 'To me to live is Christ'; or with Count Zinzendorf, 'I have one passion, it is He, and He alone'; most of our problems would disappear. Divisions and schisms and all failures are ultimately due to a failure to realize that there is only 'one Lord'. When each of us realizes that the eternal Son of God laid aside the insignia of His eternal glory, and came down to earth, and was born as a babe in a stable in Bethlehem, and endured the contradiction of sinners against Himself for thirty-three years, was spat upon, and scoffed and mocked and jeered at, and that He went through with all that while He had that right hand to hold on to, His equality with God in heaven, but made Himself of no reputation – when we know that He did all that for each of us then we are nothing, and care not what man may do unto us. Nothing matters then except that we live for Him and for His glory. Then we are prepared to sing with Isaac Watts –

> *When I survey the wondrous Cross,*
> *On which the Prince of Glory died,*
> *My richest gain I count but loss,*
> *And pour contempt on all my pride.*

As we do so we find ourselves maintaining, preserving, the unity of the Spirit in the bond of peace.

9
One Faith

'One Lord, one faith, one baptism'.

Ephesians 4:5

We come now to the next expression in the Apostle's definition of the unity of the Church – 'one faith'. And this one faith is in connection with the 'one Lord'. That is why it comes in this particular grouping – 'One Lord, one faith, one baptism'. He does not place the 'one faith' with the work of the Spirit or with the Father, but with the Lord.

The learned commentators nearly all seem to be in trouble concerning the exact meaning of the expression, and there is much disagreement among them, some taking one view, some another. These views can be divided into two main groups. There are those who feel that this 'one faith' refers to our subjective faith, to that quality in us, that capacity in us, which enables us to believe. They argue, therefore, that the character, the nature of that faith is patently and obviously the same in all Christians. It is the same action, the same consciousness, the same feeling. Everything about our faith, subjectively considered, is the same in all. It seems to me that this is an impossible explanation of this statement, and for this good reason that in a sense it is already covered by the term 'one Lord'. But there is a still more serious objection. The Apostle is endeavouring to give absolute proofs of believers' unity, so that whenever we are assailed by doubts we may have some certainty to sustain us. Now whenever we want to demonstrate or prove something, we must never appeal to that which is subjective, because the subjective is personal and cannot be defined. The subjective is no answer to an objective attack. But the Apostle is giving us objective proofs, something outside ourselves which we can apply to ourselves, and by which therefore we can test ourselves. So I argue that 'one faith' cannot be considered subjectively, because to do so removes it from the category of an objective test. All we have considered hitherto has been strictly objective.

The other idea with regard to this term is that it is something objective. But, here again, there is a difficulty. If we say that when he refers to the 'one faith' he is referring to an objective body of truth that is believed – not my act of believing but that which I and all others believe – another difficulty arises. It is that those who hold this view tend to say that the objective faith to which Paul is referring is a complete confession or compendium of faith. In the eyes of these teachers 'one faith' means that Christians adopt and subscribe to one of the great Confessions of Faith, such as the Thirty-nine Articles of the Church of England, or the West-minster Confession of Faith, or the Heidelberg Catechism. Faith here, they say, means a complete outline of what we believe, a complete compendium of theology. Once more, this does not seem to me to be a possible explanation of 'one faith'. Indeed those who adopt it have to admit, and do admit, that they are in difficulties with respect to it, and for this reason, that the history of the Church shows very clearly that all Christians have not always been agreed about everything in detail in connection with the Christian faith. There have been divergencies of opinion upon a number of matters. They admit that if you are going to define 'one faith' as a complete compendium of theology in detail, then there has never been 'one faith'. They point out that the Apostle himself seems to hint at that later on, when he says in verse 13, 'Till we *all come* in the unity of the faith, and of the knowledge of the Son of God, unto a perfect man, unto the measure of the stature of the fulness of Christ: that we henceforth be no more children, tossed to and fro, and carried about with every wind of doctrine, by the sleight of men, and cunning craftiness, whereby they lie in wait to deceive; but speaking the truth in love, may grow up into him in all things, which is the head, even Christ' (vv. 13–15). The Apostle seems to be granting that, so far, we are not all agreed about everything, but that there is a day coming when we shall all be brought together into that unity, and we shall all see everything clearly and shall be agreed about every-thing – but not yet!

*   *   *

It seems clear, therefore, that we cannot take the expression 'one faith' to mean agreement in detail about everything, agreement about a complete compendium of theology or of doctrine. The Apostle uses the expression 'one faith' as an argument for unity, and says that they all know what this one faith is. It is to him an objective test which can be applied, it is as definite as the 'one Lord' and the 'one Spirit' and the 'one God', and all the other statements. 'One faith' is clearly something which we can, and must, define, and about which we must say that all Christians must be agreed. What does this mean?

I suggest that while it is not a complete system of theology, it is something that is dealt with very frequently in the New Testament, something about which we can be quite clear. I argue that it refers to the very essence of the Gospel, that which the Apostles were specifically called to preach in their work of evangelism. It is indeed the great message of the Gospel concerning salvation, or justification by faith only. I suggest that the only possible and satisfactory exposition of this term 'one faith' is to say that the Apostle is referring to justifying faith; and that this is not only the 'one faith' but also the only faith.

To substantiate my contention let me remind you of some other statements which the Apostle makes with respect to this matter. It is customary to refer to Paul as the great Apostle of faith, and he is such. Not that the other Apostles did not preach it; they did so, as the Apostle himself argues elsewhere; but pre-eminently this was the message committed to him which he expounded to Jew and Gentile alike. Perhaps the greatest and most noble example is found in his Epistle to the Romans. He says that he is longing to meet them and to visit them (1:11). He has heard about them and he wants to visit them and to establish them in the faith. He then proceeds to tell them what is the essential message of the Gospel. He summarizes it quite early in the Epistle where he writes, 'For I am not ashamed of the gospel of Christ; for it is the power of God unto salvation to every one that believeth . . . For therein [in the gospel] is revealed the righteousness of God, from faith to faith, as it is written, The just shall live by faith' (1:16–17). That is the message, and that, I suggest, is the 'one faith' to which he is referring in Ephesians 4:5. Indeed those who are familiar with the Epistle to the Romans will know that the first four chapters of that Epistle are devoted entirely to this great message of justification, or salvation, or righteousness, by faith. This, he says, is the new message. Until the ministry of Christ, he says, the Jews were under the Law and the Law was preached, 'But now' – that is the turning point – there is something new. In the third chapter of that same Epistle he says, 'By the law is the knowledge of sin. But now the righteousness of God without the Law [or apart from the Law] is manifested' (vv. 20–21). He goes on to give a mighty exposition of this principle, this doctrine of justification by faith only. That is the 'one faith'.

The Epistle to the Galatians is devoted exclusively to the same theme. That Epistle was necessary because certain people had gone down from Jerusalem and had been disturbing the life of the churches in Galatia by saying that the Apostle Paul was right in preaching the doctrine of justification by faith, but was wrong when he said justification by faith only. They told the Galatians that, in a sense, they were Christians, but that if they desired to become true Christians they, as Gentiles, must submit to circumcision. The Apostle writes his Epistle to show that if a man makes any such addition to the faith he has 'fallen from grace' and has 'another gospel which is not a gospel'. Indeed he tells them that he had even to correct the Apostle Peter on this matter. Peter had been quite clear about this, but he had been frightened and alarmed by certain people who had come down from Jerusalem, and he had begun to dissemble and to compromise. Paul says that he had to withstand him [Peter] to the face at Antioch, and had brought him to see again that the faith principle is the centre and the glory of the Christian gospel – 'one faith'.

But perhaps the clearest statement of this truth is to be found in the tenth chapter of the Epistle to the Romans. The Apostle is comparing and contrasting the false ideas of the Jews with the true method of salvation and writes, 'But what saith it? The word is nigh thee, even in thy mouth, and in thy heart: that is, the word of faith, which we preach' (v. 8). This expression 'the word of faith' refers to what he has already said in verse 6: 'But the righteousness which is of faith speaketh on this wise'. The statement is emphasized by way of contrast with what the Law says – 'Moses describeth the righteousness which is of the law in these words, That the man which doeth those things shall live by them'.

Then he continues, 'But the righteousness which is of faith speaketh on this wise, Say not in thine heart, Who shall ascend into heaven? Or, Who shall descend into the deep? But what saith it? The word is nigh thee, even in thy mouth and in thy heart: that is, the word of faith, which we preach'. 'The word of faith' is the word of 'justification by faith'. It is the word of righteousness by faith. That is the meaning of the expression 'the word of faith'. It is the word about faith, the word about faith as the justifying principle, the word of faith in the sense that 'The just shall live by faith'. 'The word of faith' is the word that we must put over against the word of the Law.

*   *   *

We must now proceed to give further definition and description of this 'one faith'. It is most important that we should do so, for this is the only faith, this is the 'one' faith. According to Paul, whosoever says anything else is wrong; he is an enemy of the truth. This is 'the faith' that was rediscovered, or rather, revealed again and restored at the Protestant Reformation. This was 'the faith' which was preached by the Protestant Fathers; this is 'the faith' for which they died gladly at the stake. The Protestant Reformation was a re-discovery, a new realization, of the great principle that 'the just shall live by faith'. It was Luther's great message, justification by faith only – 'sola fide'. That is 'the word of faith': it is not faith in general, it is this peculiar, specific message about the way of justification. This is the 'one faith'.

I re-emphasize this, for if we do not have and hold this faith we are not Christians. I do not hesitate to say so. I repeat that we are not dealing with a compendium of faith, or a detailed list of points. I am not asserting that, if you do not subscribe to every detail of such a confession of faith, you are not a Christian. That is the way to bring divisions. I am concerned only with the 'one faith' that matters. This is the message concerning God's way of saving men. It is concerning the righteousness which is from God. It is not something that men do but what God has done. This is the message; and this is Christianity. The Apostle states this in various terms. He writes about God 'justifying him that believeth in Jesus.' In the fourth chapter of the Epistle to the Romans, he makes one of the most amazing statements he ever made, 'But to him that worketh not, but believeth on him that justifieth the ungodly, his faith is counted for righteousness' (v. 5). The fact that 'God justifieth the ungodly' proves beyond all question that this is God's act. This is God's way of making any one of us just and acceptable in His holy sight. It is the way in which we become right with God, and reconciled to God, and know that God is our Father. God alone does this, and He does so in Christ. He declares us to be righteous, He pronounces that we are righteous. It is essentially an announcement, a proclamation, a declaration, which is made by God concerning us.

The analogy which has often been used is this: A prisoner is in the dock, and the judge is sitting upon the bench. There is prosecuting counsel, the law of God, supported by a man's own conscience. The prisoner has not kept the law but has sinned against it. That is the indictment, the case against him; and the prisoner has no reply. But in view of a statement made by a benefactor, the judge on the bench makes a proclamation and an announcement; he pronounces that he regards the criminal, the prisoner in the dock, as free from the charge that has been proffered against him. He declares him to be righteous in his sight, he says that he holds nothing against him, and absolves him from all the guilt and shame. He says, I pronounce you to be just, I regard you as if you had never been guilty.

Justification is God's action, a legal action, a forensic action. Apart altogether from us, God makes a pronouncement concerning sinners, saying that He regards that particular ungodly person as now just. God pronounces him to be just and free from all sin. Justification means God declaring a man to be just in His sight.

But how does God do this? Indeed let us ask the question that Paul raises in Romans 3 verses 25, 26: How can God do this? for God is holy and just and righteous and pure. God cannot pretend or dissemble; God cannot say something one day and then take it back the next. He is 'the Father of lights, with whom is no variableness, neither shadow of turning'. Now God had said from the beginning of the creation that if man sinned he would be punished and driven out of His presence. He repeated it and made it yet more clear when He gave the Law through Moses. He said that He held the sinner responsible. God made it clear that because of His character, His being, His holiness, His righteousness and justice and equity, sin must be punished. So how can God justify the ungodly, how can He make this pronouncement with regard to any sinner? The great answer is given in a wonderful passage in the Epistle to the Romans chapter 3, from verse 21 to verse 31. God has 'set forth Christ to be the propitiation for our sins'. This means that God has taken our sins and has put them upon Christ, and He has punished them, He has dealt with them in His own Son upon the Cross on Calvary's hill. That is the doctrine, 'Whom God hath set forth to be a propitiation through faith in his blood'. This is the very heart of Christianity; indeed there is no Christianity apart from this. This is 'the faith' we must all hold and believe, namely, that 'God was in Christ reconciling the world unto himself, not imputing their trespasses unto them'; that 'He hath laid upon him the iniquity of us all'; and that God 'hath made him to be sin for us, who knew no sin, that we might be made the righteousness of God in him'. Paul tells us in 2 Corinthians chapter 5: 'We are ambassadors for Christ, as though Christ did beseech you through us: we pray you in Christ's stead, Be ye reconciled to God'. That is the way of reconciliation, that is the message of reconciliation which has been delivered unto us.

The very heart of the Christian message is that God has taken our sins and has imputed them to Jesus Christ – 'not imputing them unto us', says Paul, because He has imputed them unto Him. To 'impute' means to reckon, to put them down to someone's account. It is as if a wealthy man went into a shop or store and said, 'I want you to send the following goods to such-and-such an address, but do not send the bill to them, put it down to my account; impute it to me'. God has taken our sins and has imputed them to Christ, has put them to His account, and has punished them in Him. 'He hath made him to be sin for us' – in our stead, in our place. God smote His own Son on account of our sins. Christ bore our punishment. The Apostle Peter writes, 'Who his own self bare our sins in his own body on the tree, that we, being dead to sins, should live unto righteousness: by whose stripes ye were healed' (1 Peter 2:24).

But God has also done something beyond that, He has put Christ's righteousness to our account. The Lord Jesus Christ never sinned; He obeyed the Law of God in every detail. The Father was satisfied with Him; He had done everything the Father sent Him to do. He was described by the archangel Gabriel to Mary as 'that holy thing' (Luke 1:35). He was born full of righteousness, He kept the law perfectly, and pleased God in everything, rendering a perfect obedience. What God does is to take His righteousness and put it to our account. There is, as it were, a great transaction, a great transference in the ledgers of heaven. Our unrighteousness was put on Him; His righteousness is put on us. And so God, having taken our sins from us, and putting the righteousness of Christ upon us, pronounces us to be righteous. This is the glorious truth that enabled Count Zinzendorf to write the great hymn which John Wesley has so nobly translated:

> *Jesus, Thy robe of righteousness*
> *My beauty is, my glorious dress:*
> *'Midst flaming worlds, in this arrayed*
> *With joy shall I lift up my head.*
>
> *Bold shall I stand in Thy great day,*
> *For who aught to my charge shall lay?*
> *Fully through Thee absolved I am*
> *From sin and fear, from guilt and shame.*
>
> *Jesus, be endless praise to Thee,*
> *Whose boundless mercy hath for me –*
> *For me – a full atonement made,*
> *An everlasting ransom paid.*

The word of faith which we preach is that our salvation is all the action of God through this one Lord Jesus Christ. That is why the 'one faith' follows the 'one Lord'. The 'one Lord' was sent by the Father. He took on Him human nature, He lived a perfect life here on earth, and then 'God laid on him the iniquity of us all' and transfers His righteousness to us. This comes to us by faith, the 'one faith', the only faith. We contribute nothing at all to it. Our deeds, our actions, do not play a part, our goodness does not come in, for it is not goodness in God's sight, it is but as 'dung' and refuse in the sight of God. Our seeking it does not help, our intellectual ability does not help, nothing in us helps at all. It is all of God, it is all of grace, it is all God's doing from first to last.

Righteousness is put upon us. We were standing in our rags, as it were, as condemned criminals in the dock; but God sent Christ through the Spirit to take away the rags and to put upon us the robe of Christ's perfect righteousness. God now looks upon us and sees not us, nor our sins, but the righteousness of Christ. He looks at us 'in Christ'. Our natural birth makes no difference, our nationality does not enter in. The degree of repentance we have known does not matter, nor the amount of feeling accompanying it. If we turn our repentance into a meritorious act we are denying the faith. What we are, or what we have done or not done, does not count; nothing in us counts; our righteousness is all in Christ, and by faith, by faith alone. The Apostle has already told us in chapter 2, verse 8, that salvation is not of ourselves: 'By grace are ye saved, through faith, and that not of yourselves, it is the gift of God'. This righteousness of Christ is given to us, and becomes ours, through the instrumentality of faith which is also God's gift.

*   *   *

It thus becomes abundantly clear why the Apostle mentions 'one faith' at this particular point. He is concerned about the essential principle of unity, and this helps us to see this unity. This is the only way of salvation. Indeed the Apostle says that it has always been the only way of salvation. In the fourth chapter of his Epistle to the Romans Paul expounds this fact. He says that while, in a sense, what he preached and taught is new because of the coming of the Son of God into the world, actually it had always been God's way of justifying man. He shows how Abraham was justified in the sight of God, and that it was by faith, not by his works. He goes on to show that David had taught this same truth, saying, 'Blessed is the man to whom the Lord will not impute iniquity' (Psa 32:2). Imputation was God's method under the Old Dispensation also. For the same reason Paul says in the third chapter of the Epistle to the Galatians that Abraham is the father of us all, the father of all who believe the faith, the father of every Christian. As Christians we are the children of Abraham because we are children of faith. The eleventh chapter of the

Epistle to the Hebrews teaches that it goes even further back, to Abel, and Enoch, and Noah. This has always been God's way. It is wrong to think that there was one way of salvation in the Old Testament and now another in the New. No! God has always justified men by faith. Abraham was declared just by God, through faith. It is 'one faith', it has always been the only faith.

Once more, we must emphasize equally the way of salvation for Jew and for Gentile. Nothing else matters but faith. It does not matter whether we are Barbarians or Scythians, male or female, bond or free. We all have to come by the same way, and it is always the way of faith. We are all guilty before God: 'there is none righteous, no, not one', 'all have sinned and have come short of the glory of God'. We are all guilty under the condemnation of the same law of God. We must forget about Jew and Gentile and every other distinction. There is only one way of salvation, it is this way of faith whereby the righteousness of Christ is imputed to us after our sins have been imputed to Him and punished in Him. If we are to be Christian at all we must all become Christian in the same way. Whether you have been 'good' or 'bad' in your past life does not matter. Whether you have been brought up in a religious home, and have always gone to church, or whether your up-bringing and former life were godless, is equally irrelevant. We are all one, and there is as much hope of salvation in the second case as in the first. There is no way of salvation except by the 'one faith', the faith which receives this perfect righteousness from God through Jesus Christ and Him crucified. It is all in Christ, there is nothing in us. There must be no argument whatsoever about this. This is what makes us all one. See to it, says the Apostle, that you do not break the unity, see to it that you preserve it, 'endeavour to keep the unity of the Spirit in the bond of peace'.

*   *   *

There are, alas, many ways in which we may break the unity in respect of this faith. One way of doing so is to bring in something of our own. If we bring in our own 'good' life, and our 'good' works' we are virtually saying that we are better than others. We become like the Pharisee who went up into the temple to pray and who thanked God that he was such a good man and much better than the publican. Even if, as Christians, we begin to boast about what we are doing, or what we are, we are detracting from faith and causing division. Any boasting about our good deeds, our lives, our piety, even our faith, is a denial of the faith principle. If we boast about our understanding, and are proud of it, and despise the man who knows less, we are breaking the unity and we are violating the faith principle. How careful we must be!

Another way in which we break the unity is by denying the absolute centrality of Christ and His work. There are people who say that they are saved, that they believe their sins are forgiven, but when you ask them on what grounds they know that their sins are forgiven, they say that they believe that God is a God of love who will not send a man who asks for forgiveness to hell. They do not even mention the name of Jesus Christ; they attribute everything to the love of God alone, as if Christ had never been, as if the one Lord had never come from glory into time, and had never gone to the Cross and shed His precious blood for our sins. They believe that they have forgiveness apart from Christ. But that is not the 'one faith' and they are not in Christ. Obviously they are causing division.

A third way of breaking the unity, which is equally dangerous, is that of adding to this 'one faith'. This produced the Galatian heresy of those who said, 'faith plus circumcision'. If you add circumcision, says Paul, you have 'fallen from grace', you have denied the faith. Nothing must be added to this faith. This is the fatal heresy of Roman Catholicism, which was denounced by the teaching of the Protestant Reformation. The Roman Catholic Church had obscured the 'one faith' principle. Its teachers were adding many things to the faith, such as the church, and the idea of the transmission of grace mechanically through the sacraments. They taught that we are made Christians by baptism, that there is grace in the water as the result of a prayer by a priest, and that we receive Christ's actual body by receiving the wafer in what they called the Mass. They added also the adoration and mediation of the Virgin Mary, the works of supererogation of the saints, and many other things. By these additions they denied the 'one faith', and were thus causing division and schism. It was not Luther who divided the Church; the errors of Roman Catholicism were responsible for it.

[117]

We must be careful not to fall into this subtle heresy. Any who teach that there is anything else which is essential to salvation, whatever it might be, are denying this 'one faith', and are dividing the Church. The 'one faith' is justifying faith. That and that alone is essential. There are many other teachings which may or may not be true. We are divided in our views of prophecy, in our views concerning baptism, and on many other things. Thank God such views do not determine our salvation. The one and only way of salvation is that I come to God and I say from my heart, 'Nothing in my hand I bring, simply to Thy Cross I cling' – and

> *Just as I am, without one plea*
> *But that Thy blood was shed for me,*
> *And that Thou bidd'st me come to Thee,*
> *O Lamb of God, I come.*

That is justifying faith! You realize that you can lean on nothing in yourself, that all your righteousness is but 'as filthy rags', that if you could live another thousand years and fast and sweat and pray, you would be no nearer to salvation than you are at this moment, that there is nothing in you that counts, that it is all in Christ through the Holy Spirit, and that you rely on that alone. If you believe that, you are a Christian. If you do not believe it, you are not a Christian. Nothing else is essential; this is the 'one faith'. I do not mean that there are not other matters which are very important, and that we need to be instructed about them, but they are not essential to salvation. This is the one and only thing that is an absolute essential; and it is therefore the one and only faith.

Have you got this? I am not asking a theoretical question. Have you realized that this is the one thing that makes us all one in Christ? Are you leaning at all upon your background? Are you relying to the slightest extent upon the fact that your parents may have been Christians, and that you have always been brought up in a godly home and atmosphere, that you have always gone to church, that you have always believed in God, that you have not committed adultery or murder or any foul or vicious sins, that you have always tried to do good and have given donations to good causes? Are you relying on any one of these things? If you are, you are outside the 'one faith' and you are outside Christ. The message of the Gospel, the message of salvation, is about 'the righteousness of God by faith', 'from faith to faith'. 'The just shall live by faith', or, 'The just by faith shall live'. The 'one faith' is the faith that readily and gladly and wholeheartedly acknowledges this truth, and thanks God for it, and rejoices in it, that says with the Apostle Paul, 'God forbid that I should glory, save in the cross of our Lord Jesus Christ, by whom the world is crucified unto me, and I unto the world' (Gal 6:14). God grant that we all have the 'one faith' and rest in it, and rejoice in it, to the glory of God the Father, the one Lord Jesus Christ, God's Son, and the blessed Holy Spirit.

10
One Baptism

'One Lord, one faith, one baptism'.

Ephesians 4:5

We come now to the third statement in this second group of statements centring round our Lord – 'one baptism'. It is clear that as the Apostle makes these points he does not do so in any haphazard or accidental manner. He is not merely making a series of statements at random, still less is he repeating himself. He is really adding to the message, he is working out its meaning. Obviously he has selected the particular matters by means of which he could prove most conclusively to the Ephesian Christians the nature of the unity in the Church, the inevitability of that unity, and therefore the importance of their maintaining it. We have seen already that there is a difference of emphasis in the expressions 'one Lord' and 'one faith'. It is the Person Himself that is emphasized in 'one Lord', whereas 'one faith' emphasizes the faith concerning justification in particular, the way in which God makes and declares His people righteous.

The very mention of this term 'one baptism' undoubtedly raises a query in the minds of many, as to how this 'one baptism' promotes unity, because it is a notorious fact that the whole question of baptism has frequently led to discussion and division and separation. And yet the Apostle includes 'one baptism' in order to show the inevitability of unity among true believers. Hence, whatever our interpretation of this term 'one baptism' may be, it must show the inevitability of unity; it must be something that the Ephesians could use as an argument to persuade themselves to go on 'keeping the unity of the Spirit in the bond of peace'. So we are not merely discussing baptism in general, we must discuss this 'one baptism' in such a manner as to illustrate

[120]

more clearly than ever the particular unity that obtains in the members of the body of Christ.

We must start, however, with a number of negatives, because some have said that this is quite simple and that there is no problem here at all. Throughout the centuries there have been those who have taught that this 'one baptism' obviously refers to what they are pleased to call 'baptismal regeneration'. Baptism, they teach, is the means of regeneration, so that when anyone is baptized he is by that action given new life and made regenerate. So in their ceremony or service of baptism they say of the one whom they have baptized, 'This child is now regenerate'. They mean that he has been made regenerate by that which has been done to him. This teaching prevails in various sections of the Church; it is not confined to the Roman Catholics. This school of interpretation regards the Apostle's complete statement as meaning one Lord, one faith in that Lord, and one regeneration or incorporation into that Lord by means of, through the instrumentality of, baptism. The Roman Catholics regard baptism as something which acts 'ex opere operato', which means that it operates in and of itself. As the result of the priest's prayer there is grace in the water, regenerating grace, and therefore the child is born-again. Others who do not go as far as that believe that somehow or other the action of baptism makes the person who is baptized regenerate.

There are others who explain this expression in terms of the mode of baptism. I remember reading a sermon by a man who, referring to this phrase 'one baptism', dismissed it with the laconic remark, 'Of course this means adult baptism by immersion in water'. There was no more to be said. To him there was no problem at all. It never occurred to him that to interpret it in that manner obviously caused division in the Church, and was therefore no illustration of unity, any more than the other interpretations I have mentioned are an illustration of unity. We cannot accept the idea, therefore, that it is only a reference to the mode of baptism, for that does not show the inevitability of this principle of unity.

A third interpretation interprets 'one baptism' as a reference only to the rite of baptism. They do not believe in baptismal regeneration; they do not teach that any particular mode is essential. Their case is that there is the rite of baptism, and so the

Apostle was simply referring to the fact that when people became Christians they were baptized, and that that was their initiation into the visible body of the Church. As we shall see, there is something to be said for this third view, but we have to be careful, because there is always the danger of the making of baptism essential to salvation. Even though we reject the doctrine of baptismal regeneration, which clearly is not taught anywhere in the Scripture, but was introduced in order to establish the power of the priesthood and of the Church, there is the danger of our making the very rite itself essential. Surely we must never do that. We must not say that baptism in any shape or form is vital and essential to salvation, and that a man cannot be saved unless he is baptized. This, for the good and sufficient reason that there have undoubtedly been excellent Christians among the Quakers, the early Quakers in particular, and members of the Salvation Army today, and others. Take the case of the thief dying on the cross by the side of our Lord. Surely no-one doubts his salvation, his conversion, his regeneration; yet he was not baptized. There have been others who have come to see the truth on their death-beds and have never been baptized. Baptism is not essential to salvation; so the Apostle cannot have been emphasizing the rite in and of itself.

*   *   *

It seems clear, therefore, that we must reject those three suggestions. In their stead I hold that the Apostle is referring to that which baptism represents and signifies. It was, as we know, the custom in the infant Christian Church, as it should be still, to baptize all those who become believers. We have examples of this in the Book of the Acts of the Apostles. Take, for example, what happened on the Day of Pentecost. When certain people cried out and said to Peter, 'Men and brethren, what shall we do?' Peter's reply was, 'Repent, and be baptized every one of you in the name of the Lord Jesus Christ for the remission of sins, and ye shall receive the gift of the Holy Ghost'. Later we are told that the Philippian jailer 'believed and was baptized, he and all his, straightway'. This was done in obedience to a command of the Lord. Baptism and the Communion of the Lord's Supper should be observed; they are the two, and the only two, sacraments which we recognize, because they are the only two which are taught in the Scriptures. But it is more important that we should realize that these are simply outward representations of an inner and unseen spiritual grace. The meaning is the vital element.

I am prepared to argue, therefore, that the only conceivable meaning which this term can carry must be in the realm of this spiritual representation which is signified by the outward rite of baptism, whatever form or manner or mode you may choose to employ. It is not the mode of baptism that matters, it is the thing signified that matters. This is so because this interpretation alone is consistent with the principle of unity about which the Apostle is writing, and is concerned to emphasize. I want to show that in baptism, whether you baptize an infant or an adult, whether you baptize by immersion or by sprinkling, this unity is possible – that is to say, if the one baptized becomes a Christian. We are rejecting completely the suggestion that to baptize a child makes that child a Christian; and equally that baptism does not make an adult a Christian. The act of baptism does not achieve anything in and of itself; but it does represent and signify something, and it is this which brings out the element of unity.

The first thing to be emphasized is that baptism is into one name only, the name of the Lord Jesus Christ. I am aware that at the end of Matthew's Gospel we are told, 'Baptizing them in the name of the Father and of the Son and of the Holy Ghost' (28:19). But that need cause no confusion, because primarily baptism is into the name of the Lord Jesus Christ, and through Him, into the name of the Spirit and of the Father. Let me demonstrate this truth. What the Apostle says in the first chapter of his First Epistle to the Corinthians provides an excellent commentary on this matter for there the Apostle takes up this very question of division and disunity and schism in the Church. He says, 'It hath been declared unto me, my brethren, by them of the household of Chloe, that there are contentions among you. Now this I say, that every one of you saith, I am of Paul, and I of Apollos, and I of Cephas, and I of Christ'. Then Paul asks, 'Is Christ divided? was Paul crucified for you? or were you baptized in the name of Paul?' Clearly he is reminding them that they were baptized into the name of Christ. He proceeds to say, 'I thank God that I baptized none of you, but Crispus and Gaius, lest any should say that I had baptized in mine own name. And I baptized also the household of Stephanas: besides I know not whether I baptized any other'. Note how careful he is to put this question of the rite of baptism into its right place and into the right perspective. But the significant phrase is the question, 'Is Christ divided? was Paul crucified for you? or were you baptized into the name of Paul?' Of course not. They were not baptized in the name of Paul or of Apollos or of Cephas; every one of them was baptized into the name of the Lord Jesus Christ. One Lord, one faith in that Lord, the justifying faith, and one baptism into the same name.

But let us take some other examples. I have already quoted Peter's exhortation on the Day of Pentecost, as recorded in Acts 2:38, where he says 'Be baptized every one of you in the name of Jesus Christ'. Again in Acts 19:5 we read, 'When they heard this they were baptized in the name of the Lord Jesus'. They had previously only known the baptism of John the Baptist; they are now 'baptized into the name of the Lord Jesus'. His is the only name, and the one baptism is into His name. The tragedy is that so often in the Church that which is most important of all has been forgotten, and men have argued and debated and disputed, and, alas, even quarrelled, over the mode and method of baptism, and thereby have produced division. If they had but remembered the one name they would have been emphasizing the principle of unity.

*   *   *

We turn now to that which this baptism into the name of Christ really represents. To some the answer seems simple and obvious, and they glibly reply that it represents the washing away of my sins, the forgiveness of my sins, because of the fact that I am justified. This is true, of course, but if you stop at that point you are missing the most important thing in connection with baptism. Baptism does represent the washing away of sins, but having done so, it goes on into something infinitely more important. We note that the term used is 'baptized into' or 'baptized unto'. This gives us the key to a true understanding of this 'one baptism'. It means 'in reference to Christ', or 'into the realm of Christ', or 'into the sphere of influence which is exercised by Christ'.

There is an interesting statement, again in the First Epistle to the Corinthians, which really throws much light on this. The Apostle is writing to those Corinthians who were so ready to divide, and he uses this amazing expression: 'Moreover, brethren, I would not that ye should be ignorant how that all our fathers were under the cloud, and all passed through the sea, and were baptized unto Moses in the cloud and in the sea' (10:1–2). It is a statement about the children of Israel. God had sent Moses to deliver them out of the captivity of Egypt. They had started on their journey, but Pharaoh and his hosts were chasing them. They came to the Red Sea, and God worked the miracle of dividing the Red Sea, and the children of Israel, led by Moses, went over on dry land. The Egyptians, trying to follow them, were all drowned. It is with reference to that incident that the Apostle says that the children of Israel were 'baptized unto Moses'. That statement can have but one meaning. They were baptized into the leadership, the sphere of influence, of Moses. They had become identified with Moses and all he stood for, and the cause that was represented by Moses. In other words, they were separated from the Egyptians, amongst whom they had been living, and were now the redeemed people of God, the saved people, the protected people identified with Moses whom God had sent to deliver them. There was now a division between them and all who belonged to the realm of Pharaoh.

This is a picture of that which is true of all who are in Christ. Baptism therefore represents and signifies our being put into the realm and into the sphere and into the influence of the Lord Jesus Christ. This means that formerly we belonged to the world, we belonged to the realm of the world; but the moment we become Christian we go out of the realm of the world, and into the realm of Christ, and baptism signifies this. Paul, in writing to the Colossians, says that we have been 'delivered from the power of darkness, and translated into the kingdom of God's dear Son' (1:13). We have been taken out of the world and put into the kingdom of God, and into the kingdom of Christ. We are in a new realm, we are in a new sphere, we are under an entirely new influence. Not only so, when we are baptized we are confessing Christ, we are announcing that we have submitted ourselves to Him, that He has become our Lord and Master. Those children of Israel, if they had preferred it, could have stayed in Egypt. But they had listened to Moses and had followed him, risking their lives with him, and stepping into the Red Sea. They had submitted themselves entirely to Moses' leadership, had surrendered themselves to him; he was their leader, their master, their lord. Figuratively, they were baptized in the Red Sea unto Moses.

*   *   *

So baptism represents and signifies that you and I who are Christian no longer belong to the world, and its realm, and its interests; but that we belong now to the Lord Jesus Christ. He is to us the one Lord, the only Master whom we acknowledge. We realize that we are in a new sphere and in a new realm altogether; we have left the world and we have gone after Him. That is what is represented by baptism. Think again of Peter's congregation on the Day of Pentecost. They were Jews and proselytes, and others; they were listening to the sermon of a man filled with the Holy Spirit. They saw and they believed the truth, and they took the momentous step of being baptized into the name of Jesus Christ. They knew that it could well lead to persecution, that their families might hate them, and perhaps ostracize them because they believed in this Jesus, this Nazarene, who had been crucified as a felon. But having seen the truth they identified themselves with Him, they submitted to baptism; and in being baptized they were identifying themselves with Christ and His cause. They were declaring that Jesus of Nazareth is the Lord, that in the spiritual realm Caesar is not Lord, but Jesus is Lord, and there is no other, that He is the Messiah, the long-expected Deliverer.

All of us who say that we are 'in Christ' are proclaiming that we have forsaken all else, that He alone is our Lord and Master, that henceforth we are going to follow Him. He Himself said, 'If any man would be my disciple, let him deny himself, take up his cross, and follow me'. Baptism represents and signifies that we have done so. The importance of this in connection with unity is obvious. Before, we were individuals, every man exercising his own will, and every man going his own way; every man self-centred and selfish. In submitting to baptism we deny ourselves, we take up the cross, and we follow Christ. Obviously when we all do so truly, there can be no division, there must be unity.

Because we have all given up ourselves, we have denied ourselves, and we are looking to and following the one Lord. As the children of Israel themselves did not decide about crossing the Red Sea but listened to the call of Moses, and went after him, so we no longer are guided by our own wills, but have followed Him; and therefore we are all one. The one baptism leads inevitably to unity.

But this wonderful truth does not stop even there. There is something deeper, namely, that which we find in the sixth chapter of the Epistle to the Romans. 'Know ye not, that so many of us as were baptized into (or unto) Jesus Christ were baptized into his death? Therefore we are buried with him by baptism into death; that like as Christ was raised up from the dead by the glory of the Father, even so we also should walk in newness of life' (vv. 3–4). This statement is a part of the section of teaching which starts at verse 12 in the fifth chapter of the Epistle to the Romans, where the Apostle is showing believers, Christian people, that as they were once 'in Adam' and joined to Adam, they are now 'in Christ' and joined to Christ and a part of Christ.

Now this is the argument. Adam was the first man. In him was gathered the whole of humanity, he was the whole of the human race. Not only so, God made him the head and the representative of the whole human race. God spoke to him as such and addressed him and made a covenant with him. God told him that if he sinned he would be punished by being driven out of the Garden and would suffer death. Adam disobeyed and, as the Apostle's argument shows in the remainder of the chapter, the consequences of Adam's sin fell upon the whole of his posterity. We all sinned in Adam, because we were all 'in Adam'; we were all, as it were, in the loins of Adam. The whole of humanity has come out of Adam; so what he did we have all done. This is because of the solidity of the human race. Adam was our federal head and representative, so that what he did he did for us; and we are responsible for it, and the consequences come upon us. 'In Adam all die'.

*   *   *

The Apostle next proceeds to develop and work out his argument and to show that 'as in Adam all die, so in Christ shall all be made alive'. He makes this yet more clear in chapter 6 by dealing with the question which some might be asking, 'Shall we therefore continue in sin that grace may abound?' The Apostle replies, 'God forbid. How shall we that are dead to sin live any longer therein?' (Rom 6:1–2). But if it be asked, 'Am I dead to sin?' – of course you are, replies Paul. How am I dead to sin? You are dead to sin in that you have died to it with the Lord Jesus Christ, to whom you are now joined as you were formerly joined to Adam. You are now in Christ as you once were in Adam; and what Christ has done you have done. We can state this truth in the following manner also. In the First Epistle to the Corinthians the Apostle says: 'For by one Spirit are we all baptized into one body, whether we be Jews or Greeks' (12:13). I am not only a believer in Christ, I not only have that justifying faith which assures me that my sins are forgiven because God has punished them in Christ and imputes His righteousness to me, but I am 'in Christ', I have been baptized by the Holy Spirit into the body of Christ which is the Church. Each Christian – 'we all' – has been incorporated into Christ, has been joined to Christ and is a member in His body, the Church. As we were 'in Adam' so are we 'in Christ'. Let us look at some of the consequences of this, and see its particular importance with regard to this matter of unity.

Everything that has happened to Christ, says the Apostle, has happened to us. He was crucified; and we have been crucified with Him. 'I have been crucified with Christ', says Paul to the Galatians; and as we have just seen in Romans 6:3, 'Know ye not that so many of us as were baptized into Jesus Christ were baptized into His death'. When Adam sinned we sinned. When Christ died we died. We have died with Him. We have been buried with Him, which means that we are 'dead unto sin'. 'How shall we that are *dead* to sin live any longer therein?' The Apostle goes on to explain that 'He that is dead is freed from sin' (Rom 6:7). He says, 'Knowing that Christ being raised from the dead dieth no more, death hath no more dominion over him'. This means for us that we are dead to the realm of sin, we are dead to the whole authority of sin, we are dead to 'the world'. The Apostle says again to the Galatians, 'God forbid that I should glory, save in the cross of our Lord Jesus Christ, by whom the world has been crucified unto me, and I unto the world' (6:14).

Whether you feel it or not, if we are in Christ that is the truth concerning us. All of us by nature belong to the world and to the devil and to sin; but having been crucified with Christ we no longer belong to that realm. We have been crucified to the world, and the world has been crucified to us. Let me put it thus. I was once a man in Adam, but having died with Christ I am no longer in that position. I no longer belong to Adam's race; I belong to the new race that began in the Lord Jesus Christ who is 'the first-born among many brethren'. 'Knowing this, that our old man has been [or was] crucified with him, that the body of sin might be destroyed, that henceforth we should not serve sin' (Rom 6:6).

*   *   *

Nothing is more important than the realization of this particular truth. It affects the principle of unity in the following way. Sin always leads to division and to discord. The moment man sinned and fell, discord and disunity came into the world. You can trace the story in the early chapters of Genesis. You find Cain even murdering his brother. That is the effect of sin. Sin always divides because it leads to selfishness. Rebellious, sinful man no longer bows his knees to God, he has set himself up as a god. And each one becomes a god, and so there is discord and disunity, rivalry and strife. Such is the Adamic man always. And so the world is divided today as it has been through the centuries; and there are divisions among nations and races and groups, and alignments of nations, because of the Adamic nature that is in man. But when a man is 'in Christ' he is joined to Him; he has died with Him; the old man is dead, he is a new man. And because that is true of all who are in Christ, there should be no division and no strife and no separation.

'One Lord, one faith, one baptism'. We are no longer Adamic creatures. We should no longer be exerting our separate wills, and there should be no division, no rivalry, no jealousy, no envy. We must not begin to say, 'I am of Paul, I am of Apollos, I am of Cephas'. We must not boast in names; there is only one name – 'one Lord, one faith, one baptism'. We are in Him, we are no longer Adamic, we are Christian, we are Christ's people. We have died with Him, we have been buried with Him. The old man and his ways have been brought to an end. But thank God there is the positive also. We have also 'risen with him'. We have received new life with Him, from Him. Although we were dead in trespasses and sins we have been 'quickened together with Christ'.

So Paul goes on to argue and exhort, 'Reckon ye yourselves therefore to be dead indeed unto sin, but alive unto God, through Jesus Christ our Lord' (Rom 6:11). This means that the Christian is not only a man who believes on the Lord Jesus Christ, and that Christ has died for him and his sins. He does believe that, and he knows that his sins are forgiven because Christ has died for him. But he is much more than that! He is 'in Christ', he is joined to Christ, and the life of Christ is in him. Christ is the Head, and he is a member of the body. Christ is the Vine, and he is a branch. He is 'in Christ', a part of Christ. The life of Christ is in him, and it is the same one life in all the members. All this is true of the Christian because he has been baptized into that one body of Christ by the Holy Spirit (1 Cor 12:13). This is the true meaning of 'one baptism'. When and as we all realize this, and when we all live in the light of it, there can be no division. Christ is not divided, the body is one; it has an organic unity. There must not be schism in the body, there must not be civil war. We are each and all 'in Him' the living Head, and His life is in us, permeating our being, filling us with its power, shedding its love abroad within us.

Thus we see what the Apostle means by this 'one baptism'. He is not thinking in terms of the rite; it is not anything magical; it is this realization that there is only one name and one Lord, there is only one life, the life of the Son of God, who has redeemed us, who has ascended into heaven, in whom we have been incorporated, and whose life is our life. In writing to the Colossians Paul says, 'When Christ, *who is our life*, shall appear . . .' (3:4). He is our life. When each one of us can join in saying, 'I live, yet not I, but Christ liveth in me', we shall all be one in this living spiritual unity. The old self will have disappeared and we shall be one in Him, the living Head.

II

One God

'One God and Father of all, who is above all, and
through all, and in you all'.

Ephesians 4:6

These words complete the Apostle's great statement which began
in verse 4: 'There is one body, and one Spirit, even as ye are
called in one hope of your calling; one Lord, one faith, one
baptism, one God and Father of all, who is above all, and through
all, and in you all'. It is also the climax of Paul's appeal to the
Ephesian Christians to 'endeavour to keep the unity of the Spirit
in the bond of peace'. As we have seen, he gives them these seven
reasons for doing so, and he divides these into three main groups.
The first three centre on the Holy Spirit (one body, one Spirit,
one hope of your calling); the second three on the Son (one Lord,
one faith, one baptism); and now he comes to the climax – 'one
God and Father of all, who is above all, and through all, and in
you all'.

Nothing is so characteristic of the way in which the Apostle
writes to the various churches as the way in which he always rises
to this climax. We find, for instance, another example of this in
the eleventh chapter of the Epistle to the Romans, where after
outlining the course of the Church's history, and showing how a
temporary blindness had fallen upon Israel, he asserts God's
great and sure purpose, and ends by saying, 'O, the depth of the
riches both of the wisdom and knowledge of God! how unsearchable are his judgments, and his ways past finding out! For
who hath known the mind of the Lord? or who hath been his
counsellor? or who hath first given to him, and it shall be
recompensed unto him again? For of him, and through him, and to
him, are all things; to whom be glory for ever. Amen' (vv. 33–36).

[131]

The Apostle does not stop at the Spirit or the Son, as so many Christian people are tempted to do; he always goes on to the Father.

We must remind ourselves of the fact that the Apostle arranges these truths in an experimental order. As members of the Church we naturally think first of the work of the Holy Spirit. But the Holy Spirit brings us to the Son, because He was sent to glorify the Son. And the Son's chief desire and purpose was to glorify the Father. This needs to be emphasized at the present time because there is a tendency to fail to remember this. There is a popular school of theology which emphasizes the Christocentric aspect of salvation. In a sense it is correct in doing so; but we must never stop at the Son. The Apostle Peter in his First Epistle reminds us of this when he writes: 'For Christ also hath once suffered for sins, the just for the unjust, that he might bring us to God' (3:18).

The Apostle is concerned to show that everything in connection with our Christian salvation suggests the element of unity; and nowhere is this seen more clearly than in the doctrine of the Persons of the blessed Holy Trinity. Each Person in the Trinity is concerned about us and our salvation; each One deals with a particular aspect of this work, and each One co-operates with the Others. The Apostle is encouraging the Ephesian believers to remember this always. He does not begin by immediately talking to them about themselves; he reminds them, rather, of the great objective truth concerning their salvation. This is the key to most of our problems. I find more and more that most troubles in the Christian life are due to the fact that we are too subjective, and spend too much time in looking at ourselves and feeling, as it were, our spiritual pulses. The cure for most of the ills and diseases of the soul is to look at the grand objective truth, the glory of our redemption and salvation. Were we but to realize that the three blessed Persons in the Holy Trinity are intimately and actively concerned about us and our salvation, our whole situation would be entirely changed. The biblical teaching concerning salvation is that, even before time, in an eternal Council between Father, Son and Holy Spirit our salvation was planned and purposed; and in the fulness of time it was put into operation. As members of the Church, the Apostle teaches, we are in relationship to the Spirit and the Son and the Father. And this relationship makes the question of unity inevitable.

This is also the only way to maintain that unity; not the setting up of vast organizations in order to try to produce it. The way to unity is to preach the Gospel, not to set up new offices and organizations. Unity results from a comprehension and understanding of the truth.

*   *   *

And now we come to the particular truth concerning 'one God and Father of all'. For some strange reason we are constantly in danger of forgetting that the Church, after all, is 'the church of God'. There are cults which talk about 'the Church of Christ' – and there is a sense in which the Church is the Church of Christ – but the term used in the Bible is 'the church of God'. We read, for instance, of 'The church of God which is at Corinth'.

How does this help us to understand this principle of unity? The first expression is, 'one God'. This means that as Christians we realize that there is only 'one God'. The pagan world to which the Ephesian Christians had once belonged did not believe this truth. As the Apostle reminds the Corinthians, 'We (Christians) know that an idol is nothing in the world, and that there is none other God but one. For though there be that are called gods, whether in heaven or on earth (as there be gods many, and lords many), but to us there is but one God, the Father, of whom are all things, and we in him, and one Lord Jesus Christ, by whom are all things, and we by him' (1 Cor 8:4–6). Here, also, in the interests of unity, the Apostle is producing the argument of the 'one God'. Belief in a multiplicity of gods always leads to division. One man worships Jupiter, another Mercurius, another Mars, or some other god. The towns and cities of the Pagans were cluttered with altars to the various gods, as Paul found at Athens. That, Paul taught everywhere, was the result of the work of the Devil; for there is only 'one God'. And because there is only one God there must be essential unity among those who believe in Him.

The Apostle is not only teaching that there is only one God, but is also emphasizing the fact that God is one. This is a great mystery, but it is the essence of the doctrine of the Trinity. We

[133]

do not believe that there are three Gods; there is one 'God in three Persons, blessed Trinity'. The one great doctrine which the Jews had to preserve and to protect was this truth and doctrine concerning the unity of God, that 'God is one'. This explains why some of the Jews at first found it difficult to believe in the Lord Jesus Christ, who claimed that He was one with the Father. This seemed to suggest that there are two Gods, but it is not so. Do not try to understand this; no one can understand this ultimate mystery. But it is the truth which we find in the Scriptures. God is One – there is one Godhead. But there are three Persons in the Godhead. This does not imply three Gods, not Tri-theism but Monotheism – three Persons in the one and Eternal Godhead. This truth is clearly in the mind of the Apostle here. We recognize the Spirit; we recognize the Son; we recognize the Father: but we say that the Three are one God.

This is taught throughout the Scriptures. We read that the Spirit is in us, that Christ is in us, that God is in us. We read that the Spirit has done certain things, we read elsewhere that Christ has done the same things, and again that the Father has done the same things. That is but a way of emphasizing this truth that the Three are One in the Eternal Godhead – 'God in three Persons, blessed Trinity'. It is a Trinity in Unity, it is a Tri-unity. This again enforces and emphasizes the principle of unity. in the Church. As the three blessed Persons are one, so we who worship and belong to God are likewise of necessity one. We are to remember, therefore, to 'maintain the unity of the Spirit in the bond of peace' by looking at, and believing, and by being amazed at, this doctrine of the Trinity.

*   *   *

Certain practical conclusions can be deduced from this. The end and object of salvation is 'to bring us to God'. Is it not extraordinary that one has to go on repeating and emphasizing this? The end of salvation is not to bring us to the Lord Jesus Christ. The Lord Jesus Christ came into this world, and did all He did, 'to bring us to God', to God the Father. That is why we pray to God the Father rather than to the Lord Jesus Christ. We come to God through the Lord Jesus Christ; but the end of all is 'to bring us to God'. We see this to be quite inevitable when we really understand the message of the Bible. At the beginning we find that God made man in His own image, and that man was subject to God. But sin and rebellion came in; and that led to the Fall, the effect of which was to separate man from God. So as sin is that which separates us from God, salvation is that which brings us back to God. The grand end and object of salvation is not only that we should be happy and have certain experiences and benefits. It does all that, of course, but if I do not realize that the chief end of my salvation is to reconcile me to God and to bring me to God and to enable me to enter into the presence of God, I have not understood it truly. It is at this point that Christianity differs from all cults and from all other religions. They always centre on man, and some benefit for man; but the Christian faith and teaching starts with God, and everything leads to God – 'one God'.

This being the great end and object of salvation, all of us who are Christians therefore obviously come together to the same God; and if we come to the same God there can be no divisions. We all have one and the same object of worship. The Apostle has already dealt with this several times in earlier portions of this Epistle. In chapter 2, verse 18, he says, 'For through him [Christ] we both [Jew and Gentile] have access by one Spirit unto the Father'. The Jew was formerly a worshipper of God, while the Gentile was a worshipper of one of the pagan deities; but now all that has gone, and both Jew and Gentile 'have access by one Spirit unto the Father'. If we realized this, unity would be quite inevitable.

In heaven everything centres around God. We are taught this clearly in chapters 4 and 5 of the Book of Revelation. The beasts and the elders and all the holy angels worship and bow before and centre on God the Eternal Father. Before Him the angels veil their faces. There is perfect harmony in heaven. Indeed this is what makes heaven heaven; there is no disunity, there is no discord. Everything is in unison, everything is in harmony. God is all, and all are worshipping Him and bowing before Him. God is the centre. And therefore all is bliss and joy and perfection. But Paul reminds us that even here on earth we are all worshipping this one God, and as we realize the presence of God, all distinctions and all schisms immediately vanish and disappear. In the presence of the glory of God everything else pales into insignificance, and we are 'lost in wonder, love and praise'. One God! We worship Him, the only God, and we all do so together. There is no need to argue about unity; the realization of the presence of God creates unity.

Furthermore we can and should remind ourselves that we are all going to this one and the same God. We are now on earth and are together as members in the Church. Our salvation reconciles us to God, and enables us to worship Him. But we are not static; we are but 'strangers and pilgrims' in this world, we are 'marching to Zion'. We are all going to meet and to see the same God. 'Blessed are the pure in heart, for they shall see God'. We are going to the same eternal home. As the hymn from which we have already quoted reminds us:—

> *One the gladness of rejoicing*
> *On the far eternal shore,*
> *Where the one almighty Father*
> *Reigns in love for evermore.*

O that we might realize that we are all under the eye of God and all going to God! There is only one God, and nothing else matters.

*   *   *

The Apostle, however, does not leave it at that; he says, 'One God and Father of all, who is above all, and through all, and in you all'. It is most important for us to note that the word *all* is not in the neuter gender, but in the masculine gender. This is important because when he says 'One God and Father of all' he does not mean all things – the creation, the universe, the cosmos and all it contains – but all persons. However, we must hasten to add that that does not mean every single individual that has ever lived or ever will live. There are those who are prepared to say that that is the meaning, and that they find in this verse an argument for what they call the 'Universal Fatherhood of God'. God, they assert, is the Father of all, and we as Christians must not confine God's Fatherhood to ourselves only. A careful analysis of the statement shows that this cannot be its meaning. The Apostle is writing about the Church; he is not writing about the world. He is writing to those who belong to a 'body', those who are 'in Christ'; he is writing to Christian people whom he is exhorting to endeavour to 'keep the unity of the Spirit in the bond of peace'. He is not thinking about the world in general, but about those who have been gathered out of the world, incorporated into the body of Christ, and who are members of His mystical body. The entire reference is to Christian people only; the 'all' covers all Christian people and no-one else.

Not only so, for the very last phrase here, 'and in you all', is itself sufficient to settle the matter once and for ever. This phrase is never used about the unbeliever, the non-Christian. God is only 'in' the believer, 'in' the Christian. But we can go further and give a clinching final proof. The next verse – verse 7 – establishes our contention beyond any doubt whatsoever, that the Apostle is talking about the Church – 'But unto every one of us is given grace according to the measure of the gift of Christ' – and he proceeds to deal with the division of gifts and of labours within the body, the Church. So from the very beginning he is confining his attention to the Church, to Christian people, and is not saying anything whatsoever about those who are outside.

God is not the Father of all men. Our Lord said of some men, 'Ye are of your father the devil, and the lusts of your father ye will do' (John 8:44). God is the creator of all, and there is a kind of general fatherhood in that respect; but God's fatherhood, as stated here, is limited to those who are in Christ and in the Church. So while we do not believe in the Universal Fatherhood of God, and the Universal Brotherhood of man, we do and should believe in the Fatherhood of God in the case of all who belong to Christ. The Apostle began this Epistle by saying, 'Blessed be the God and Father of our Lord Jesus Christ', and his entire argument is that, through Christ, God has become our Father also. The stupendous fact that we must try to grasp is that God, this great, glorious and eternal God, is our Father. Paul has repeated this in chapter 2, saying, 'Through Him we both have access by one Spirit unto the Father' (v. 18). Then in chapter 3 he refers to the 'Father of our Lord Jesus Christ, of whom every family in heaven and earth is named' (vv. 14, 15), and he is but repeating it here. Were we but to see and understand by the Spirit that we are the children of God it would revolutionize our whole thinking and our entire living. The Apostle Peter, using a different expression, says that we have become 'partakers of the divine nature' (2 Peter 1:4). This does not mean that we have become gods, but that we have been given a principle of life which comes out of God Himself.

This is what it really means to be a Christian. A Christian is a man who is born-again, born of the Spirit, born of God. This principle of divine and eternal life is put into him; he is therefore a child of God. God is his Father. This of necessity introduces the principle of unity. As Christians we are all the children of God, children of the same Father, who belong to the same family. We belong to the household of which Paul has reminded us at the end of the second chapter where he says, 'Ye are no more strangers and foreigners, but fellow citizens with the saints, and of the household of God'. We have been adopted into God's family, and He has sent the Spirit of His Son into our hearts, crying, Abba, Father' (Gal 4:6). How little we think about these things, and how infrequently we speak about them! How concerned we are about externals and things that are on the periphery and the circumference of our Christian life. If we came back to these centralities, if we but realized the meaning of this particular statement that God is our Father, and that we belong to His family, and that He looks upon us as His dearly beloved children, our entire outlook would be changed and unity would follow inevitably, as night follows day.

*   *   *

The Apostle was a wise teacher; he knew these Ephesians, and he knows us. Therefore he does not leave this as a general statement, he goes on to particulars, adding, 'Who is above all, and through all, and in you all.' This addition is no mere rhetorical flourish or vain accumulation of words. It is the working out of what he has already been saying in detail, knowing that if they grasp this it will solve their problems, and help them to guard 'the unity of the Spirit in the bond of peace'. He divides up the general statement into three particulars. Some have interpreted this as meaning that the Apostle is again obviously referring to the doctrine of the Trinity. They say that the 'one God and Father of all, who is above all', refers to God the Father; the 'through all' refers to

God the Son; 'and in you all' refers to God the Holy Spirit. Many great and learned commentators have argued thus, probably tending to repeat one another. But surely that is a totally impossible explanation and exposition for the good and sufficient reason that the Apostle is dealing here with God the Father only, with the 'One God and Father of all, who is above all and through all, and in you all'. He has already dealt with the Spirit, and with the Son; he is dealing now with the Father, and these three statements undoubtedly refer to the Father.

I suggest that Paul has already given us in the first three chapters an exposition of what he means here. The first thing he says about God the Father is that He is 'above all'. This means that God is over all. It is a reference to the supremacy of God the Father, to the exalted position of God the Father, to the fact that in the 'economic' Trinity God the Father is supreme. In the work of salvation the Son has subordinated Himself to the Father, though He is co-equal and co-eternal with Him; and the Spirit has subordinated Himself to the Son and to the Father. The Father is 'over all'; His is the ultimate supremacy. Does this refer to the fact that God is the Creator, that God is supreme over the whole universe and cosmos? That is true; but the Apostle does not have that in his mind here. He is thinking in terms of the Church. And when he says that God, the one Father, is above all, he means above all in the Church, and to the Church of the redeemed. The meaning surely is that in this whole matter of the Church, in the matter of the redeemed, in the case of you and myself and all of us who are in the body of Christ, and in this blessed unity, God the Father is the originator of it all. The Church is His grand purpose and design. The Apostle has already been saying this and expounding it in chapter 1, 'Blessed be the God and Father of our Lord Jesus Christ' (v. 3). That is where he begins, and that is where we must begin in our thinking. He is about to expound Christian doctrine, he is about to unfold the amazing thing that God has done in bringing the Church into being, and he begins with 'Blessed be the God and Father of our Lord Jesus Christ'. But he continues to stress the same thing in the following verses: 'According as he [God the Father] has chosen us in him [God the Son] before the foundation of the world, having predestinated us unto the adoption of children by Jesus Christ to himself [God the Father].' The Father conceived the idea, He has planned it, He has purposed it. Then note the significant phrase at the end of verse 5, 'according to the good pleasure of his will' – the will of God.

The same truth is found yet more explicitly in later verses: 'Having made known unto us the mystery of his will, according to his good pleasure which he hath purposed in himself' (v. 9). The great eternal God, in His glory and infinity and ineffability, has 'purposed in himself' to look upon you and me and to redeem us, to take us out of the dominion of sin and Satan and hell, and put us into 'the body of Christ' and adopt us into his own family. God the Father did it Himself, 'according to the purpose of his own will', 'according to his good pleasure which he purposed in himself'. It is in this sense that God the Father is 'above all' or 'over all'. The purpose is stated clearly in the words, 'That in the dispensation of the fulness of times he [God the Father] might gather together in one all things in Christ, both which are in heaven and which are on earth; even in him' (v. 10).

Of these things the Apostle is reminding us here in chapter 4 in dealing with the question of unity. His argument is that there is 'one God and Father of all, who is above all', and being above all, His plan and purpose is to re-unite, to gather together in one all things in Christ. There is no need to argue or to appeal about unity if you realize that the purpose of God the Father, who is above all, is to re-unite, to head up again in one, that which has been divided and sundered by sin. Disunity and schism become utterly impossible for us if we rejoice in such a truth as this; we would never allow ourselves to be in a position in which we cause division. God's whole purpose is to re-unite. He is 'above all', and He has planned and purposed this gathering together again.

*   *   *

But Paul says, secondly, that God is not only 'above all' but also 'through all'. By this he means that He acts through all, or He is 'energetic' in all. This may be regarded as a description of God's providence. In other words, Paul is saying that God pervades the whole life of the Church and sustains it. It is the energy of God that has brought the Church into being, and keeps the Church in being, and will hold it in being until the final consummation. The

Apostle expounds this himself at the end of chapter 1 where, having thanked God for the Ephesian Christians, he tells them that he is praying for them thus: '. . . the eyes of your understanding being enlightened; that ye may know what is the hope of his calling, and what the riches of the glory of his inheritance in the saints, and what is the exceeding greatness of his power to us-ward who believe, according to the working of his mighty power, which he wrought in Christ' (vv. 18–20). His desire for them is that they may realize the exceeding greatness of God's power, 'the energy of the might of his strength', toward all who believe. It is this power which brought them out of darkness and deadness into light and life, when they were 'dead in trespasses and sins'. He had quickened them, He had raised them from the dead by this energy. No man would or could be saved but for God's energy; it is He who quickens and raises us from the death of sin.

This is worked out in chapter 2. God did not stop at quickening us. He maintains us and sustains us. Nothing is more important, says Paul to these Ephesians, than that we should know this 'exceeding greatness of his power to us-ward who believe'. And this power is in all of us. The same energy, the same life, the same power is in us all. The familiar hymn on the nature of the Church reminds us of this:—

> *One the light of God's own presence*
> *O'er His ransomed people shed,*
> *Chasing far the gloom and terror,*
> *Brightening all the path we tread.*

> *One the object of our journey,*
> *One the faith which never tires,*
> *One the earnest looking forward,*
> *One the hope our God inspires.*

With the same idea in his mind, Paul, in writing to the Philippians says, 'Work out your own salvation with fear and trembling, for it is God that worketh in you both to will and to do of his good pleasure' (2: 12–13). The energy of God is seen in sanctification as in every part of our salvation. He is 'above all', and He is 'through all'.

Finally, He is 'in you all'. This, the most amazing thing of all, means nothing less than that God the Father, as God the Son and God the Holy Spirit, is in us all. The Apostle has said in chapter 2: 'Ye are no more strangers and foreigners, but fellow-citizens with the saints, and of the household of God; and are built upon the foundation of the apostles and prophets, Jesus Christ himself being the chief corner stone; in whom all the building fitly framed together groweth unto an holy temple in the Lord: in whom ye also are builded together for an habitation of God through the Spirit' (vv. 19–22). The Church is the habitation of God; He dwells in her, and therefore in us. Our Lord Himself had already taught this, as we find in John's Gospel: 'Jesus answered and said unto him, If a man love me, he will keep my words: and my Father will love him, and *we* will come unto him, and make our abode with him' (14:23). These words state the truth in all its wonder and amazement and glory. We cannot contemplate it and realize it without being one. It is not surprising that our Lord in His 'high priestly prayer' should have prayed thus: 'That they all may be one; as thou, Father, art in me, and I in thee, that they also may be one in us: that the world may believe that thou hast sent me. And the glory which thou gavest me I have given them; that they may be one, even as we are one: I in them, and thou in me, that they may be made perfect in one; and that the world may know that thou hast sent me, and hast loved them, as thou hast loved me' (John 17:21–23). 'One God and Father, who is above all, and through all, and in you all'.

*   *   *

Have you contemplated this great truth? Have you considered the fact that God the Father, God the Son, and God the Holy Spirit are concerned in your redemption? Have you seen that to realize this alone makes us one? The end of all doctrine is to lead to the knowledge of God, and the worship of God; any knowledge we may have is useless if it does not bring us to that point. If your spirit is not humble, if you are not loving, if you are not concerned about this unity of God's people, you have nothing better than intellectual knowledge that is barren and may indeed be even of the Devil. Our Lord said, 'If ye know these things, happy are ye if ye do them' (John 13:17). Are you striving to realize that there is 'one body and one Spirit, even as ye are called in one hope of your calling; one Lord, one faith, one baptism, one God and Father of all, who is above all, and through all, and in you all'? The Apostle Peter tells us that the angels desire to look into this. Are you looking into it?

12

'One ... every one'

'But unto every one of us is given grace according to
the measure of the gift of Christ. Wherefore he saith,
When he ascended up on high, he led captivity
captive, and gave gifts unto men. (Now that he
ascended, what is it but that he also descended first
into the lower parts of the earth? He that descended is
the same also that ascended up far above all heavens,
that he might fill all things.)'

Ephesians 4:7–10

Although this great statement starts with the disjunctive word
'but', it is obvious that the subject with which it deals is related
very closely to the one with which we have been dealing. In other
words, 'but' is, after all, a conjunction. It implies a contrast, but
at the same time it refers us back to that which has gone before.
Clearly the Apostle is still continuing with the subject of the
unity of the church; he is still working out the exhortation to
'maintain the unity of the Spirit in the bond of peace'. But he is
now going to do so in a slightly different manner; he is going to
look at another aspect of the subject. That is why he employs
this particular word 'but'. It is essential that he should do this, for
had he not done so there would be a very real danger of our
having a false sense and conception of what this unity means.

There is always the danger of our conceiving of unity in terms
of uniformity. Our tendency is to think of unity as consisting of
a number of things which are absolutely identical in every single
respect, with no difference at all, such as a sheet of postage
stamps. But the Apostle is at pains to show us that that is not
true unity, but a dull, drab uniformity. Unity, he shows, is much
bigger than that, a much grander thing. Any conception of unity
which equates it with uniformity detracts from the essential
greatness and glory of unity. In other words unity is not some-

thing mechanical; it does not mean sameness. It is very difficult for us, living at the present time, to grasp this point. We are accustomed to mass-production – articles coming out of a machine one after another, all exactly the same. And they are meant to be identical. This is not only true of machinery and manufactured goods, there are obvious tendencies in the world today to think in the same manner of human beings. This is not entirely new; it has characterized certain educational establishments which have produced a mass product, a distinct type of individuals, all of whom conform to the same behaviour pattern in deportment and speech and other respects. Each one has the stamp upon him, and one is more aware of the type than of the individual himself, except in certain unusual individuals. This is not surprising, because the herd-instinct is powerful in all of us by nature. The Apostle discountenances this notion and shows that unity is something living and vital, something which is almost staggering in its variety. This indeed is the very special and most glorious aspect of spiritual unity. Let us follow the Apostle as he works out this principle.

In studying verses 4, 5 and 6 we saw that the Apostle uses the word 'one' seven times – '*one* Spirit, *one* body, *one* hope of your calling, *one* Lord, *one* faith, *one* baptism, *one* God and Father of all', and thereby establishes the great principle of unity. But the Apostle's conception of unity, and the New Testament teaching about unity, is such that having emphasized the oneness seven times, he can immediately go on to say, 'But unto every one of us'. He seems suddenly to have shattered the unity by this 'every one of us'. But he has not done so, for we have not become merged into a solid and undifferentiated mass; we have not lost our identity. We are still our individual selves. We are being regarded again as single personalities, and must think of ourselves as units in a whole. The amazing and astonishing fact is that, though we are all 'one', we can nevertheless be addressed in the phrase 'every one of us'.

The explanation is this. We are all 'one' in Christ. We are all one in the matter of our salvation, and as children of God. We are all one as members severally of the body of Christ. This is what the Apostle has been emphasizing and stressing. Every individual Christian has been saved in exactly the same manner as everyone else. The Apostle Paul's salvation is no different *qua* salvation from any other Christian's salvation. All conversions are essentially the same. The special and peculiar circumstances, the particular details, are really irrelevant. That is why it is so wrong to make so much of them as is frequently done. Regeneration is the work of the Spirit of God, and Him alone. It is a miracle in every single case, and it is always the same miracle. Furthermore, as children of God, and as members of the household of God, there is no difference. Think of a family, a large family; some may be boys, some girls, but all are equally children. The boys are no more children than the girls, and the girls no more so than the boys. They may differ greatly in many respects, but that does not make the slightest difference to their relationship, to the fact that they are children, to the fact that they are in this peculiar relationship to their father. The image and illustration of the body clearly conveys the same notion and idea.

In those aspects we are all identical, we are all one, and we are all the same. But – and this is what the Apostle is now going to deal with – our unity does not mean that we are identical in every single respect. A thousand times no! 'Every one of us'. In this expression he is introducing the diversity and the difference and the variety and variation. The special glory of the unity is that it is a unity in diversity, a unity that comprehends variation and variability. We are essentially one, but in many respects we differ. We must keep these two principles together in our minds constantly. The diversity does not break the unity; and the unity does not do away with the diversity. This is the special glory of redeeming grace; this is the miracle of redemption. This is the peculiar phenomenon which the Christian Church is to manifest and demonstrate to the world, and which nothing else can do.

*   *   *

The Apostle now proceeds to emphasize these obvious differences in the members of the body, that is, in the members of the Church: 'Unto every one of us is given grace according to the measure of the gift of Christ'. The question which confronts us is, How can this great unity which Paul has emphasized so much be possibly preserved in the light of this diversity and variation? It is a question he answers immediately, beginning at verse 7 and

[146]

continuing to the end of verse 16. In these verses he paints a picture of the Church, and showing how the Church is character- ized by these twin elements of unity and diversity. The two elements are held together throughout in a marvellous manner. We are led into the secret of it all, and shown how it comes to pass in the experience and activity of the Church.

The Apostle lays down the great principle in the words: 'Unto every one of us is given grace according to the measure of the gift of Christ' (v. 7). The controlling principle is that the Lord Jesus Christ Himself is the Head of the Church and is the Giver of the variety of gifts which are enjoyed by the Church as a whole and by every single member in particular. This is the principle which guarantees the unity in the diversity. The Apostle works out this same principle in the twelfth chapter of his First Epistle to the Corinthians. He does so in that instance in terms of the Spirit. It amounts to the same thing, because, as he tells us here, it is the Lord Jesus Christ who gives the Spirit, and He gives His gifts through the Spirit. To the Corinthians he says, 'Now there are diversities of gifts, but the same Spirit. And there are differ- ences of administrations, but the same Lord' (1 Cor 12:4–5). There we have precisely the same central and controlling principle.

*　　*　　*

But now a question arises which insists upon our attention. It is something which is very characteristic of this Apostle, and which he is going to work out: 'Unto every one of us is given grace according to the measure of the gift of Christ'. We anticipate that he is about to say immediately, 'and he gave some apostles, and some prophets, and some evangelists, and some preachers and teachers'. But he does not do so. It is what he eventually does say, and clearly intends to say; but he interrupts himself and inserts the contents of verses 8, 9 and 10. These verses constitute a kind of parenthesis, and it is that which is so characteristic of Paul's method as a writer. But why does he follow this method? There is but one answer to the question. He had mentioned the name of Christ: 'But unto every one of us is given grace according to the measure of the gift of Christ'. Mention of the blessed name immediately inflames him and fires him. He cannot restrain

[147]

himself, and he pours out these three verses with this tremendous statement about our blessed Lord and Saviour. I emphasize this because it illustrates the fact that the Apostle Paul so loved the Lord Jesus Christ that the very mention of His name always moved him to the depths of his being. He could say in a yet higher degree what Bernard of Clairvaux said –

Jesus, the very thought of Thee
With sweetness fills my breast.

The very mention of the name causes him to interrupt his particular thought and to set forth His glory once more. In doing so he becomes guilty of perpetrating a literary crime known as an anacoluthon. The purists comment on this. These anacolutha which are very characteristic of Paul's style constitute an interruption of an argument or a statement by another statement and then a return to, and a continuation of, the original idea. In the Authorised Version verses 9 and 10 are placed in brackets, and rightly so in a sense. Indeed the first bracket should appear at verse 8. I suggest that what led to the parenthesis was something like this. Paul has mentioned in the original statement in verse 7 that the Lord Jesus Christ is the Head of the Church and that He is the Giver and the Dispenser of all the gifts. This leads him not only to ascribe all glory to the Lord but also to show us how the Lord Jesus Christ ever came into the position to be able to do this. Why is Christ the Head of the Church? Why is He the Giver of all the gifts? How has the Son of God ever arrived at the particular position which entitles Him to do this? This is the question which is answered in verses 8, 9 and 10.

We can analyse the statement in the following manner. The first thing the Apostle says is that the statement he has just made should not surprise us, for it has all been foretold and prophesied of old – 'Wherefore, He saith', meaning that the Holy Ghost, or God, so speaks in the Scripture – and immediately he quotes from the 68th Psalm: 'When he ascended up on high he led captivity captive, and gave gifts to men' (v. 18). His point is that his statement about the grace given to each one of us as Christians by the Lord Jesus Christ must not be thought of as something which had suddenly come into the mind of God. On the contrary it was always a part of God's plan of redemption, and of His purpose with respect to the Church. God had actually revealed it to the Psalmist some ten centuries previously.

I emphasize this matter because there is a teaching known as Dispensationalism, which tells us that God sent the Lord Jesus Christ into the world to set up the Kingdom of God, but that when He found that the Jews rejected His Son and His teaching, and would not receive the Kingdom, He then decided upon the way of salvation through the Cross and the setting up of the Church. The Church, say the Dispensationalists, is an afterthought, a parenthesis; it was not a part of the original plan, and is but a temporary phase until the Kingdom will again be preached to the Jews and introduced. But in verses 8, 9 and 10 we have a complete denial of this dispensational teaching, for it is disproved beyond any question in Psalm 68, verse 18, where we have this prophecy concerning the Church, and the Lord Jesus Christ as the Head of the Church.

But the Apostle goes further, for he proceeds to make a comment on his quotation. He does so in verses 9 and 10. These three verses 8, 9 and 10 are extremely interesting and important. Anyone who is at all familiar with the history of the Church, and especially the history of the doctrine and of theology, will know that they have often played an important part in discussion and in controversy, and have frequently been misunderstood. It therefore behoves us to consider them carefully and to take time to understand them, not only in their general import, but also in their particular teaching, and even in a technical sense.

*   *   *

The first thing we note is that the quotation in verse 8 from the 68th Psalm is obviously a reference to God Himself, the Lord, Jehovah. This is true of the entire psalm. For instance we read in verses 4 and 5, 'Sing unto God, sing praises to his name: extol him that rideth upon the heavens by his name JAH [which is short for Jehovah], and rejoice before him. A father of the fatherless, and a judge of the widows, is God in his holy habitation'. Again, 'The chariots of God are twenty thousand, even thousands of angels: the Lord is among them as in Sinai, in the holy place' (v. 17). And in the eighteenth verse, which the Apostle quotes: 'Thou hast ascended on high, thou hast led captivity captive: thou hast received gifts for men; yea, for the rebellious also, that the Lord God might dwell among them'. In this psalm David is extolling the name of God; and he does so because of a great victory God had just given him. His own victory reminds him that it is not the only victory which God has given His people. That sends him back to the story of the children of Israel coming out of Egypt and crossing the Red Sea, the destruction of Pharaoh and his hosts, and the journey through the wilderness and the entry into Canaan. All these, says the Psalmist, are the victories of God. God's people have been in trouble, and God has, as it were, come down and delivered them; and having done so He has, as it were, ascended into heaven again. That was what David was setting out to say. But here in this eighth verse of this fourth chapter of his Epistle to the Ephesians the Apostle Paul ascribes it all to the Lord Jesus Christ. He is referring to the gift of Christ. 'Wherefore when he ascended up on high, he led captivity captive and gave gifts unto men'. Paul is talking about Christ and the Church, whereas the psalmist is talking about Jehovah. How do we reconcile these things?

The difficulty reminds us of something which we must always bear in mind when we read the Bible. If we fail to do so our reading will often be unintelligent and confused. It is that we will often find a double meaning in statements in the Old Testament. This is so in many of the psalms; it is equally true of many of the Prophets and their writings. In the 68th Psalm the first thing in David's mind was a local historical event, a contemporary happening about which he desires to write. But because he is under the influence of the Holy Spirit, and thereby an inspired man, he is led on to something beyond the time then present. David himself may not have realized this, but he is led by the Spirit to a higher truth. Inspiration leads David to describe the local circumstance in such a way that it becomes also a perfect foreshadowing of that which is going to happen later. It is a prophecy of Christ; it is an accurate and exact description of what happened to the Lord Jesus Christ Himself. Similarly the prophets wrote for their own day and generation; they had a local and an immediate message; but it did not stop at that. Coupled with it was the larger, the greater message, the prophetic message concerning the coming of the Messiah. The immediate and the local also contained the remote and the greater. Our first principle, then, is that the psalmist, under divine inspiration, saw in the local event a picture and an adumbration of the coming of the Son of God and what He was going to do. This is one of the great proofs of the inspiration of the Scriptures.

In the second place it is equally clear that the teaching of the Apostle here, as indeed in all his writings, is that the Lord Jesus Christ is Jehovah, the JAH of whom David writes. In the Old Testament there are references to 'the Angel of the Covenant', and of his coming down to help the people. Undoubtedly these are references to the Lord Jesus Christ. We recall also how Paul, in 1 Corinthians chapter 10, says that Christ was the Rock that followed the children of Israel, the Rock which gave them water. The martyr Stephen likewise, in his great address when he was on trial, says that Christ was with the children of Israel, 'the Church in the wilderness'. In other words the teaching is that Christ is Jehovah.

You cannot say of the Father that He received gifts for men. You cannot say of the Father that He ascended, because He is always in heaven and always has been there, and always will be there. There is only one of whom we can say that He ascended up on high – the Lord Jesus Christ. So we deduce this great truth which is at the very heart and centre of the Christian message. Jesus of Nazareth is the Son of God. He is not a created being. He is co-equal, co-eternal with the Father, equal with Him in might and majesty. The truth concerning the Father, Son, and Holy Spirit, the whole doctrine of the Trinity, is found here. The Son subordinated Himself for the work of salvation; but He is not subordinate in Himself. It is at this point that the Arian heresy arose in the early Church, and threatened her very life. It taught that Christ is a created being, created before time, but still a created being. This is where Unitarianism is equally wrong. Christ is Jehovah, Christ is the Lord. The term 'Lord', used in the Old Testament of God, is the same term which is applied and ascribed to the Lord Jesus Christ in the New Testament. Our second deduction, therefore, is that Jesus Christ is Lord, that Jesus Christ is Jehovah.

There is yet another matter for our consideration. The 18th verse of the 68th Psalm is not identical with the quotation in this

8th verse of Ephesians chapter 4. Here we read, 'Wherefore he saith, When he ascended up on high, he led captivity captive, and gave gifts unto men'. But in the 68th Psalm we find, and he 'received gifts for men' (v. 18), not that He *gave* them, but that He *received* them. This again is important. In the Hebrew of the Old Testament the word is indeed *received*, and in the Septuagint, the translation of the Seventy, it is also rightly translated *received*. But here the Apostle Paul writes *gave*. This seems to conflict with the doctrine of the inspiration of the Scripture. How can we say that the Apostle is definitely writing as one inspired when he mis-quotes an Old Testament Scripture? The clever critics argue that this disposes of our claim for the authority of the Scripture and especially of the infallibility of the Scripture. But our answer is quite clear, and it is that there is no contradiction here. It is true to say of the Lord Jesus Christ that He both *received* and *gave*. The Apostle Peter said on the Day of Pentecost at Jerusalem, 'Therefore being by the right hand of God exalted, and having received of the Father the promise of the Holy Ghost, he hath shed forth this, which ye now see and hear' (Acts 2:33). He has *received*, and He has *given*; it is one action. The same Person receives and gives; the giving presupposes the receiving. But granting that, says someone, 'what about the question of the authority and inspiration of the Holy Spirit?' The answer is that it is the same Holy Spirit who inspired David when he wrote the Psalm as inspired the Apostle Paul when he wrote the 4th chapter of this letter to the Ephesians; and what He does in both cases is to show that all the gifts that come to the Church come from and through the Lord Jesus Christ. In the one instance He emphasizes that it is the Father who gives them to the Son, in the other he emphasizes that it is the Son who gives them to the Church, and her individual members. There is no contradiction; both state-ments are true. Indeed it is precisely here that we see so clearly the lordship and the sovereignty of the Holy Spirit. There are other examples in the New Testament where Old Testament statements are quoted but not in the absolutely identical words. What matters always is the meaning. The Holy Spirit is concerned about meanings, and He brings out the same meaning in both cases, which is that the gifts are given to the Church in and through and by the Lord Jesus Christ. The Apostle Paul was well aware of what is stated in Psalm 68, verse 18, both in the original Hebrew and in the Septuagint translation, and yet, under the inspiration of the Spirit, he says 'gave'. He desires to emphasize the one action, receiving and giving. The Son is ever, always, the great Mediator.

*   *   *

This brings us to a final comment on what we may call the mechanical aspect of this great statement before we go on to draw out the great doctrine which is taught here. The final phrase reads, 'he led captivity captive'. There has been a teaching which regards 'captivity' as referring to the Old Testament saints. It maintains that they were children of God, that they were saved, but that they were held in a kind of captivity. What the Lord Jesus Christ did after His death, they argue, was to go down into Hades and bring them out of their captivity and introduce them to a higher sphere. That is the teaching of the Roman Catholics at this point. They talk about what they call a 'limbus patrum', where the fathers remained until Christ brought them out of their captivity. I reject that as an entirely false interpretation here, because the picture is one of triumph over enemies, one of the leading of enemies in triumph. In ancient times, if a king or a prince or a great military captain waged successful warfare, when he came back to his own country there was always a kind of victory parade. The conquered kings and princes and military chieftains and captains were all made to walk in the procession in their chains. The conqueror was 'leading captivity captive'. He had taken his foes captive and was now making a public display of them. At the same time he threw gifts to his own people. He was riding in his chariot distributing his largesse among the acclaiming people, and he was leading these conquered men as captives at the same time. That is undoubtedly the picture here. So we must not interpret this in terms of some liberation given to the redeemed saints of the Old Testament. It is a picture of the Lord Jesus Christ leading in His triumphal train the devil and hell and sin and death – the great enemies that were against man and which had held mankind in captivity for so long a time. The princes which had controlled that captivity are now being led captive themselves. The Apostle is telling us that the Lord

Jesus Christ came into the world to deal with and to conquer our enemies, and having finished His campaign, and having routed them, He has returned to heaven leading all these enemies captive, and showering His gifts upon us, His acclaiming people. The Apostle was not content to leave it at that point, as we shall see; but the great thing we must hold in our minds is that the principle of unity is emphasized by the fact that Christ is the dispenser, the giver of all the gifts. He is the great heavenly Captain and we are His people. Having routed His enemies, He dispenses and showers His gifts upon us. But all the gifts, ever, always, come from Him.

13

The Drama of Redemption

('Now that he ascended, what is it but that he also
descended first into the lower parts of the earth? He
that descended is the same also that ascended up far
above all heavens, that he might fill all things.')

Ephesians 4:9–10

In these verses the Apostle proceeds to prove and to demonstrate
that the statement which he has quoted from Psalm 68, verse 18,
must be applied to our blessed Lord and Saviour. In the Authorised
Version, as we have observed, these two verses are placed in
brackets to indicate that they are a part of the whole statement
and are an exposition of what he has just said, as is indicated by
the word 'Now'. He is really expounding that verse; and we shall
follow him as he does so. 'Now', he says; and then asks the
question 'what is it but'? Then he concentrates on the word
'ascended'. This word, he argues, proves that He must also have
descended first into the lower parts of the earth.

As we have seen, Psalm 68 is a great hymn of praise to
Jehovah, who has given David a marvellous victory, as He had
of old given a notable victory to the children of Israel over
Pharaoh and his hosts when He took them through the Red Sea.
But David says that Jehovah had 'ascended'. The question is,
How can Jehovah, the 'I am that I am', the eternally existing
One, without beginning, without end of days, ascend? The
Apostle's answer is that there is but one way in which it can be
explained. It is that the very use of the term 'ascend' implies a
prior descent – 'Now that he ascended, what is it but that he also
descended first into the lower parts of the earth?' There is but
one way in which we can speak of a descent of the Godhead and
that is in respect of Jesus of Nazareth, the Son of God. It is in
Him and in Him alone that God, Jehovah, has descended. So the
Apostle argues that the statement of Psalm 68, verse 18, can only

be a reference to our blessed Lord and Saviour Jesus Christ. He is not doing any violence to the Scripture as he applies all this to our Lord. There is no other conceivable explanation, there is no other possibility, it is the only way in which God has ever descended to earth and again has ascended back into heaven.

We come now to the statement which has proved to be more difficult in the history of interpretation – 'that he also descended first into the lower parts of the earth'. As those who are at all familiar with the history of doctrine in the Church will know, the expression 'the lower parts of the earth' has provoked much discussion and has led to the propounding of certain doctrines. Many explanations of it have been suggested with which we cannot deal exhaustively. But we must glance at some of them because they are repeated thoughtlessly by many Christians. In churches where it is customary to recite Creeds people recite Sunday by Sunday the phrase, 'He descended into hell'. We may well wonder how many of them know exactly what they mean as they do so. It is based upon a particular exposition of this statement in Ephesians 4, and as it is our business to worship intelligently we are forced to consider the exposition of this particular phrase.

Some have maintained that it is a reference to our Lord's birth of the Virgin Mary, that He was born 'of the Virgin's womb'. There is some support for this suggestion in Psalm 139, verses 13–15: 'For thou hast possessed my reins; thou hast covered me in my mother's womb. I will praise thee; for I am fearfully and wonderfully made: marvellous are thy works; and that my soul knoweth right well. My substance was not hid from thee, when I was made in secret, and curiously wrought in the lowest parts of the earth'. Others say that Paul's words make reference to the grave. 'Earth' is the earth, they argue, but the 'lower parts of the earth' indicating something beneath ground level therefore must be the grave. Others, who go yet further, say that the words in question refer to hell. Hell is down, heaven is up; so 'the lower parts of the earth' is a reference to hell or to Hades.

With regard to the first two suggestions, all I need say is that obviously in the 139th Psalm, verse 15, the reference is to something that happened on earth; it certainly did not happen in the deep places of the earth. Man is not formed in some pit or well in the depths of the earth. It is simply a pictorial phrase describing how man is born in his mother's womb. So there is no reference to going down in a physical or material sense. The same applies, of course, to the grave. The important interpretation for us to consider is the third, for this is the one that has figured most prominently in the history of the Church and the history of doctrine.

*   *   *

There are those, I say, who believe that Paul's words teach that our Lord, after His death and burial, went down into hell and did certain things, and in particular that he conquered there the Devil and all his hosts. Others say that what he did in Hades was to set at liberty the saints of the Old Testament who had been held in a kind of captivity ever since their death. Our Lord, they say, went down and brought them out and raised them up with himself. Others believe that what our Lord did when He descended into hell was to proclaim salvation to certain persons who were there. They base that idea, not only on this text, but also upon what we find in the First Epistle of Peter chapter 3; 'For it is better, if the will of God be so, that ye suffer for well doing, than for evil doing. For Christ also hath once suffered for sins, the just for the unjust, that he might bring us to God, being put to death in the flesh, but quickened by the Spirit: by which also he went and preached unto the spirits in prison; which sometime were disobedient, when once the longsuffering of God waited in the days of Noah, while the ark was a preparing, wherein few, that is, eight souls were saved by water' (vv. 17–20). The important phrase is 'the Spirit; by which also he went and preached unto the spirits in prison'. This, they maintain, can only carry the meaning that our Lord, after His death and burial, went down into hell and there preached the Gospel to the people who were destroyed in the Flood in the days of Noah, in order to give them 'a second chance', another opportunity of repenting and believing. There are some who go even further and teach that there will be 'a second chance' and a further opportunity for everyone after this life, in Hades. Such is the most popular of the suggested explanations of the expression 'the lower parts of the earth'. It is the same explanation as that given of 1 Peter 3:19, namely, that it is an indication that our Lord went after his death and preached to or evangelized those 'spirits in prison'.

Another explanation is that what our Lord did was not to preach the Gospel to them in the sense that he was giving them the opportunity to believe it, but that he went down and proclaimed His resounding victory over the Devil and hell to all the inhabitants and the inmates of hell. He told them how he had overcome all the enemies of God everywhere and that he was Lord over all.

Such are the statements which have been put forward from time to time in the long history of the Church. It is my conception of the business of preaching and teaching that we should face these matters honestly and not skip over, or leave them unconsidered, because obviously this expression has some meaning. I therefore suggest that it carries none of these meanings whatsoever, but that the meaning of the phrase 'the lower parts of the earth' is simply the earth itself. I say so for the following reasons. As I have already suggested, the statement in Psalm 139, verse 15, obviously means the earth. When a man is born and comes into being he enters into life on earth; although the psalmist's term is the 'lower parts of the earth'. A similar expression in Psalm 63, verse 9, may have the meaning of 'the grave', but again it is very uncertain.

But the crucial matter is the exposition in 1 Peter 3:19. Is the Apostle Peter saying that our Lord went and preached to the people who had been destroyed in the Flood in the time of Noah? I reject that explanation by asking a question: Why should they be given a 'second chance' or opportunity more than any other sinners? Why should *they* be the only people to whom He preached? There were many of earlier generations who had sinned before the people alive at the time of the Flood; and there have been myriads who have sinned since that time; why then are they alone given this further opportunity? Why not the people of Sodom and Gomorrha also? why not many other people who have been suddenly killed and destroyed by the action of God? Why are these singled out? Those who teach that our Lord preached in Hades to these people have no answer to these questions. Their position as sinners is no different from the position of all other sinners. The fact of the matter is that the

Apostle Peter is not saying any such thing. In this section of his Epistle Peter is reminding his readers that they were living in a time of judgment. In the following chapter he says, 'Judgment must begin at the house of God'. He is warning them of the coming of judgment and he tells them that there is only one way to be saved, the way he mentions in the verses that follow. He reminds them that Noah and his family were saved by means of the ark; and then tells them that we are saved by a similar kind of ark, namely, by baptism into Christ. In Christ who is our Ark we are saved.

Peter's contention is that the position of Christians in the world is similar to the position that obtained immediately before the Flood. Christ is speaking in the Spirit through the Apostles (Peter and others) and warning God's people, and others, to 'flee from the wrath to come'. He had done precisely the same 'in the Spirit' through Noah before the Flood. There are only two great universal judgments in the history of mankind – the first was the Flood; the second will be when the Lord comes again and the elements will melt with fervent heat at the final judgment. So Peter is saying that there is a parallel between those who are living in the age and era before the second great judgment, and those who lived before the first great judgment. The parallel is perfect: Christ preaches 'in the Spirit' now through the Apostles, as He preached 'in the Spirit' then through Noah to those ancient people. This is not only the true exposition; it is the only one which avoids the suggestion that the Gospel was preached only to certain particular sinners and not to all.

It follows, therefore, that if we propose to buttress our exposition of verse 9 in Ephesians 4 by adducing 1 Peter 3:19, we find that it does not help us at all. We have no evidence for saying that our Lord ever preached in hell. It is a supposition, mere speculation, and a theory. There is nothing in the Scriptures to substantiate it, not a word to suggest that He liberated people who had been held captives. There is no indication whatsoever that our Lord finally conquered the devil and his powers in hell after His death; indeed we are told, positively, that that work was done upon the Cross. Paul teaches in the second chapter of the Epistle to the Colossians: 'And having spoiled principalities and powers, he made a show of them openly' – not 'in the lower parts of the earth', but 'openly' – 'triumphing over them in it' – namely, in His death upon the Cross. It was on the Cross our Lord cried out, saying, 'It is finished'. Nothing was left to be completed in hell; the work was completed upon the Cross.

*   *   *

Finally, to end this exposition, there are other statements in Scripture which, when taken together with this statement, lead to the conclusion that what we are dealing with is nothing but a graphic and pictorial manner of describing our Lord's coming down to earth. It is not His going down into some depths, but His coming from heaven to earth. Take, for instance, what our Lord says in John 3:13: 'No man hath ascended up to heaven, but he that came down from heaven, even the Son of man which is in heaven'. There again we have the ascending and descending, the descent and the ascent; not in terms of going down to hell but of coming down to live on earth. Our Lord was on earth and He was speaking to Nicodemus on earth, and claiming unique authority for His teaching. No man has ever gone up into heaven to speak to God and to listen to God's secrets, he says, but I have come down from heaven. 'We speak that we do know, and testify that which we have seen'. I have come down from heaven and still I am in heaven. Or take what is found in John 8:23: 'You are from beneath; I am from above'. He did not mean that they were down in some pit under the earth; they were on the earth but, as compared with the 'above' from which He came, they were 'from beneath'. 'Ye are of this world: I am not of this world' conveys exactly the same contrast. It is a contrast between being from above, from heaven, and being on earth, not under the earth.

As a final quotation take Acts 2:19. Peter is preaching on the Day of Pentecost and he quotes from the prophet Joel, 'And I will show wonders in heaven above, and signs in the earth beneath; blood and fire and vapour of smoke'. We must not literalize the expressions 'beneath', or 'lower parts' or 'under'. The contrast patently is between heaven above and earth beneath. The Apostle says that this Jehovah has ascended 'far above all heavens'. There again we have a pictorial phrase, for 'far above all heavens' means in the highest heaven, in the highest place conceivable. The Apostle does not say 'in the highest place conceivable' but 'far above all heavens'. There is nothing 'far above all heavens' because heaven is heaven; it is an expression used for the sake of emphasis. As the heavens are the higher, the highest parts, so earth is the 'lower parts'. The contrast is between heaven and earth.

So the Apostle is asserting that what puts our Lord into the position in which He is the Giver of all these gifts to the Church, and is the Head of the Church, and is Lord of all over the Church, is the work which He did when He was here on earth. He has ascended, and He is in the position to dispense gifts because He first descended and came down on earth to dwell and did certain things while He was here. This exposition and explanation avoids all confusion and unnecessary speculation about what our Lord may or may not have done after His death and before His resurrection. These speculations have even crept into the Creeds, but they have no real Scriptural warrant.

*   *   *

What we have here is a description of the whole movement of salvation. Indeed we can use a stronger term and say that the Apostle is describing the great drama of salvation. He is saying, in effect, that the verse which he has quoted from Psalm 68 is a description of how our Lord has achieved salvation and redemption, and, as the mighty Victor, is now giving gifts to His people in the Church.

Let us examine the terms the Apostle employs. Why is there any need of salvation at all? The answer is, because mankind in sin is in a condition of slavery. An enemy has entered the world. The Devil, the enemy of God, pretending to be the friend of man, was man's greatest enemy. He conquered man, and he has held man in bondage and in captivity ever since. This is taught in the second chapter of the Epistle to the Hebrews: 'Forasmuch then as the children are partakers of flesh and blood, he also himself likewise took part of the same; that through death he might destroy him that had the power of death, that is, the devil; and deliver them who through fear of death were all their lifetime subject to bondage' (vv. 14–15). Man in sin is a slave of the Devil;

[161]

he is under the dominion of Satan. When the Apostle Paul on the road to Damascus was given the command by the Lord Jesus Christ to preach the Gospel, he was told to go to the people and to the Gentiles 'to open their eyes, and to bring them from darkness to light and from the power of Satan unto God'. Satan the arch-enemy is the commander of the hosts of hell; and he has attacked and defeated mankind, and has taken it captive. He exercises a terrible dominion and power over mankind. Sin is likewise a terrible bondage – 'The way of the transgressor is hard'.

People think that a life of sin is a life of freedom but it is the greatest slavery of all. Think of the masses of people in the world today who are slaves to drink and drugs, to sex and a thousand and one other things. They talk about their marvellous liberty and life, but they are poor benighted slaves, as they soon discover when they try to set themselves free. Anyone who has ever tried to break free from a long-continued or long-practised habit knows something about the slavery and the power and the bondage of sin. In addition mankind is under the curse of the Law. 'The handwriting of ordinances which was against us, which was contrary to us', says Paul in Colossians (2:14). The Law of God is against us because of our sin and is pronouncing a judgment upon us. We are 'under law' by nature. This is the condemnation, and we cannot escape it. And then there is the fact of death. 'The last enemy that shall be destroyed is death' (1 Cor 15:26). This is the mighty enemy that holds mankind in bondage all their lives; the fear of death. Satan controls it and uses it to keep us in bondage. Mankind in sin hates this awful spectre that comes ever nearer to us. It would do anything to avoid it, but it cannot. These are the enemies that have conquered man. The Son of God came into this world in order to conquer these enemies and to set all believers in Him free. Christ came to redeem the Church, to redeem His own people out of this bondage, this captivity, this tyranny. He came with that specific object, and He has carried it out.

Our Lord is now in glory, seated at the right hand of God, having put all enemies under His feet. But as we think of Him we must think of something else also – 'what is it but that He descended first into the lower parts of the earth?' He is in high heaven now, but He was once on earth. He 'came down on earth to dwell'. The children's hymn reminds us of it:

> *I love to tell the story*
> *Which angel voices tell,*
> *How once the King of Glory*
> *Came down on earth to dwell.*

He left the courts of heaven, He 'humbled himself': these are other ways of saying, 'What is it but that He first descended?' These are ways of describing the Incarnation. As John Henry Newman expressed it:—

> *O loving wisdom of our God!*
> *When all was sin and shame,*
> *A second Adam to the fight*
> *And to the rescue came.*

He could not lead captivity captive until He had first come down and dealt with the enemy. But He has come, He has descended.

*   *   *

The classic description and elaboration of this is found in the second chapter of the Epistle to the Philippians: 'Let this mind be in you, which was also in Christ Jesus: who, being in the form of God, thought it not robbery to be equal with God'. He did not hold on to this equality which He had with God as a prize He would never let go, 'but made himself of no reputation'. He was still God in all His fulness; but he laid aside the signs, the insignia, the pomp and the glory of it all. He came down to earth as it were incognito. 'He took upon himself the form of a servant and was made in the likeness of men'. 'He that ascended, what is it but that He first descended?' means that He came from the highest courts of heaven to the Virgin's womb, to earth, in the form of a man, in the form of a servant, with all the poverty and all that characterized the home into which He came. Give rein to your inspired spiritual imaginations and contemplate this drama of redemption. He has come down to meet the enemies who have conquered us, and especially the mighty foe who holds us in bondage.

But He not only took upon Him the form of a servant and was

made in the likeness of men, for we read on: 'And being found in fashion as a man, He humbled Himself, and became obedient unto death'. We pause here for a moment to emphasize this element of obedience which characterized the whole of His life. He came to engage in a terrible conflict; even when He was a Babe King Herod tried to kill Him. 'A second Adam to the fight, and to the rescue came'. Consider also His conflict with the Devil. Then think of His obedience to His parents. He became obedient, although He was the Son of God. Recall how at the age of twelve in the Temple His mother and Joseph found Him 'sitting in the midst of the doctors, both hearing them and asking them questions' and upbraided Him (Luke 2:46). He said, 'Wist ye not that I must be about my Father's business?' Though He knew His Father's 'business', He was obedient to Joseph and Mary. 'He became obedient'. He did so because it was part of the fight. He submitted Himself to baptism, though He had done no wrong, and had no need to be baptized. Recall what John the Baptist said to Him. But He was identifying Himself with His people for whom He was going to fight. He was tempted of the Devil. For forty days and forty nights in the wilderness He was in single, mortal combat with the chief enemy. Think of the opposition of the Pharisees and scribes and Sadducees and the doctors of the law. It is all part of the drama of redemption, and of the fight, the conflict to deliver His people. He 'descended' in order to do this. 'He became obedient'. He never failed; He rendered a perfect obedience to His Father's will. Then came that terrible moment in the Garden of Gethsemane when He saw clearly what our redemption was going to involve, and He cried, 'Father, if it be possible let this cup pass from me, nevertheless not my will but thine be done'. Obedience! Yes, 'obedient unto death, even the death of the cross'. He went even to the Cross in order that this victory might be complete.

Consider again Paul's word to the Colossians: 'And having spoiled principalities and powers' (2:15). At Calvary they brought out their last reserves. The Devil assumed that if he killed Him he would get rid of Him and thus defeat Him. But as they were killing Him He was destroying them. 'Having spoiled principalities and powers, he made a show of them openly, triumphing over them in it'. It was by dying and rising again that He finally

[164]

defeated the Devil and all his hosts. At the same time He dealt with the Law, 'Blotting out the handwriting of ordinances that was against us, which was contrary to us, and took it out of the way, nailing it to his cross'. In doing all this He died, and they took down His body and they buried it in a grave.

Was He defeated at last? We know the answer, thank God. There was no defeat; it was still victory all along the line. He died and was buried; His friends rolled a great stone over the mouth of the grave and His foes set soldiers to guard it. The enemy seemed to be triumphant, and all seemed to be lost. But He 'burst asunder the bands of death' and rose triumphant o'er the grave. 'Death is swallowed up in victory'. He conquered death and the grave, so that we can say with Paul, 'O death, where is thy sting? O grave, where is thy victory? The sting of death is sin, and the strength of sin is the law; but thanks be unto God, which giveth us the victory through our Lord Jesus Christ' (1 Cor 15:55–57).

Our Lord conquered the last enemy. Every enemy that has ever enslaved man, and kept him in bondage, has been routed and defeated. Thus, having completed the work, He rose and ascended from earth to heaven. The disciples were with Him on mount Olivet and they saw Him ascending into heaven. 'He passed through the heavens'. As the Apostle says, 'He that descended is the same also that ascended up far above all heavens, that He might fill all things'.

The Apostle's assertion is that it is because He has done all He came on earth to do, that He is now 'far above all heavens'. He expresses the same truth in the Epistle to the Philippians: 'Wherefore God also hath highly exalted him, and given him a name which is above every name: that at the name of Jesus every knee should bow, of things in heaven, and things in earth, and things under the earth' (2:9–10). It is because of what He has done that God has exalted Him to this supreme position. Our Lord Himself stated this when He said, 'All power is given unto me in heaven and in earth. Go ye therefore and teach all nations ... and lo, I am with you always and [shall be with you] unto the end of the age' (Matthew 28: 18–20). Then turn to the Book of Revelation, chapter 5, with its account of a book with seals on it, the book of history, and take note of the weeping and wailing because no man is strong enough to tear off the seals; no-one in heaven or on earth is big enough to control history. Again all seems to be lost and hopeless; but 'the Lion of the tribe of Judah hath prevailed to open the book, and to loose the seven seals thereof'. The Lion of the tribe of Judah! Jesus, Son of God! The One who 'descended' has also 'ascended' and is big enough and great enough! The Book is handed to Him, and He tears off the seals. He is the Lord of history! He is seated at the right hand of God and 'waiting until all His enemies shall be made His footstool'. Lord of creation, Lord of history, Lord of everything!

* * *

The Apostle has already said all this in the first chapter of our Epistle. He wants us to know the exceeding greatness of God's power to us-ward that believe, 'according to the working of his mighty power, which he wrought in Christ when he raised him from the dead, and set him at his own right hand in the heavenly places, far above all principality, and power, and might, and dominion, and every name that is named, not only in this world, but also in that which is to come: and hath put all things under his feet, and gave him to be the head over all things to the church, which is his body, the fulness of him that filleth all in all' (vv. 19–23). 'When he ascended up on high, he led captivity captive, and gave gifts to men'. 'To every one of us is given grace according to the measure of the gift of Christ'. And it is all because He who ascended and is in the position to give gifts first descended, and conquered all our enemies and captors, and led them in His triumphal train. He has earned the right to be the Head of the Church, and has all power. Thus He dispenses these gifts to His people in the Church according to the measure that He Himself has determined.

Surely we must all join in thanking God that the great Apostle broke off his argument and gave us this exposition, and thereby gave us this astounding view of the drama of redemption – from heaven to earth, to the grave, and back into heaven. But let us remember that He has taken our human nature back with Him into the glory. The One who is on the throne is 'touched with the feeling of our infirmities'. He carried His human nature, our nature, with Him to glory! And in a sense we are there with Him,

[166]

seated with Him 'in the heavenly places'. Such is the Apostle's picture of Christ as the Head of the Church, imparting and distributing the graces and the gifts to His people in the Church 'which is his body, the fulness of him that filleth all in all'.

14
Differing Gifts

'But unto every one of us is given grace according to
the measure of the gift of Christ.' 'And he gave some,
apostles; and some, prophets; and some, evangelists;
and some, pastors and teachers'.

Ephesians 4:7 & 11

We must turn our attention now to these two particular verses.
We have been considering the parenthesis in verses 8–10 because
it is essential that we should grasp its teaching if we are truly to
understand the teaching of these two verses which surround it.
The Apostle, having written the statement which we have in
verse 7, namely, that 'Unto everyone of us is given grace according
to the measure of the gift of Christ', instead of going on immediately to explain what exactly the Lord Jesus Christ does give,
first of all explains how He is in the position to do this. We must
also remind ourselves once again that the fundamental theme of
the entire section is that of the unity of the church. He is also
concerned to show that this unity does not imply a drab mechanical sameness, but is a unity in variety, a unity in diversity, the
result of the work our Lord, as the Head of the Church, has done
on behalf of His people.

In these two verses the Apostle begins to work out this
principle in detail and as we see it, or should see it, in the life and
the activity of the Christian Church. This theme is a most important one, and particularly important at the present time when there
is so much talk and writing about the church and œcumenicity
and unity. Never perhaps has it been more important that we
should consider and try to understand the Apostle's teaching with
regard to this essential matter. As we do so let us be careful to
observe that the Apostle does not lay down a rigid system of
church order. Indeed it is questionable whether any such thing is

[168]

to be found anywhere in the Scriptures. Nevertheless it is important to observe that certain principles are laid down which we are meant to observe and to practise. We must therefore be careful to avoid two dangers. The one danger is to go beyond the Scripture and to impose some rigid, legal, mechanical system of order upon the church. The other is, that in our fear of doing so, we should have no system at all, making it impossible to do everything 'decently and in order' according to the apostolic injunction. We must turn, therefore, to an examination of these principles.

The first is that Christ, and Christ alone, is the Head of the Church. There is only one King in the Church, it is King Jesus, as the Scotsman Andrew Melville said in the 16th century. The Pope is not the head, neither is any earthly prince or monarch. No man or woman can ever be the head of the Church. Church history shows that this has often been forgotten, and many a battle has had to be fought concerning it. Christ in the Church is the Head of the Church, and wherever two or three are gathered together in His name He is there in the midst. We must re-assert this central truth in these days when all these principles seem to be again in the melting pot in the minds of the vast majority of people. Did our forefathers fight in vain about these matters? Is it of no consequence that we say that there is no Head of the Church but the Lord Jesus Christ, and that no man must ever be placed in that position? Christ is the Head, and we are the body, and members in particular.

The second principle is that the Church consists of members, each having a function under the Head. This is what is stated in verse 7, 'But unto every one of us is given grace according to the measure of the gift of Christ'. When the Apostle says 'grace given' he is not referring to the grace of salvation, because he has already dealt with that subject. He is concerned now with the functioning of the Church as the body of Christ. Obviously we have all been given the grace of salvation, otherwise we are not in the Church at all, but now, as the expression 'and He gave some, apostles' indicates, his theme is the grace given to every single member of the Christian Church enabling him or her to perform some particular function. A particular function is given to each one and with it He gives the ability to exercise that

[169]

particular function. The analogy of the body makes this quite clear. Every particular part in my body has some function to perform. We do not always know what the function is; but the fact that we may not know does not mean that it does not have a function.

Scientists have often fallen into error concerning this matter. A hundred years ago, and later, there were those who, believing in the theory of Evolution, were saying quite dogmatically that the thyroid gland had no function, but that it was one of a number of vestigial remains. They spoke similarly concerning various other ductless glands. But today we know that these glands perform vital functions. Such people are still saying that the appendix has no function, but what they really mean is that they do not know what it is, and they will probably discover that it has a most important function. The point I am stressing is that there is nothing in the body, nothing even in a single smallest cell, not a hair, but has a function, a purpose. It may appear to be very insignificant in and of itself; but it is in the body and it works with the other elements, and has its part to play.

As we look at this truth and test ourselves by it, how do we find ourselves as members of the Christian Church? A fatal tendency has come in to think and to say that the vast majority of people in the Church are meant to be entirely passive. Many seem to think of the Church as just a building to which they come to sit and listen to sermons and addresses, and in which they do nothing. This is a denial of the fundamental proposition that to every one of us is grace given in the Church and as parts of the body of Christ. Every one of us has a function, and we are not meant to be entirely passive. The whole secret of the working of the human body is that every part and particle has a particular function which it is meant to fulfil.

The first thing we have to do, therefore, is to discover what our function is. As we realize this we discover what a privilege it is to be members of the Christian Church. The glory of our position is that in this body which Christ is forming through the Spirit we all have a part and a place. In 1 Corinthians chapter 12 we are reminded of some of these functions, but Paul does not supply us with an exhaustive list. There is some particular position that every one of us is called to occupy, and in which to work. So as we believe in Christ, and in the Church, and as we believe that the Church is the custodian and guardian of the only message which can save man in this terrible modern world, our first duty is to discover what our function is and to exercise it. This function may *appear* to be unimportant, as I am going to show, but that does not matter; the vital thing is that there is something for every one of us to do – 'Unto every one of us is given grace according to the measure of the gift of Christ'.

The third principle is that it is Christ Himself who gives each one of us this particular grace. The Apostle emphasizes this point in the 7th and 11th verses. The grace is given to us 'according to the measure of the gift of Christ'. In verse 11, unfortunately, the Authorised Version does not bring out the meaning and reads, 'And He gave some, apostles'. But the right and better translation is, 'And He Himself gave some to be apostles'. It is emphatic; not 'He' but 'He Himself', lest we might fail to realize and to remember that it is the Lord Himself who gives all these various gifts.

*   *   *

We come next to the most important practical aspect of this whole matter. From the standpoint of the activities in the Church today it is certainly one of the most important questions. In other words, we are going to consider what is known as the doctrine of the Call. Men and women in the Church are called to given functions and given the ability to perform them by the Lord Himself. This is a difficult subject and one that is frequently mis-understood. We can but deal with some of the principles involved in it.

The first principle is that one does not call oneself. We are not to decide to do this or that in the Church, as has often been done. For example, a man decides that he is going to preach, and he does so. He is not interested in the doctrine of the Call; he has never heard of it. He does what he wants to do. But according to the Apostle's teaching a man does not call himself; still less, of course, does he enter the ministry, or any other office in the church, as a profession. The history of the dead periods in the annals of the church shows how the idea of entering the ministry as a profession tended to prevail. The tradition and the custom in great families was for the eldest son to join the Navy, the second son went into the Army, while the third son entered the ministry of the church as a clergyman. The son who went in for ministry did so in exactly the same way as his brothers went into the Navy or the Army. This has frequently accounted for the sad state of the Christian Church. And let us not imagine that this custom is confined to the past; there are still those who go into the ministry in exactly the same way. A man who may be a poet and who desires a quiet life in which he will have time for reading literature and time to compose poetry or to write novels, or other types of literature, may enter the ministry for these reasons. This explains why the Church is so often weak and ineffective. Men have forgotten that it is Christ who calls, and that we ourselves do not decide what we do in the Church in any capacity.

We must go yet further and emphasize that the need is not the Call. This is an important negative, because a popular evangelical teaching has urged that the need is the Call. The reply to that is that it is the Lord who calls. He may of course call us to do something because of a certain need; but the need cannot be the Call, for the good and sufficient reason that if the need constitutes the Call, then every one of us should be responding to that need, and that is patently ridiculous. The need is not meant to be the Call. The Lord Himself sees the whole field, and is the Head of the whole body. He sees a need here and a need there, at the same time. He does not see, as we see, in a partial manner; He sees perfectly. We must emphasize this principle, that simply because I see a need in a given place I must not thereupon conclude that it is incumbent upon me to satisfy it. It may not be the Lord's will that I should do so. He may have something else for me to do, and He may will that someone else should perform the work that I unwisely rush to undertake. The teaching that the need is the Call is not only unscriptural, it is a denial of the teaching that the Lord, as Head of the Church, is the only one who can give the Call, and that He gives it directly to us.

In the third place we must emphasize that the Church alone does not give the Call. I am not putting forward my own opinion or interpretation of what the Apostle says here – 'Unto every one of us is grace given, according to the measure of the gift of Christ . . . And he himself gave some, apostles; and some,

prophets; and some, evangelists; and some, pastors and teachers'
– for Christ Himself gave the same teaching in the oft-quoted
statement found in Matthew 9: 'The harvest truly is plenteous, but
the labourers are few'. Is the church therefore to lay hands upon
people and thrust them forth into the harvest? Our Lord's reply
is, 'Pray ye therefore the Lord of the harvest, that he will send forth
labourers into his harvest' (vv. 37–38). We do not thrust forth
labourers; He does so; and all we do is to pray to Him to send
them forth. In our carnal zeal and enthusiasm we often deem it to
be our business to call people to tasks in the church, and we do so
in different ways. We suggest to young men that they should
enter the ministry, or preach, or teach. How scandalous this is!
We have no right to suggest to another what his function may be
in the church or what he ought to do. There are many men in the
ministry for one reason only, namely, that at a given point an old
minister or some elder or deacon went to them and asked them
whether they had ever thought of entering the ministry and then
persuaded them to do so.

*   *   *

Forgive a personal reference which may help to illustrate this
matter. Some thirty years ago when I felt called of God to enter
the ministry and to preach the Gospel, I received a letter from the
General Secretary of a certain Foreign Mission Society. In his
letter he suggested to me that instead of preaching the Gospel in
this country I should be a Medical Missionary in India. It seemed
so obvious to him. At the time there was a man needed very badly
in a certain hospital in India, and here was I going to preach the
Gospel in Great Britain when obviously I was the man to fill that
post in India. My reply to that good man – whose motives, of
course, were excellent and with whom I had great sympathy – was
simply to ask him a question. I asked him whether he believed in
the biblical doctrine of a Call, whether he believed that the Lord
of the harvest still chose the men and chose where to send them?
I told him that, for myself, I not only believed it but acted upon it,
and hence I did not go to India.

There is indeed an element which is almost impertinent,
spiritually impertinent, in this false teaching about the need being
the Call. We think we understand, and so we often blunder in our

[173]

own efforts. In our ignorance we do not hesitate to legislate for the Church and decide what men are to do. It is not the business of the Church to suggest, or to call, still less to bring pressure upon men as is so often done and in an emotional atmosphere. The need is outlined and impressed upon young people; then an appeal is made for all to be ready to volunteer. It is a most unscriptural procedure.

I am emphasizing this, not only because it is a matter of theological interest, but also because tragedies have often followed this practice. There are people whose whole life has been ruined by this teaching which proclaims that it is the business of every young Christian to go to the Mission Field. Do not trouble about absence of feeling, it says, the need is the call; go to the Mission Field and if you find when you have arrived there that you are not meant to be there, well then, go home! That is the exact opposite of our Lord's teaching and also of the Apostle's teaching. Thus confusion enters the Church and many a life is ruined simply because of failure to apply the teaching of the Scripture.

Each one of us is to be willing to do anything that the Lord may call us to do – to go to the Mission Field, and equally perhaps, not to go to the Mission Field. Sometimes it may be easier to go than not to go. There are people who comfort and satisfy their consciences by doing something heroic, such as going to the heart of Africa and building a hospital. But it may not be God's will that they should do so. It may be His will that they stay doing something drab and ordinary in this country. As Christian people, as members of the body of Christ in particular, we are to be at His disposal, to be ready to do anything He calls us to do. Those whom He calls to go and sends do a faithful work and bring glory to His name.

There has been much confusion in connection with this whole subject of Foreign Mission work, and Christ's name has often been brought into disrepute. People who rush emotionally into the work discover their mistake when they get to the Field, and when they come home on furlough they do not go back again, and this becomes known to those who are outside the Church. I have heard that in some countries only about one in three return to the Mission Field after their first furlough. This is so because they have been called by men and not by the Lord; the need has been regarded as the Call, or the Church has given the Call. They have never realized that we are but individual parts and members of a body, and that it is the Head who decides and calls, and that this is His prerogative, and His alone.

*   *   *

But someone may ask as to how we are to know when this Call comes. They ask whether the Church has anything to do with this. What is to be done with a man who comes forward and says that he has been called of the Lord to do some particular work? The Scripture provides an answer to the problem. It starts, as we have stressed, with the great central doctrine that the Lord Himself is the One who calls. But in addition, the Scripture shows that what any one of us may regard as a Call is to be tried and tested. It is just here that the Church comes in; but the function of the Church is mainly negative. The Church is to apply certain tests to a man who claims that he is called by the Lord to a task. Such a man should not act immediately, he should come to the Church and make his statement; and then the Church should consider the matter.

Take for instance what we find in the sixth chapter in the Book of the Acts of the Apostles, and also in the Pastoral Epistles. There we find detailed rules and regulations with regard to elders and deacons and about those who preach and teach. It is the business of the Church to apply these tests to any candidate. There are two sides to this question. I can illustrate this by repeating a well-known story about Charles Haddon Spurgeon who had his own way of applying these principles. A young man once went to him and said that he had been called, and told by the Spirit that he was to preach the following Thursday in Spurgeon's Tabernacle. Spurgeon replied that this was very odd because the Spirit had not told him (Spurgeon) anything about it. When the Lord calls through the Spirit He not only tells the young man, He tells Charles Haddon Spurgeon also! 'Everything must be done decently and in order', says Paul, lest the ministry be blamed. There must be no confusion in the Church: and when the Spirit acts He always does it in an orderly manner. So we are given these instructions to the Church, and thus have a check which makes sure that we are not misled by a passing impulse. We are all so frail, and the enemy is so subtle. He can 'turn himself even into an angel of light' in order to confuse us. A man who is truly called is a humble man who does not set himself up; he goes to the Church and says that he believes he has been called by Christ. He presents himself before the Church; and the Church examines him.

It is most important, of course, that the Church should do this correctly; and there are errors and dangers and pitfalls on all sides here. The Church must do this testing in a spiritual manner. She herself must be sensitive to the leading of the Spirit. She must not act in a legalistic manner nor in a rigid manner nor in a merely formal manner. The Church has made tragic mistakes at times. There have been men who have been truly called of God, and who have gone to the Church only to be told that they were not Called. The Church has rejected them. But in some instances the Church has been entirely wrong. The Church is not infallible and must not act in a legalistic manner; she must respect the liberty of the Spirit, and the balance of the Spirit. So it behoves us all to keep ourselves in the Spirit and under the influence of the Spirit so that we may 'judge righteous judgment' (John 7:24).

Church history shows very plainly that whether we like it or not it is the Lord Himself who calls. The treatment meted out to George Whitefield and the Wesley brothers by the Church of England two hundred years ago supplies us with a perfect illustration of this point. The Anglican Church at that time was blind, and could not see that it was the Lord who had called these men and sent them out on their mighty ministries. The Church could not see it; and the Church was wrong. It is the Lord who gives His gifts to the Church; and nothing is more fascinating in Church history than to observe the way in which He does so. How unexpectedly He acts at times! He lays His hand on an immoral philosopher like Augustine of Hippo, He takes hold of a monk like Martin Luther, or a great legal brain like John Calvin. Thus we see Him giving His gifts. He calls and He gives. The Church does not always understand; but that does not mean that we must ignore the Church and say that the Church does not matter. She may make mistakes because she is not scriptural and not spiritual, but He is the Head and can over-rule even her errors.

Nothing is so far removed from the Apostle's picture of the Church as institutionalism and ecclesiasticism. These 'isms' are not to be found anywhere in the New Testament. Institutionalism is a denial of the picture of the Church as the body of Christ, and of Christ alone as the Head, and of the Holy Spirit making and preserving this blessed unity. Ecclesiasticism is as much a denial of the scriptural teaching as is the chaos that is seen in other circles at the present hour where men set themselves up and recognize no authority whatsoever. We must be guided by the whole of Scripture and endeavour, as we are given grace and strength by the Spirit, to preserve a true balance.

*   *   *

This brings us to the fourth principle, which is still more practical. This grace which the Lord gives to every one of us differs and varies from case to case. 'He gave some to be apostles, and some to be prophets, some to be evangelists, some to be pastors and teachers'. It is He who appoints the various offices and functions in the church; therefore anyone who does not believe in any organization at all is in an entirely unscriptural position. There are people who imagine that it is very spiritual to have no organization, but to have a loose, free fellowship. But our Lord has determined upon specific offices in the Church. This is not a man-made device; it has all come from Him through these inspired apostles. He has not only appointed that there should be offices and functions, but has also determined their nature and variety. This is taught clearly in 1 Corinthians chapter 12. Some offices are more important than others, and yet every one of them is essential. As in the physical body some parts are not as comely as others, yet these uncomely parts are necessary and we bestow the more abundant honour upon them. The various functions differ from each other and they are meant to be different; yet they are all essential to the harmonious working of the whole.

Furthermore, we are also told that our Lord also appoints the men to these offices. 'He gave some to be [or as] apostles'. It is the Lord Himself who chose the apostles, the prophets, and all others. He establishes these different offices, calls men to them, and gives them the ability to exercise the functions they are meant

[177]

to exercise in that particular office. Here again there is obvious inequality. The Scripture itself teaches that exceptional honour is to be given to those elders who preach and teach, for that function is exceptionally important. There is a gradation of offices in the Church; some are more important and others are less important, but all are essential. So we are to hold these two things constantly in our minds at the same time – the division of offices, the gradation in offices, and yet the fact that they are all equally essential, and are all appointed by the Lord Himself.

The carrying out of this teaching in practice is highly important. We start by recognizing the inequalities; and far from being disturbed or upset at the inequalities we recognize that they are of His appointing, and that they are for the full and harmonious functioning of the Church. Then, having recognized these differences and gradations, we must respect them. Hence James teaches in the third chapter of his Epistle, 'My brethren, be not many masters' (v. 1). There were people in the early Church who claimed that all were equal, that all were teachers, all preachers, all able to do the same things. We are not all meant to be masters! We must recognize that there are different functions, different offices, different abilities, different callings in the Church. But I must add immediately that we must not harden this into a rigid, absolute division. There is nothing in the Scriptures to support a monarchical idea of Church government. We are to call no man lord in the Church. There is no monarchical or papal authority.

It is interesting to observe that it is the Apostle Peter of all men who wrote, 'Neither as being lords over God's heritage, but being ensamples to the flock' (1 Peter 5:3). Our Puritan and Free Church forefathers shed their blood for this principle; but there is a tendency today to say that these things do not count at all. We must recognize that there are different functions and callings and offices; but they are not to be hierarchical in character. The man in a lower office is not to bow the knee to one in a higher office and call him 'My Lord'. We have all received the same grace, and although we have been given different functions, we are all equally essential. I call no man lord, and I call no man master, in the Church. I recognize the divisions, and I look up to a man who has a higher function to perform than I have, but not in a slavish manner, not as a subject to a lord or king or one who has

some monarchical authority. The monarchical idea is a denial of
what is plainly taught here.

*   *   *

We must learn how to regard these things aright both in ourselves
and in others. As regards ourselves, if you feel that you have been
called to a high office or that you have been given some remarkable
gift, do not be proud, do not boast of it, and do not despise
another brother. As Paul argues, 'Who maketh thee to differ from
another? and what hast thou that thou didst not receive? now if
thou didst receive it, why dost thou glory, as if thou hadst not
received it?' (1 Cor 4:7). If you are in an exalted position, be
humble; what you have has been given to you; the office has been
given, the gift has been given; the ability has been given. You
have nothing but what you have received; do not boast, therefore,
and do not despise others. On the other hand, if you are the man
in the humbler position, do not be envious, do not be jealous.
Do not look at another and say, Why has he got this, and not I?
Read 1 Corinthians chapter 12 and be corrected. We must all be
content with the function which we have been given, the task to
which we have been called. I care not how lowly, or how insignificant it is; I care not if I am not lauded by men, and if my name
is never in the newspapers; that is quite unimportant because it is
the Lord who has called each one, and my function is essential.
I do all to His glory; I rejoice in it; I praise God that I am in the
body at all, even though I may be one of the less comely parts
which does not seem to be necessary. 'I am what I am by the
grace of God'. It is He who has called me, it is He who has given
me the appointment and the ability.

We must apply this also with regard to our view of others. This
is what they had failed to do in Corinth, with the result that the
church was divided up into sects and schisms and groups, each
following a particular man and boasting of a particular gift. They
had forgotten that 'Paul is nothing, and Apollos is nothing, but
ministers of Christ', and that not one of them would have had any
gift whatsoever if the Lord Christ had not given it to him. So
Paul tells them not to glory in man, but to glory only in the Lord,
the Giver of the gifts, the Head of the Church.

Is it not increasingly obvious that it is our failure to study the

Scriptures that leads to the troubles and the confusion, the divisions and the schisms, the heart-rendings, the heart-breakings, the jealousy, envy and rivalry, and all the muddle and confusion in the churches, and that causes Revival to tarry? How can the Lord honour such a Church, such a collection of people? We must return to the biblical teaching concerning the Church. This is not something theoretical for church elders and leaders only, not only something to be discussed in Church councils. This Epistle was written to every member of the church at Ephesus. We must all have clear ideas about these things so that when we read about them we may have opinions and express them. It is our duty to see that the Church functions as her Lord intended her to do. Let us therefore, all of us, humble ourselves before Him, let us confess our pride or our jealousy, our envy or failure, our self-seeking, our self-importance, our feelings that we are neglected. Let us return to Him, I say, and humble ourselves before Him; let us ask Him to forgive us, to cleanse us; let us ask Him to make plain and clear to us what He has called us to do, what He desires us to do: and then let us rise up and do it with all our might, relying upon the might and the authority and the power of the Holy Ghost Himself.

15
Apostles, Prophets, Evangelists, Pastors and Teachers

'And he gave some, apostles; and some, prophets; and some, evangelists; and some, pastors and teachers'.
Ephesians 4:11

We have already seen that verse 11 is a continuation of what the Apostle begins to say in the seventh verse. It was essential that we should have taken them together. But having done so we can now consider the particular message and statement of this verse by itself, but only on condition that we continue to bear in mind that the Lord Jesus Christ is the Giver of every gift in the church. We must also continue to bear in mind that God's ultimate object and purpose is to re-unite in one all things, and that one of the chief functions of the Christian Church is to manifest this to the world. That is why we must be careful always to preserve the unity and to guard it. The Apostle explains how our Lord Himself has done certain things to that end, and in order to safeguard this unity.

Having laid down his doctrine, his principles, the Apostle now proceeds to illustrate this and to give some examples of how He does this: 'And he gave some, apostles; and some, prophets; and some, evangelists; and some, pastors and teachers'.

It is important that we should realize that in verse 11 the Apostle is simply illustrating his great theme. He does so by pointing to something with which his readers were quite familiar in the life of their own churches and in the life of other churches. But he is not setting out a full and an exhaustive account and description of Church order. There are offices which he does not mention here. His object is simply to illustrate his principle. What he is saying in effect is that in the life of the Church there are different offices and different gifts, but that each and every one of them is designed to lead to the same end of unity. He proceeds to work that out in detail in verses 12–16: 'For the perfecting of the saints, for the work of the ministry, for the edifying of the body of Christ: till we all come in the unity of the faith', and so on.

This is mainly a matter of instruction which may at first seem remote from the life of the individual Christian, but there are many pressing reasons why we should study it. The history of the Church throughout the centuries shows that nothing, perhaps, has been more prolific in causing trouble, dispute, schism, and grave damage in the Church, and consequently to the name of Christ and His salvation, than a failure to understand this very matter. This has been particularly true in the case of the Roman Catholic Church; but it is not confined to them. There have been other sections of the Church, and movements within the Church in general, which are equally guilty of confusion in this respect and we shall be referring to some of them.

The difficulty has been with respect to the definition of 'apostles and prophets' and other offices. But this is not only important from the standpoint of understanding Church history, it is of practical importance at this present time with all the emphasis on œcumenicity. We are being told constantly that the one important question is the coming together of the various sections of the Christian Church in one great world Church. We are told that this is the greatest need, and there are those who assert that the promoting of it is the greatest movement of the Holy Spirit since the age of the Apostles. The danger is that those who lack a firm grasp of scriptural teaching may be ready to make concessions to grievous error. In their desire for unity Christians may jettison certain principles for which our forefathers not only fought but even died. For instance, there is a general agreement among the larger religious bodies that episcopacy is essential to the well-being of the Church. It is important, therefore, that we should have an intelligent understanding of these matters. As Christian people it behoves us to have an opinion about them, and we are failing in our duty if we cannot speak about them intelligently. It is very wrong for any Christians to say that they do not bother about these matters, that they are simply evangelicals who are concerned only about saving souls. We have no right to dissociate ourselves from the Church, no right to ignore the teaching of the Scripture. You may imagine you are being very spiritual in so doing, but actually you are failing to submit yourself to the Word of God. We have no right to remain babes; we are to grow, as the Apostle will remind us. It is those who pose as being unusually spiritual, and who cannot be bothered with these things, who, as the Apostle says, are most liable to be 'carried about with every wind of doctrine' and find themselves eventually in positions which they never imagined for a moment would ever become true of them.

*   *   *

The offices mentioned by the Apostle are apostles, prophets, evangelists, pastors and teachers. Concerning these there has been much writing and discussion and disputation throughout the centuries. I suggest that these can be divided into two groups. First there are certain offices which were temporary and extraordinary in the church, certain functions which were only meant to be in use for a certain period and which since then have disappeared. Obviously the second group therefore consists of the permanent offices in the life and witness of the Church. In order to establish and to prove that this classification is a sound one, we must now look at these different offices.

In the first group, the extraordinary and temporary, we have apostles and prophets and evangelists; and in the second permanent group we have pastors and teachers. We begin with 'apostles'. It is our Lord Himself who created the office, and it is He who appointed men to the office. As Paul reminds us in the first verse of his Epistle to the Galatians, 'Paul, an apostle, (not of men, neither by man, but by Jesus Christ, and God the Father, who raised him from the dead)'. He is not an apostle 'of men'; he had not been called or appointed by men; 'but by Jesus Christ'. 'He gave some to be apostles', and He gave these apostles to the Church. Certain things are made quite plain in the New Testament Scriptures with regard to the office of an apostle. An apostle was a man of whom the following things had to be true. First and foremost, he must have seen the risen Lord, he must have been a witness of the resurrected Christ. We cannot deal with all the scriptural proofs, but one of the most important is 1 Corinthians

9:1, where Paul writes, 'Am I not an apostle? am I not free? have I not seen Jesus Christ our Lord?' Likewise in 1 Corinthians 15, in giving a list of the people by whom the risen Lord had been seen, he mentions the fact that 'Last of all he was seen of me also, as of one born out of due time. For I am the least of the apostles, that am not meet to be called an apostle'. A man could not be an apostle unless he could be a witness to the Lord's resurrection, unless he could say that he had seen the risen Christ. We shall see the importance of emphasizing that.

The second essential is that he must have been called and commissioned to do his work by the risen Lord Himself in person; not by the Church, not by any delegation. This, again, is seen in Galatians chapter 1. Indeed Paul generally starts his epistles by describing himself as 'Paul, called to be an apostle', or 'a called apostle'. He thereby differentiates himself from other men who claimed that they were apostles but who had never been called by the Lord. They had called themselves, or certain sections in the Church had called them. Paul was 'called' on the road to Damascus. The risen Lord appeared to him; and Paul saw Him. This was not a vision, let us remember; Paul actually saw the risen, glorified Lord with his naked eyes. He saw Him as definitely as each of the other apostles saw Him in the Upper Room and elsewhere. The Lord commissioned him there and said that He was going to make him 'a minister and a witness both of these things which thou hast seen, and of those things in the which I will appear unto thee' (Acts 26:16). He said that He had 'appeared' to Paul 'for this purpose'. Without actually having seen the risen Lord a man could not be an apostle.

Thirdly, an apostle was a man who had been given a supernatural revelation of the Truth. The apostle has already dealt with this in the third chapter of this Epistle where he says, 'If ye have heard of the dispensation of the grace of God which is given me to you-ward: how that by revelation he made known unto me the mystery' (vv. 2-3). He had received 'by revelation' the knowledge of the truth he was to preach. In the first chapter of the Epistle to the Galatians, where he is defending his apostleship and pronouncing anathema on anyone, even an angel from heaven, who preached any other gospel than that which he had preached to them, he justifies his strong language and claims in the following words: 'Do I now persuade men, or God? or do I speak to please men? for if I yet pleased men, I should not be the servant of Christ. But I certify you, brethren, that the gospel which was preached of me is not after man; for I neither received it of man, neither was I taught it, but by the revelation of Jesus Christ' (vv. 10–12). This is what gives an apostle his authority and competence as an exceptional teacher.

Fourthly, the next desideratum follows logically from the third, namely, that an apostle is a man who has been given power to speak not only with authority but infallibly. The apostles were the ambassadors of Christ, and a unique authority was granted to them. The early Church recognized this authority. When, later, the early Church had to decide on the canon of Scripture in the New Testament under the guidance of the Holy Spirit, this was the ultimate test, that a book should have apostolic authority. It had to be traced either to an apostle himself, or it must be proved that it derived from the teaching of an apostle. Apostolicity was a test of canonicity, because an apostle, and an apostle alone, could speak infallibly and with divine authority. This explains why the Apostle Paul could write to people and say, 'Be ye followers of me' (1 Cor 4:16; Phil 3:17). This was not egotism or conceit; it was the humility of an apostle who always made it clear that his words were not his own but those of the Lord Himself. The importance of emphasizing this is self-evident.

The fifth and last test which must be emphasized is that an apostle was a man who had the power to work miracles. This is stated in Hebrews 2:4, where we are told that the word was first spoken by the Lord, and by them who heard Him, 'The Lord also bearing them witness with signs and wonders and divers miracles'. The Lord had said to His disciples, 'Greater works than these shall ye do' (John 14:12). This refers to miracles; the performing of miracles was one of the marks of an apostle, as we see abundantly in the Book of the Acts of the Apostles.

All this is important because even in the days of the early Church and of the apostles themselves there were men, claiming to be apostles, who were setting themselves up as apostles and teachers. They are referred to by Paul in the Second Epistle to the Corinthians. These men were troubling the church at Corinth and other churches; and this is what Paul says about them, 'For such are false apostles, deceitful workers, transforming themselves into the apostles of Christ. And no marvel; for Satan himself is transformed into an angel of light' (11:13–14). That there were false apostles makes it vitally important for us to understand what an apostle truly is. False apostles had not seen the risen Lord, they had never been called and commissioned by Him. They did not understand the truth, they had never received the revelation, they did not work miracles. They were imposters who gave to, and received 'letters of commendation' from one another (2 Cor 3:1). By definition this office of apostle was clearly an extraordinary and a temporary office. It is impossible that it should continue, were it merely for this fact, that no man has seen the risen Lord with the naked eye, or could possibly have claimed to see Him in that manner, since the Apostle Paul. Some have claimed to have seen visions, but visions belong to an entirely different category. Paul did not see a vision on the road to Damascus, he actually saw the Lord Christ.

*　　*　　*

There is thus no successor to the apostles. By definition, there never can be or has been a successor to the apostles. That this is taught in the New Testament itself can be proved thus. Recall how, because of the defection and the suicide of Judas Iscariot, the apostles decided that they must appoint a successor to him; and they appointed Matthias, as we are told in the first chapter of Acts. But then there is this interesting case of the Apostle Paul and how he was brought into the apostolate. He would never have been accepted by the other apostles had he not been given that sight of the risen Lord on the road to Damascus. He tells us himself that his case was unusual and exceptional, saying that he was 'as one born out of due time', a kind of ectopic (1 Cor 15:8). The risen Christ was revealed last of all to him. He had not been present at the time of the resurrection.

There is also a very interesting negative proof of the matter. In the twelfth chapter of the Acts of the Apostles we are told that James, the brother of John, one of the Apostles, was put to death by king Herod. But no successor to him was appointed. If Apostles were to be appointed by the Church, undoubtedly the

Church would have appointed a successor to James there and then. But that was not done. All this evidence taken together proves beyond any doubt that the apostolate was a temporary office and that its continuance was never intended by the Lord. How frequently has this not been understood! The whole structure of the papacy is based on a misunderstanding of this. It is based on the theory that Peter became the fixed and settled apostle and bishop in Rome, and that he appointed a successor, and that that process has gone on ever since. Roman Catholicism teaches that Peter transmitted to these successors the same power which he himself possessed. The claim is not only unscriptural, it is even wrong historically. There is no valid evidence that such a position was ever accorded to Peter or that he was the first bishop of Rome. That fabrication was invented in subsequent centuries. But it is ultimately based on a complete misunderstanding of the office of an apostle. The Church-appointed popes do not claim that they have seen the risen Lord; but we have seen that that is the first essential qualification of an apostle.

This fallacy, alas, has not been confined to the Church of Rome. Apart from the teaching in Catholic sections of the Church of England and certain other Churches about 'apostolic succession', there have been others in the Church who have claimed to be apostles, and that what is taught in 1 Corinthians chapter 12 should be perpetuated in the Church. This is seen for instance in the extraordinary story of Edward Irving and the Irvingites and the so-called Catholic Apostolic Church which he established in London about 1830. Irving was a brilliant young Scottish preacher, who had been assistant to Dr Thomas Chalmers, and who by many was thought to excel even Chalmers in his eloquence and oratory. He came to London and was the fashionable preacher there for a number of years; but suddenly to everyone's consternation and amazement, he began to say that the whole Church system was wrong, that he was an apostle, and that the apostolate was something that should be perpetuated in the Church. So he set up what he called the Catholic Apostolic Church, with apostles and prophets and other offices. His life ended in tragedy. The account can be read in a book entitled *Edward Irving and his Circle*, by A. L. Drummond. Since then there has been a church calling itself The Apostolic Church. It is all based upon a misunderstanding of the New Testament teaching concerning the office of an apostle.

*   *   *

We come next to the term 'prophets'. In the New Testament prophets are generally coupled with the apostles, as in the second chapter of this Epistle: 'And are built upon the foundation of the apostles and prophets, Jesus Christ himself being the chief corner stone' (v. 20). But though coupled with the apostles, prophets are obviously different. For instance, it was not necessary that a prophet should have seen the risen Lord. Indeed he need not, in general, have most of the qualifications of the apostle. Essentially a prophet was a man who spoke under the direct inspiration of the Holy Spirit. It is clear also that sometimes a prophet was a woman. We are told in the second chapter of Luke that Anna was a 'prophetess'. Likewise we are told in Acts that Philip the evangelist had four daughters who 'did prophesy' (21:9). There are many references to prophets in the New Testament. For instance, in Acts we are told that there were several prophets in the church at Antioch some of whom had come down from Jerusalem (11:27; 13:1). One of them named Agabus prophesied that a dearth was about to come upon the earth and he warned the Christian people about it. There is specific teaching about the prophets in the fourteenth chapter of the First Epistle to the Corinthians. The whole question of prophets is a difficult subject, and one must not speak too dogmatically about it. We can and must be absolutely dogmatic about the apostles, but as regards prophets we must be more cautious, because the teaching is not clear-cut.

We can say, however, that a prophet was a person to whom truth was imparted by the Holy Spirit. Indeed we can say that he received a revelation of truth, and was given power also to speak and to utter this truth in a more or less ecstatic manner. This becomes evident from the fact that one of the problems in the church at Corinth was that these ecstatic utterances of the prophets were tending to cause confusion. Some who prophesied there were excusing themselves by saying that they were helpless under the power of the Spirit. Paul counters that by saying 'and the spirits of the prophets are subject to the prophets'. He teaches that prophets can and should control themselves, and that they must speak one at a time and not interrupt one another.

We must emphasize that a prophet is a person to whom a revelation of truth has come. This is made plain in Paul's teaching in 1 Corinthians 14, where he says, 'Let the prophets speak two or three, and let the other judge. If any thing be revealed to another that sitteth by, let the first hold his peace' (vv. 29–30). A revelation or message or some insight into truth came to them, and, filled with the Spirit, they were able to make utterances which were of benefit and profit to the Church. Surely it is clear that this again was temporary, and for this good reason, that in those early days of the Church there were no New Testament Scriptures, the Truth had not yet been expounded in written words.

Try to imagine our position if we did not possess these New Testament Epistles, but the Old Testament only. That was the position of the early Church. Truth was imparted to it primarily by the teaching and preaching of the apostles, but that was supplemented by the teaching of the prophets to whom truth was given and also the ability to speak it with clarity and power in the demonstration and authority of the Spirit. But once these New Testament documents were written the office of a prophet was no longer necessary. Hence in the Pastoral Epistles which apply to a later stage in the history of the Church, when things had become more settled and fixed, there is no mention of the prophets. It is clear that even by then the office of the prophet was no longer necessary, and the call was for teachers and pastors and others to expound the Scriptures and to convey the knowledge of the truth.

*   *   *

Again, we must note that often in the history of the Church trouble has arisen because people thought that they were prophets in the New Testament sense, and that they had received special revelations of truth. The answer to that is that in view of the New Testament Scriptures there is no need of further truth. That is an absolute proposition. We have all truth in the New Testament, and we have no need of any further revelations. All has been given, everything that is necessary for us is available. Therefore if a man claims to have received a revelation of some fresh

[189]

truth we should suspect him immediately. The Church has often had to do this. In the second century a sect arose called the Montanists who made this very claim. They were denounced as heretics by the Church; and rightly so. They were good and sincere people, as heretics often are, and much of their criticism of the state of the Church was correct. They were spiritually-minded people, but they pressed a particular truth too far, and the Devil came in and urged them to go beyond the Scripture, and so they became heretics. But ironically enough the Roman Catholic Church is herself the chief heretic in this matter, as in the matter of the Apostolate. The Roman Catholic Church in the past has often not hesitated to claim and to assert that she has received fresh revelations of truth beyond what is found in the New Testament. This applies to most of her teaching about the Virgin Mary. It is not to be found in the Scripture, but they claim to have received it through fresh revelations. On the whole they do not teach this at the present time in the former bald fashion, but say that these things were latent in the Scriptures. However, when the Pope speaks 'ex cathedra', and pronounces the doctrine of the so-called Immaculate Conception or that of the Assumption of the Virgin, it is claimed that he is speaking with the authority of the apostles and prophets and as the Vicar of Christ. This is all due to a misunderstanding of these offices of apostles and prophets. Is it not right that we should be aware of these things when many urge us to join with Rome to form one great world Church?

Furthermore, we must remember that this has not been confined to Roman Catholicism. At the time of the Protestant Reformation certain sects arose – they are often classified somewhat unfairly under the general heading of the Anabaptists – on the continent of Europe, which caused much trouble to Martin Luther in particular, and also to Zwingli and Calvin. These people, called 'Zwickau prophets', claimed that they were prophets, and that they were receiving revelations from heaven. Some of the more fanatical went so far as to dismiss and ignore the written Word and to replace its authority by what they claimed to be direct revelations of the Spirit. The same tendency is found in England in the case of Quakerism which arose in the seventeenth century at the time of the Puritan revival. George Fox, their founder, was undoubtedly a saintly man of God, but increasingly he emphasized the 'inner light' and direct leading and guidance as superior to the written Word, and his followers did so still more. They were really claiming to be prophets in the New Testament sense.

The answer to all this is that the need for prophets ends once we have the canon of the New Testament. We no longer need direct revelations of truth; the truth is in the Bible. We must never separate the Spirit and the Word. The Spirit speaks to us through the Word; so we should always doubt and query any supposed revelation that is not entirely consistent with the Word of God. Indeed the essence of wisdom is to reject altogether the term 'revelation' as far as we are concerned, and speak only of 'illumination'. The revelation has been given once and for all, and what we need and what by the grace of God we can have, and do have, is illumination by the Spirit to understand the Word. The preacher should not enter his pulpit claiming to have received a revelation; his claim should be that he is a man who reads the Word and prays and believes that the Holy Spirit illumines and enlightens his understanding, with the result that he has a message for the people. In other words he is a man who prays constantly for himself what Paul tells us he was praying for the Christians in Ephesus (chaps. 1 and 3).

*   *   *

I suggest also that the same is true of the term 'evangelist'. If any are surprised that I place the evangelist and his office in the same extraordinary and temporary category as the apostles and prophets, the probability is that they are thinking of an evangelist in terms of the modern use of the term. This is something essentially different from its use in the New Testament, where we are not told much about the evangelists. Philip who is mentioned in the eighth chapter of the Book of the Acts, was an evangelist. He is mentioned again in the twenty-first chapter. It is quite clear also that Timothy and Titus were evangelists. The Apostle Paul reminds Timothy to do the work of an evangelist. It seems clear from these references that an evangelist was a very special man who was in close association with the apostles. Some of the Early Fathers in the church tended to say that the evangelists were those who wrote the Four Gospels; but that cannot be the case in the light of what we are told in the places already mentioned. The evangelist is a man who had been given a special ability and power to make known, and to expound, the facts of the Gospel. Generally he was a man appointed by the apostles themselves, and can be described as a kind of understudy to the apostles. He was one sent by the apostles to do a given work. Sometimes he was sent ahead of the apostles, as Philip was sent to Samaria, but generally he followed the apostles.

The apostles, prophets and evangelists were itinerant. They travelled around and established churches and laid the foundations of the Christian Church. Frequently, therefore, you will find that the evangelist was left by the apostle to build upon the foundation that had been established, to expound and explain the truth more fully. Or, as I have said, sometimes he was sent ahead of the apostle to prepare the way and to introduce the general message of the Gospel. That was his particular task. He had not seen the risen Lord, he could not witness to the resurrection in that manner. The story of Titus and Timothy proves that beyond any doubt. But he was a man whom the Holy Spirit had led the apostles to choose. He had been given certain abilities; he knew the facts, he knew the truths of the Gospel, and he could present them in a clear manner and with unction and authority and power from the Holy Spirit. He thus supplemented the work of the apostles and extended it and caused it to spread and to become established. Thus the evangelist was a man whose office was temporary, and as the churches were established and became more settled, this office likewise disappeared.

This does not mean that there may not be men since then, and in the Church today, who are given a special call to preach the Gospel in a particular way and manner, but strictly speaking they are not evangelists in the New Testament sense of the word. It would be better to call them 'exhorters', as they were called at the time of the evangelical awakening of the eighteenth century.

* * *

Here, then, are three offices which were extraordinary and temporary. The permanent offices are described as those of 'pastors and teachers'. This group is much simpler to understand, although there has been much dispute as to whether pastors and teachers are two different offices. I agree with those who say that they are one. Were they two separate offices we would expect to read, 'He gave some, apostles; some, prophets; some, evangelists; some, pastors; some, teachers'; but the apostle writes, 'some, pastors and teachers', linking the two together; and generally speaking, these two offices are found in the same man. They apply to a more settled state of the Church, and have persisted throughout the centuries. The office of a pastor is generally concerned about government and instruction and rule and direction. It is borrowed, of course, from the picture of a shepherd. The shepherd shepherds his flock, keeps the sheep in order, directs them where to go and where to feed, brings them back to the fold, looks after their safety and guards them against enemies liable to attack them. It is a great office, but unfortunately it is a term which has become debased. A pastor is a man who is given charge of souls. He is not merely a nice, pleasant man who visits people and has an afternoon cup of tea with them, or passes the time of day with them. He is the guardian, the custodian, the protector, the organizer, the director, the ruler of the flock. The teacher gives instruction in doctrine, in truth. The Apostle proceeds to elaborate this, showing that we need to be built up, and that we must not remain 'babes'. We must be protected against 'every wind of doctrine', and the way to do so is to give instruction and teaching.

Although I say that these two offices generally go together and have done so throughout the long history of the Church, sometimes one man has had more of a pastoral gift than a teaching or preaching gift, at other times a man has more of a teaching and preaching gift than a pastoral gift. This is a matter of individual variation according to the gift of the Spirit. But in the Church you have these offices, these men who teach and preach and care for the souls of the members of the church. The Roman Catholic Church has tended to divide these offices, and the Puritans in the 16th and 17th centuries appointed 'lecturers' who had no pastoral charge. But these are exceptions to the general rule.

* * *

In the Christian Church we hold the wisdom of the Head, our

Lord and Saviour Jesus Christ. He has given apostles and prophets to lay the foundation. The Church is built 'on the foundation of the apostles and prophets' (Eph 2:20). They were men whom He called in special manner to do this. The Apostle Paul, looking back, can say, 'He separated me from my mother's womb'. He did not know this for years and was a blasphemer who hated the Church and persecuted it. Nevertheless the time came when He revealed Himself to Paul and called him. Oh the wisdom of the Head of the Church! You and I would probably never have called most of the apostles who were fishermen and unlearned men. We would have called a series of men noted as philosophers. But our Lord, as the Head of the Church, chose some very ordinary men as well as this unusual and remarkable man Paul. It was He who chose them all. He knew how to lay the foundation. The Church has often forgotten this, as for example when the Roman Emperor Constantine became a Christian and turned Christianity into the official religion of the Roman Empire in A.D. 313. At once there was an alliance between Church and State. Members of noble families began to be appointed to church offices by emperors and councils; and thus it has continued ever since. The un-Christian term 'patronage' came in, and has persisted and continued. So that, generally speaking, men have not been called to these high offices because of their spirituality or understanding of truth, but rather because of their natural birth, their natural ability or secular learning, obtained in the universities to which they belong, and for similar reasons. The Christian Church is constantly in danger of forgetting the teaching of the apostles, the foundation on which we are built, with the result that the world does not even look at the Church but ignores her. The world sees this worldliness in the Church, sees the office-seeking, the rivalries and scheming and manipulating with which it is so familiar in its own sphere, and says that it is therefore not interested in the Church. In other words, one of the most urgent needs of the hour is that we should demonstrate to the world that the Church is still the body of Christ, that she is still spiritual, that everything about her, and especially these offices, is determined by the Lord and not by astute ecclesiastics. As the true Church remains the body of Christ, it is only as the Head calls and appoints men to these offices that the world will listen to the Church and her message and be delivered out of the thraldom of sin and Satan and become saints in the Church of the Living God.

May God grant us wisdom and understanding in these matters, that we may play our rightful part in all the dangerous discussions of this present time. Let us not be afraid to take our stand on the Scripture, and let us not be carried off our feet and swept away by vague generalities about unity that oftentimes are made at the expense of the truth itself.

16
Edifying the Body

'For the perfecting of the saints, for the work of the
ministry, for the edifying of the body of Christ: till we
all come in the unity of the faith, and of the knowledge of the Son of God, unto a perfect man, unto the
measure of the stature of the fulness of Christ: that we
henceforth be no more children, tossed to and fro,
and carried about with every wind of doctrine, by the
sleight of men, and cunning craftiness, whereby they
lie in wait to deceive; but speaking the truth in love,
may grow up into him in all things, which is the
head, even Christ: from whom the whole body fitly
joined together and compacted by that which every
joint supplieth, according to the effectual working in
the measure of every part, maketh increase of the
body unto the edifying of itself in love'.

Ephesians 4:12–16

That is all one great statement, and what a mighty statement it is!
Its purpose is to tell us why our Lord and Saviour Jesus Christ
has appointed in the Church the various offices and the men to
fill those offices. It is in order to perfect the Church, to make her
entire and complete in every respect.

It is well for us to start by making a general analysis of the
statement. In verses 12 and 13 the Apostle gives a general positive
statement of the object in view. All this has been done, he says,
'for the perfecting of the saints, for the work of the ministry, for
the edifying of the body of Christ, till we all come in the unity of
the faith, and of the knowledge of the Son of God, unto a perfect
man, unto the measure of the stature of the fulness of Christ'.
That is what we are meant to be, that is the goal, but wise teacher
as he was, he states it negatively in verse 14: 'That we henceforth
be no more children, tossed to and fro, and carried about with
every wind of doctrine, by the sleight of men, and cunning

craftiness, whereby they lie in wait to deceive'. Then he returns to the positive in verse 15: 'But speaking the truth in love, may grow up into him in all things, which is the head'. It is all designed to the building up of the body and its harmonious functioning as he works it out in some detail through the analogy of the Church as the body of Christ in verse 16.

Once more we are looking at a wonderful picture of the Church. It is only as we who are in the Church have a right view of the Church that she will begin to function truly. For instance the first question with regard to the problem of evangelization is not the state of the world outside, it is the condition of the Church. Defective views of the Church and her functioning lead to the employment of worldly and carnal methods. If we saw the Church as she is depicted by the Apostle, everything would be changed. The real problem is still the nature of the Church.

* * *

We must begin with the general statement in verses 12 and 13 with respect to the purpose of all offices in the Church. In verse 12 Paul states it objectively and in general. In verse 13 he states it somewhat more particularly and subjectively: the end itself in general in verse 12, the way in which it affects us in verse 13. There are apostles and prophets and evangelists, and pastors and teachers in the Church for three main reasons: for the perfecting of the saints, for the work of the ministry, for the edifying of the body of Christ. The question that arises is the relationship of these three offices to one another, and the learned commentators spend much time in discussing it. The question is, are these three things absolutely parallel and exactly co-ordinate?

The answer is provided by the word 'for' – '*for* the perfecting of the saints, *for* the work of the ministry, *for* the edifying of the body of Christ'. The same word is used three times in the Authorised Version, but if we go back to the original we find that in the Greek the first *for* is a different word from that employed in the second and third cases. The first *for* is more general than the others. I entirely agree with those who say that the difference is that the first *for* has reference to the ultimate purpose, whereas the second and third refer to a more immediate purpose. There is a grand end to which the two intermediate ends lead.

We can state the matter thus: The ultimate purpose of all these offices and divisions of labour in the Church is the perfecting of the saints; and the way in which the saints are to be perfected is through the gift of the ministry, the function of which is to edify the body of Christ. There is an ultimate objective, and there are more immediate objectives.

I call attention to the way in which believers are described here. Each one is a saint – 'for the perfecting of the saints'. Every member of the Christian Church is a saint. The New Testament epistles make this plain and clear; they are addressed to 'the saints which are at Corinth' or 'the saints which are in Rome', or elsewhere. It is much to be regretted that Christians have allowed this word to be misused, and in particular that we have allowed the Roman Catholic conception of a saint to influence us so much. In our folly we say, 'Ah, I am not a saint', or 'I would not like to say that I am a saint'. But we should say that we are saints. What is a saint? A saint is a man who has been separated from the world. The actual word means 'a holy one' – 'for the perfecting of the holy ones'. 'A holy one' is a person who has been taken out of where he was and set apart. The term is constantly used in the Old Testament. A mountain was made holy and separated in this sense for God's use. The vessels in the temple were made holy when blood was sprinkled upon them. They were sanctified in that way and set apart. The way in which we are to conceive of ourselves as Christians and as members of the Church, therefore, is that we have been separated from the world, that we are no longer profane, and no longer belong to that realm. God has moved us, and separated us, and has set us apart for Himself. We are a 'chosen generation, a royal priesthood, an holy nation, a peculiar people' – a people for His own peculiar possession. We have been segregated and separated. Once more I assert that the Church is as she is because this idea has been forgotten. This separation is no longer in evidence; we are too much like the world. The world has come into the Church, and it has become difficult to tell the difference between a Christian and a non-Christian. The word 'saint' reminds us of the whole process of calling out and separating and putting on one side for God. Let us rejoice in the fact that we are saints and let us glory in our high calling.

We turn now to the word 'perfecting'. Essentially this word means that we have to be made fit to serve the end and object aimed at. The picture is that something which we desire to use is not yet perfect, so we have to do certain things to it in order to fit it for that end and object for which we desire to use it. This means the supplying of certain deficiencies or the mending and adjusting of certain parts that are wrong. The original idea at the back of this word is that of 'fitting together into one body'. Actually it was a term that was used for the setting of bones which had become dislocated. When bones are dislocated, the particular limb to which they belong is not perfect. When they are set or re-set and put again into the right alignment the limb becomes perfect again. So the idea in the word used by the Apostle is that all these different parts and portions of the body of Christ should be put into the right alignment, should be properly adjusted, and that each one should be fully developed. The Apostle is still thinking in terms of the Church as the body of Christ. We are all together the body of Christ, but we are members in particular; and every one of us has to be perfected; and as every one is perfected the whole will be perfected. So the work is being done in every one of us, we are being made to fit in properly into our particular place in the Church, with the result that the whole body will function in an harmonious and satisfactory manner. Everything that our Lord has appointed for the Church has that end and object in view, namely, that this body of Christ in all its members may be made perfect and entire.

* * *

Turning now to the next question as to how this is to be accomplished we come to the second statement – 'for the work of the ministry'. This is one of the subsidiary ends. Here again there is much dispute and discussion as to the meaning of this particular phrase. Some argue that it means 'for the doing of service', that our Lord has set all these offices in the Church in order that we all may be rendered fit or 'furnished out for' the doing of our service, whatever that service may be. Some contend that it means that the Apostle is saying that all these offices are designed to enable us as members of the body to serve one another. But it seems to me that this is quite untenable as an exposition. Of course, there is a sense in which it is true, but the question is whether this is what the Apostle is emphasizing here. I suggest that it is not, for the reason that the whole context is against it, and that the Apostle's idea in the entire context is that of the ministerial offices in the Church. To that end he has been specifying them – 'apostles, prophets, evangelists, pastors and teachers'. He is not thinking of the ordinary, average members of the Church; he is deliberately illustrating his theme by picking out certain offices and certain special callings. In other words he is emphasizing that the Lord has appointed a form and an order of ministry in the Christian Church. That is the entire context; and he includes those, and those only, who hold ministerial offices. Indeed in the New Testament this word for 'ministry' is generally used in that sense and connotation. Take, for example, what the same Apostle says in 1 Corinthians 3:5: 'Who then is Paul, and who is Apollos, but ministers by whom ye believed, even as the Lord gave to every man?' What he means by 'even as the Lord gave to every man' is 'even as the Lord has appointed his office to every man'. He goes on to say, 'I planted'; that was the work given to him; 'Apollos watered'; that was the task given to him. But note that the Apostle describes himself and Apollos as 'ministers'. He does so again in the following chapter in 1 Corinthians 4:1: 'Let a man so account of us as of the ministers of Christ, and stewards of the mysteries of God'. Again he is dealing with the ministerial office.

The risen Lord Jesus Christ in all His glory has sent down these gifts into the Church. They are not of human institution, He Himself has ordained them and appointed them, He has decided the nature of the offices, and He has decided on the men who are to occupy these offices. They are thus 'ministers' in the Church. The Apostle is a minister. Prophets, evangelists, pastors, teachers are all ministers of Christ, and stewards of the mysteries of God. What ministers do in the Church Sunday by Sunday is not something which man has evolved over the centuries; it was originated by the Lord Himself and we do it because it is our duty to do it, because we are called to do it. 'The perfecting of the saints' cannot happen apart from the work of the ministry.

This work of the ministry is 'for the edifying of the body of Christ'. This word 'edifying' means 'building up'. The Apostle has already used this word at the end of the second chapter where he says that we are 'built upon the foundation of the apostles and prophets, Jesus Christ himself being the chief corner stone; in whom all the building fitly framed together . . .' Indeed it is the same idea as our Lord Himself used when He said, 'Thou art Peter, and on this rock I will build my church'. So we are concerned here with the idea of building. The Apostle seems to be mixing his metaphors, as he seems to be doing also in the second chapter. His controlling idea is that of the body, but he speaks of building up the body. He combines this idea of constructing a building with the growth of a body, and so he writes about building up the body. We do something similar when we talk today about 'body building' foods. Paul teaches that the work of the ministry is 'body building'.

The work of the ministry, the Apostle says, is to promote spiritual growth and development. Let no-one think that this subject is only appropriate for a theological seminary or for a gathering of ministers, and that it has nothing to do with members of the Church who are not called into any ministerial office. This matter is important for all Church members, for this good reason, that far too often the pew has controlled the pulpit, and great harm has come in the Church. The Apostle warns Timothy that a time is coming when people 'will not endure sound doctrine'. This is frequently the case at the present time, and has been so during this present century. So it is important that every member of the Church should have a true conception of the Church and the office of the ministry in particular.

There are churches in the world today which appear on the surface to be very flourishing. People crowd into them and they display much zeal and enthusiasm. But on closer examination you will find that most of the time is taken up with music of various types, and with clubs and societies and social activities. The service starts at 11 a.m. and must finish promptly at 12 noon. There will be real trouble if it does not! There is but a brief 'address' of some quarter of an hour's duration, twenty minutes as a maximum. The unfortunate minister, if he does not see these things clearly, is afraid to go against the wishes of the majority, his livelihood depends upon church members, and the result is that everything is made to conform to the desires and wishes of the pew. I have been told on excellent authority that there is a

[201]

church which is attended at certain seasons of the year by most distinguished personages, in which instructions are given to the preacher that he is not to preach for more than seven minutes. It is most important, therefore, that every member of the Church should understand that the purpose and the function of the ministry is 'for the edifying of the body of Christ'. The history of the Church shows clearly that it is when the pew, the listeners, exert such powerful influence and when ministers lacking courage have been so bound, that the Word of God has not been truly preached and the Church has become dead and lifeless. The pew does not dictate to the minister as to what he is to do.

But let me add that the minister also must not dictate. It is the Lord Himself who determines, He who is seated at the right hand of God and who has given 'some, apostles; some, prophets; some, evangelists; and some, pastors and teachers'. He has given them for the edification of the members of the Church, and it is His message that is to be preached without fear or favour. We need to recapture something of the spirit of John Knox whose preaching caused Mary Queen of Scots to tremble.

The work of the ministry is to build up the body of Christ. It is the business of the ministers to build up the Church, not to build up themselves! Alas! they have far too often built up themselves, and we read of princes of the Church living in positions of great wealth and pomp. What an utter travesty that is of Paul's teaching! Let us note also that ministers are called to build up; not to please and to entertain. The way in which they are to do this is summed up perfectly in that most lyrical passage in Acts 20. The Apostle Paul was bidding farewell to the elders of the church at Ephesus, at the seaside, and this is what he said: 'And now, brethren, I commend you to God, and to the word of His grace, which is able to build you up, and to give you an inheritance among all them which are sanctified' (v. 32). 'The word of His grace, which is able to build you up'! The Apostle expresses the same idea in writing to the Colossians: 'Whom we preach, warning every man, and teaching every man in all wisdom; that we may present every man perfect in Christ Jesus: whereunto I also labour, striving according to his working, which worketh in me mightily' (1:28--29). We find the same teaching also in the Second Epistle to Timothy: 'All scripture is given by inspiration

[202]

of God, and is profitable for doctrine, for reproof, for correction, for instruction in righteousness: that the man of God may be perfect, throughly furnished unto all good works' (3:16-17). Again in the fourth chapter of the same Epistle we read: 'Preach the word; be instant in season, out of season' (4:2). In his First Epistle to the Corinthians the Apostle says: 'I have fed you with milk, and not with meat; for hitherto ye were not able to bear it' (3:2). Then in the Epistle to the Hebrews we find: 'Of whom we have many things to say, and hard to be uttered, seeing ye are dull of hearing. For when for the time ye ought to be teachers, ye have need that one teach you again which be the first principles of the oracles of God; and are become such as have need of milk, and not of strong meat. For every one that useth milk is unskilful in the word of righteousness: for he is a babe. But strong meat belongeth to them that are of full age, even those who by reason of use have their senses exercised to discern both good and evil' (5:11-14).

All these passages instruct us as to the work of the ministry. They show the way to build up the body of Christ. It is to 'preach the Word' – 'the Word of his grace which is able to build you up'. The work of the ministry does not consist in talking about current affairs or events, the minister is not to find his message in newspapers, he is not to be entertaining the people by telling them stories, or provoking laughter. He is to 'preach the Word'. This is the only Word which can build up the Church, and build up every member of the body of Christ.

*   *   *

Turning now to the practical question as to how this Word is to be preached, the first rule is that purity of doctrine must be the rule. The Apostle Peter in his First Epistle writes: 'As newborn babes, desire the sincere milk of the word, that ye may grow thereby' (2:2). 'Sincere' means 'unadulterated', 'pure', without admixture, up to standard, passing the test – the sincere, unadulterated milk of the Word. And this is not 'the word of man', it is 'the word of God'. It is not surprising that the Church is as she is today; she has been given philosophy and entertainment. By those means a minister may attract and keep a crowd for a while; but they cannot 'build up'; and the business of preachers is to build up, not to attract a crowd. Nothing builds up but the unadulterated Word of God. There is no authority apart from this; and it must not be modified or trimmed to suit the fashion of modern science, or some supposed 'assured results of criticism' which are always changing. It is the 'everlasting gospel', it is the 'eternal Word', the same Word which Paul and the other apostles preached, the same Word which the Protestant Reformers preached, and the Puritans, and the great preachers of two hundred years ago, and likewise Spurgeon in the last century without any modification whatsoever. It is because this has been so largely forgotten in the last hundred years that things are as they are today.

But, secondly, it must be the appropriate word, the appropriate food. We have seen how the Apostle Paul says, 'I did not feed you on meat, I fed you on milk', and how the author of the Epistle to the Hebrews says exactly the same thing. We do not give strong meat to a babe; the babe has to be fed on milk. This means that the minister must have discernment and judgment in these matters. The child does not decide what particular diet is best for his growth. The child wants to decide, of course, the child always wants to have what it likes; but it does not know what is good for it. It is not the business of the child to decide; it is the business of the parent. In spiritual nurture there is milk, and there is strong meat; and it is a part of the business of the preacher to know the difference between the two. He must vary the diet according to the people's need – not only milk, and not only strong meat – otherwise his preaching will not be edifying. Then again, there are varying circumstances; and this Word is to be applied to every conceivable circumstance. Some of the listeners are happy, and some are sad; there are those who may be enduring persecution and tribulation; some may be celebrating a victory. There is a word for all; and a full ministry of the whole Word will meet every condition and every conceivable circumstance.

Furthermore, this diet that builds up must not only be un-adulterated and appropriate, it must also be full and it must be balanced. This can be illustrated by what is true in the natural realm. We read in the newspapers about the importance of having a balanced diet of protein, fat and carbohydrates, and also vitamins. One of the great discoveries of this present century, and especially during the second World War, was the importance of having a balanced diet. People are often ill, not only because they are not taking sufficient food, but also because their diet is not balanced. This is equally true and vital with respect to spiritual food. It must be a balanced diet, as our quotations have told us. It is to consist of teaching and doctrine. This always comes first. '. . . give attendance to reading, to exhortation, to doctrine' says the Apostle to Timothy (1 Timothy 4:13). And again in the same chapter: 'Take heed unto thyself, and unto the doctrine' (v. 16). Unless we are established in the doctrine of the Christian faith we cannot possibly grow.

*   *   *

The history of the Church shows clearly that her great and glorious periods, such as during and after the Protestant Reformation, always follow the mighty preaching of doctrine. It is unintelligent to admire great heroes of the faith such as the Covenanters unless you understand them. What made those men the men they were was the fact that they knew the great doctrines of the Christian faith. This is the protein and the iron which give strength. The great doctrines of the faith must be the basis of the Christian diet. Following the doctrine must come the teaching which applies the doctrine. The Apostle was careful to say that he 'warned every man'. And we need to be warned in days and times such as these. There is far too much complacency in the Church. The position is really desperate, and 'judgment must begin at the house of God'. Do we realize our responsibility for the state of the Church, and the state of the world? We shall be held accountable.

Following warning comes reproof and correction. We do not like this, and desire something that makes us feel happy. But the Bible is full of reproof, full of correction; and we all need to be reproved and corrected as to our lives and our mode of living; for example, our use of money, our use of time, our very dress, and many other things. Then we need 'instruction in righteousness'. We need to be told how to live a godly and holy and pure life. In this very Epistle we are studying the Apostle goes on from the middle of this fourth chapter to the very end to give this instruction in righteousness. He also tells Timothy to 'exhort with all longsuffering'. This means that the truth has to be applied. A ministry which merely states the truth without applying it has failed. The true preacher of righteousness urges the people to put it into practice. In other words, if we are concerned about the growth of a child or an adolescent we stress the need of exercise. This will help growth and development.

Here, again, we must be careful that our teaching is balanced. A friend was telling me recently that he and many of his fellow-members were feeling discouraged because they were constantly being exhorted to do various things without being given the reason for doing so. A ministry which consists only of exhortation and appeals to people to take decisions constantly, generally becomes barren and futile. Action and activity should result from the doctrine. A balanced ministry does not confine itself to doctrine only or to exhortation only, but combines both and places them in the right order. There must always be something for the mind, for the heart, and for the will. Truth involves practice as well as theory. The preacher is not to treat and to analyse a portion of Scripture as if he were handling a play of Shakespeare. The Word is God's Word, it is holy truth, and it is meant to move the heart, and to influence and affect the will. So the one who ministers the Gospel must preach in a lively and warm manner under the power of the Spirit. In a sense nothing is more devastating than a ministry which is only intellectual, and which never disturbs. There have been times in the history of the Church when ministers have preached very orthodox sermons, but the Church was dead. The explanation is that the preaching was purely intellectual, the heart was never moved.

A man said something to me not long ago which encouraged me more than anything I have heard for years. He was a man over eighty years of age. I happened to be preaching on justification by faith, and with tears in his eyes he said to me, 'I have known that doctrine all my life; but I have never known it to move me before'. He had held the doctrine intellectually; he had belonged to a section of the Church where these things are regarded objectively in a purely intellectual manner, but it had not moved him. What we may call spiritual vitamins should always be a constituent of the diet if there is to be a life-giving quality in the ministry.

Finally, it must all be done in an attractive manner. When a person is ill and has lost his appetite, his food must be presented in an attractive manner. You do not, as it were, throw it at him; you cook it as well as you can, and you serve it as attractively and as tidily as you can. In other words, if a minister does not have a concern about people's souls, if he is not troubled about them, and is not careful to observe whether they are growing and developing, he is not exercising an edifying ministry. I emphasize again that this does not mean that he should be entertaining people. Paul emphasizes, in his pastoral epistles particularly, that it must be done with gravity and with sobriety. The Apostle writes of himself and his ministry in these terms: 'Knowing therefore the terror of the Lord, we persuade men' (2 Cor 5:11). He felt responsible for the souls of men, and he knew that he and his work would be judged at 'the judgment seat of Christ' partly by the condition of the people. The truth must be presented attractively, that is to say, in a spiritually attractive manner, not in a carnally attractive manner, not as entertainment.

A further instruction to the minister is that he is to show himself a pattern in his life and ministry. He himself is to manifest spiritual growth, understanding of the doctrine, and concern about it, in his own life, and in the whole of his demeanour. The Apostle could challenge the people at Thessalonica in this respect: 'You are witnesses, and God also, how holily and justly and unblameably we behaved ourselves among you that believe' (1 Thess 2:10). And he urges upon Titus the importance of showing himself a pattern of all godliness and righteousness and holy living (2:7–8).

As we have seen, the Lord Himself has appointed these offices, 'for the perfecting of the saints'. His desire is that through the ministry we may all be built up, that the body of Christ may be built up, that every part may be strong and powerful and a credit to the Head, and all in conformity to His will and pleasure. The living Head, knowing what is needed, appoints the offices and the men to fill them and to do His work.

God have mercy upon all of us who are called to preach if we fail in the exercise of this ministry. We are left without excuse, for we are told here plainly what we are meant to be and to do. What we all need to know is 'the word of his grace which is able to build us up'. Are you being built up? Are you 'growing in grace and in the knowledge of the Lord'? Are you strong, are you virile? Are you able to stand up against the dangerous infections that are epidemic in this modern world? Are you healthy? Are you being perfected, being truly edified as a member of the body of Christ? It is a solemn matter. 'Let every one examine himself'.

17
Faith and Knowledge

'Till we all come in the unity of the faith, and of the
knowledge of the Son of God, unto a perfect man,
unto the measure of the stature of the fulness of
Christ'.

Ephesians 4:13

In this thirteenth verse, the Apostle explains how the various
offices in the ministry and the work of the ministry lead to the
edifying, the building up, of the body of Christ. Nothing, therefore, is more important for us, as nothing was more important
for these Ephesian Christians, than to understand this picture and
conception of the Christian Church which the Apostle places
before us. It is our failure as Christian people to understand what
our church membership means – the dignity, the privilege, and
the responsibility – that causes most of our troubles. Our greatest
need is to recapture the New Testament teaching concerning the
Church. If only we could see ourselves in terms of it, we would
realize that we are the most privileged people on earth, that there
is nothing to be compared with being a Christian and a member
of the mystical body of Christ.

The offices in the Church have been introduced and men have
been called to function in them in order that the body of Christ
might be built up. But there are difficulties about this, as stated in
this thirteenth verse, as there are about the subsequent statements
in verses 15 and 16. The Apostle has returned to his favourite
analogy of the Church as the body of Christ. He is so concerned
about this that he interrupts his own thought with the negative
statement in verse 14, and then he returns to it again, and in
doing so almost mixes his metaphors. Nevertheless the main
essential picture is quite clear. The ultimate object of these offices,
and of the work of the Church, is that the saints be made perfect.

This is described, firstly, in terms of unity – 'Till we all come into the unity of the faith' – and then secondly in terms of 'the knowledge of the Son of God'. Through these we shall attain 'unto a perfect man, unto the measure of the stature of the fulness of Christ'. The final objective can be described as 'the perfect man', or 'until we attain unto the measure of the stature of the fulness of Christ'.

The word 'perfect' means 'pure', 'full grown', 'fully developed', or 'complete'. The danger with regard to the use of the word *man* is to regard it as something which refers to us one by one, individually, as if the Apostle were saying 'until we all come to be perfect men'. Now, while in a sense, as I am going to show, this is true, it is not exactly what the Apostle conveys by this particular picture, for as has been pointed out, if that were so, the question as to where women come in would arise. Indeed, on account of that difficulty, some of the early fathers got into great trouble at this point. But the 'perfect man' means the Church, with Christ the Head and ourselves, males and females, as members of the body. So the 'perfect man' means Christ and His Church, He as the Head, and the members making up the different parts of the body. Thus 'the perfect man' can be regarded as the Church in a perfect condition, the body corresponding to the perfection of the Head.

We can justify this interpretation by referring to the fact that the Apostle again uses this term concerning our Lord in the First Epistle to the Corinthians where we read, 'For as the body is one, and hath many members, and all the members of that one body, being many, are one body: so also is Christ' (12:12). 'Christ' here obviously stands for the Church. What is true of the body, the natural human body, is also true of 'Christ', by which he means Christ and His Church, Christ and the Church making up one body. So the Apostle is saying that we must always think of ourselves in this manner and realize that God's grand purpose and programme is that the Church should be perfect – Christ as the Head and we as members in particular of that body. This is to be the final state of the Church, and it is to that end that apostles, prophets, evangelists, and pastors and teachers are ordained. A day is coming when this body, the Church, will be complete, mature, full grown, fully developed. It is not so yet; but it will be.

The Apostle then states this matter in other terms, 'unto the measure of the *stature* of the fulness of Christ'. The learned commentators spend much time in arguing whether this should be translated 'stature' or 'age'. Ultimately it makes no difference whatsoever to the meaning, for the two ideas of age and height obviously go together. The picture is that of the development of a child into adolescence and into manhood. We can think of this in terms of height or in terms of age; because it is when the child attains a certain age that he or she attains permanent height and stature. What is important is that the Apostle helps us to see how this perfection of the body is going to be attained. The perfect man consists not only of the Head Himself, Jesus Christ, who is always perfect, but also of us who form the limbs and individual parts of the body. So what Paul is really saying is that the perfect man will only have arrived when every single one of us who is a member of the body will have grown up to the full stature and development that God has appointed for us. That body, that 'man', the Church, is not going to be perfect until every single part and portion is perfect. If there is a blemish or a lack of development or an immaturity in any part or portion, you cannot say the whole is perfect.

Think, for instance, of an apple. You may have what appears to be a wonderful specimen; but if there is one blemish in it, the slightest bit of decay, it will not be awarded the first prize in a competition in a horticultural show. Though it stands out from all the others as regards size and shape and colour it is no longer a perfect specimen. So this 'perfect man' will not have arrived until every single part and portion will be fully developed and absolutely perfect.

But once more, this does not mean that we shall be absolutely equal and identical. The figure of the body makes that quite impossible. The toe and the finger are different, the fingers and the hand are different; all the various parts are different: there will be variations in ability and in function; nevertheless each single part will have attained fully that which it was meant to be and that which it was meant to do.

The idea which constitutes the central glory of the Christian Church can be regarded negatively in this way. We can say that any presentation of Christian truth that tends to produce a sameness in its people is, by that test, wrong and false. The cults, as we have seen, always reproduce a type; their members are almost identical, and all conform to a pattern. They use the same expressions, they speak them in the same manner. There is no suggestion of this in the New Testament; and it is never a characteristic of a true work of the Holy Spirit. This analogy of the body should have saved us from that particular error. Counterfeits are always mechanical and they show that they are such by reproducing people who are identical in most respects. The glory of the Church lies in this extraordinary variety and variation; there is not only unity but also the perfection of each of the parts. In other words, the body will not be perfect until every toe is perfect, until every nail is perfect, until every hair is perfect, until every detail is absolutely perfect.

What matters in the church, therefore, is not what our peculiar calling or office is, or the particular grace which has been given to us according to the measure of the gift of Christ; what matters is that every one of us should be perfect in that position. Each one of us is meant to be filled with His life. Each member does not contain the same amount, but each is full. If you go to the ocean with a tumbler in your hand and dip it in, you say 'My tumbler is full', and if you then take a great tank and fill it you say the tank is full. There is a great difference in the amount of sea water in the tumbler and the tank, but both are full, and both can be overflowing. So what is taught here is not identity in amount, but the enjoyment by each one of the fulness that is meant for him or her.

When the Church is complete, when this 'perfect man' will have arrived, not a single saint will be wanting; all will be safely gathered in. 'The fulness of the Gentiles' and 'all Israel' shall be saved. Known unto God is the number and the completion and the fulness. I do not know it, and no-one else knows it; but 'God knoweth them that are his', and when the perfect man shall have arrived, not a single member of the body will be absent or missing, nor will the slightest degree of grace be wanting in any part. The whole body will be proportionately full and perfect.

We can look at this in two ways. There is a sense in which you and I will be parts of that which makes up Christ's fulness. There is a sense in which He is not complete without us. It is a part of

His self-abnegation and of His self-humiliation that He has subjected Himself to this, that He has joined Himself to this body and is now a part of it, namely, the Head. In this sense He is not complete without us, because this fulness which belongs to Him as the Head of the body will not be complete until we are all sharing His fulness and are perfect. But now, and until we are perfect, it means that His fulness is in every one of us.

It is at this point we see that the analogy of the body is so valuable. The whole organization of the body, its organic nature, and the organic nature of its unity, makes this absolutely vital. The life is in the blood and the blood courses through every part of the body, even the most distant members of the body. The same blood courses through each part carrying the same life. The fulness of the head is in the fingers and in the toes. His fulness is in us. But it is equally true that our being filled makes up *His* fulness. This is how we should view ourselves as Christian people.

It is failure to realize this, and the privilege and the glory that is involved, that leads to the miserable position in which many pastors and preachers have to appeal to their people to attend church on Sunday and to persuade them to do various duties in the church. Such people have never seen themselves as members of the body of Christ. They think that they are conferring an honour upon the church by being even loosely attached to her and honouring her with their fitful attendance. They do not see that they are to strive to make up His fulness, that there is no time to waste, and that they must purge themselves of sins, and seek holiness and growth in grace in order that they may arrive at this fulness. We must meditate more and more on this 'perfect man' that is coming, this attaining 'unto the measure of the stature of the fulness of Christ'.

Let us not concentrate upon our place or position in the Church, for no-one is unimportant in the Church. We tend to go wrong (and certain sections of the Church encourage us to go wrong) if we over-stress the distinction between clergy and laity. As we have seen, it is right to emphasize particular offices and we must not detract from them; but we must never so regard them as to say that we do not matter or count, and that we are unimportant church members. The body is not yet perfect, nor is it complete while we are imperfect or have some imperfection about us. The goal which is going to be arrived at for all of us is this 'perfect man' and 'the measure of the stature of Christ'. Haste then on 'from grace to glory'. There is no time to waste, for as the Apostle John says, 'Every man that hath this hope in him purifieth himself, even as he is pure' (1 John 3:3).

*   *   *

Let us now consider how this objective is to be attained. The Apostle's teaching is that the whole work of the ministry is to bring us to it. There are two things to which we have to attain. The first is the 'unity of the faith'. He says, 'Till we all come in the unity of the faith, and of the knowledge of the Son of God'. 'The unity of the faith' is the faith of 'the Son of God'. The grammarians are all agreed about this. So we may read, 'Till we all come in the unity of the faith of the Son of God, and of the knowledge of the Son of God'. We have to come unto the unity of the faith concerning the Son of God. This is the way to arrive at that perfection. We see how practical the Apostle is. He does not leave anything to chance. The perfection of which he writes is not some kind of esoteric or mystical experience; the way to attain unto it is first and foremost to grasp this unity of the faith concerning the Son of God.

What does this unity mean, and how do we reconcile it with what Paul said in verse 5 about 'one Lord, one faith, one baptism'? He says in that verse that we already have 'one Lord, one faith, one baptism', yet here he says that we shall attain unto the unity of the faith. There appears to be a contradiction, but obviously there is not a contradiction. When we were studying verse 5 we suggested that it meant that there is an irreducible minimum in the matter of saving faith, without which one is not a Christian. I ventured to suggest that that really meant justification by faith only. This doctrine is the heart of the faith; any introduction of works means that it is no longer Christianity. 'The faith' is the beginning, the first step; the 'one faith' means that we are justified by faith alone. But this is only the beginning and not the whole of the matter. It is that first step which is absolutely essential, it is also the first step which leads on to the final stage in which our faith will be perfect and entire and full and balanced, with nothing lacking in it, and nothing missing

from it. But while I say that here and now we must all be clear
about the one first truth without which there is no Christianity,
there are many aspects of the faith concerning the Son of God
about which we are not clear, and about which Christians differ.
When, however, we attain unto this perfection of faith, we shall
all be saying the same things and believing the same things; for
then we shall know Him and see Him as He is. It will then be a
perfected faith.

Hence, while we talk about the 'one faith' we can also talk
about attaining unto 'the unity of the faith of the Son of God'.
This faith is large and comprehensive and we cannot hope to deal
with it in any exhaustive manner; but it means in the first place
that there must be unity of faith concerning our Lord's Person.
The very term used by the Apostle stresses this: 'Until we attain
unto the unity of the faith of the Son of God'. Later Paul refers
to Him as 'Christ'. There must be no doubts or uncertainties
concerning His Person. He is the Son of God; but He is also
Man. The unity of the faith embodies both. Some emphasize only
the man in Him, and they see nothing else. That is not 'the faith'.
Others emphasize the God in Him and do not seem to be clear
about the fact that the Incarnation was real and that He did not
take on Him a phantom body, but did really take unto Himself
human nature and was born of the Virgin. He was both Son of
God and Son of Man. 'The faith' holds these things in the right
proportion, and gives each its relative value. We all have to be
careful constantly not to become guilty of a false emphasis. Some
of us may tend to over-emphasize His eternal and unique deity,
and to forget to emphasize as we should that He was a man
amongst men, truly Man as well as truly God. Others may be
guilty of the opposite over-emphasis, while really holding the
truth about the two natures. But when we really attain unto this
'unity of the faith' we shall see it all clearly, and we shall see it all
in proportion. We are to press on towards that perfection.

That involves the whole wonder and marvel of the Incarnation
and all that led to it. It is a part of 'the faith of the Son of God' to
know that God, before time, purposed all this and appointed His
Son heir of all things and gave Him the Church to be His people.
And so the Son came, accepting the plan and His part in it
voluntarily. The way to attain unto that final perfection is to look

into these things, to grasp them, to understand them, and to meditate upon them. We must believe in the plan of redemption, the scheme of salvation, as the prophets foretold it. It is all a part of this faith of Jesus Christ, the Son of God. The Old Testament with its types and shadows is essential to our well-being. The more we know about them, the more we shall be growing and maturing.

Then we must think of our Lord's offices – Prophet, Priest, King. We must look at His teaching, and grapple with it. We must believe that 'No man hath seen God at any time; the only begotten Son that is in the bosom of the Father, he hath declared him' (John 1:18). We must read the four Gospels and look at this manifestation and revelation of God's glory, and look at Christ's teaching. We neglect these things at our peril; we must live on them. We must listen to the Prophet in the Sermon on the Mount, and to all His other teaching, because that is a part of 'the faith of the Son of God'. Then we must look at Him as the Priest. We must look at Him making His offering of Himself. He made His soul an offering for sin. He laid down His life, He gave Himself unto death. He submitted as God 'laid upon him the iniquity of us all', as God smote Him with the stripes that you and I so richly deserve. As our great High Priest He offered Himself; and then took His own blood and presented it in the Holiest of All in heaven. This great High Priest 'passed through the heavens' and took His place at the right hand of God. To meditate upon these things is the way to mature and to develop. This is the way to attain eventually 'unto that perfect man, unto the measure of the stature of the fulness of Christ'.

Then think of our Lord in His kingly office. He is already the King of the Church. He came to found a Kingdom. The Church is the present form of the Kingdom. But He will come again and establish His Kingdom in a visible manner. He will set up that eternal state in which we shall be with Him in glory, with our very bodies glorified, judging the world and judging angels. We must also consider His sending His Spirit upon the Church, His appointing all these offices, and all the work of the Spirit in perfecting us, sanctifying us, purifying us. It is all a part of this 'faith of the Son of God', and the knowledge of this brings us to the ultimate perfection.

*　　*　　*

The Apostle not only speaks of the faith of the Son of God but also of 'the knowledge of the Son of God'. There has been much discussion concerning this knowledge. There are those who say that we should read the statement thus: 'Till we all come unto the unity of the faith, that is, of the knowledge of the Son of God' – the faith which leads to the knowledge. We cannot accept this, because the Apostle said 'and' and not 'that is'. He is referring to something additional. I emphasize this because it is the most precious thing of all. Faith, of course, does lead to knowledge, and there is always an element of knowledge in faith. It is difficult to differentiate between these things, but it is vital that we should attempt to do so. You can have 'the faith of the Son of God' without having this particular 'knowledge' about which the Apostle is speaking. You can be a Christian without having much of this knowledge of which he is speaking. I repeat that you cannot have faith without having a certain knowledge. You cannot believe the things to which I have been referring without, in a sense, knowing them. There is that element of knowledge, that kind of knowledge, in faith which, to use a technical term, is called 'the knowledge of cognition'. But here we are not dealing with cognition but with recognition. This is something experimental. The Apostle uses a very strong word (epignosis) which means 'full knowledge', something over and above that other kind of intellectual knowledge and apprehension. This is something deeper, something profounder, and as I say, something experimental.

It is a vital part of the work of the ministry to bring us to this fuller knowledge; and may God forgive us that we are liable to neglect it and that we are not as aware of it as we should be! It is an essential part of the building up of the body that we come to this knowledge of the Son of God. This 'knowledge' is what Paul meant in the third chapter of his Epistle to the Philippians. He had been clear for years about justification by faith. He was no longer interested in his own righteousness which is 'after the law'; he had come to see it as 'dung' and refuse and worthless. He desired and had 'the righteousness that is of God by faith' in Jesus Christ. Nevertheless he had a still greater longing, namely, 'That I may know him' – not only know the doctrine about Him – 'and the power of his resurrection, and the fellowship of his sufferings, being made conformable unto His death; if by any means I might attain unto the resurrection of the dead. Not as though I had already attained' (vv. 10–12). He had not got this yet as he desired it. Of all men he had received much and thanked God for it, but he was still trying 'to apprehend that for which also I have been apprehended'. His desire was to know Christ Himself, he was not content with only believing about Him and on Him. There is possible to Christians this further intimate knowledge of the Son of God, an appropriation of His love to us personally, a true knowledge of the Lord Himself.

The Apostle has already dealt with this deep knowledge in the previous chapter where he has expressed his desire that the Ephesians might 'be able to comprehend with all saints what is the breadth, and length, and depth, and height; and to know the love of Christ, which passeth knowledge, that ye might be filled with all the fulness of God' (vv. 18–19). The 'knowledge' of which the Apostle speaks again is the knowledge of His personal love to us; our confidence in Him, and devotion to Him in a personal sense. It means knowing Him directly, and having communion and fellowship with Him personally. This is something which is possible to all Christians; it is a part of the process of our development. It means that we know what it is to receive of His fulness, as John's Gospel expresses it: 'We beheld his glory, the glory as of the only begotten of the Father, full of grace and truth; and of his fulness have we all received, and grace upon grace' (1:14–16). It means receiving something of His strength and power and grace; and literally knowing that we are receiving it, knowing that we are in Him as a branch is in the vine, and receiving of His life.

This is what our Lord Himself meant when He said to the woman of Samaria, 'The water that I shall give him shall be in him a well of water springing up into everlasting life' (John 4:14). It means never hungering, never thirsting again, knowing His fulness and receiving of it. In other words it means living on Him in accordance with the words of our Lord Himself in this connection, as found in the Gospel of John: 'He that eateth my flesh, and drinketh my blood, dwelleth in me, and I in him. As the living Father hath sent me, and I live by the Father: so he that eateth me, even he shall live by me' (6:56–57). Do we know

[218]

what it is to partake of Christ in that manner spiritually? Are we eating His flesh and drinking His blood spiritually? Are we living by Him? are we living on Him? Can we say with Paul, 'To me to live is Christ'? All this is a part of the 'knowing' of the Son of God. We are meant to be filled by Him. We are meant to experience what we say and what we pray for when we sing together –

> *Fill Thou my life, O Lord my God,*
> *In every part with praise.*

It means to receive of the fulness of the Head and thus to be filled in every part and portion of our being.

We are not only to attain unto 'the faith of the Son of God', but also unto 'the knowledge of the Son of God'. Do you know Him? Is He real to you? He has said that He will manifest Himself to those who keep His commandments. When He manifests Himself we know Him; it is no longer the preliminary faith, as it were. This is a personal knowledge, an intimate knowledge of Him, that is offered to His children, that is a part of the life of His people.

* * *

These are the ways in which we are to be built up. The business of the Church is not just to tell us that we can be happy, and how we can find a Friend, or how to overcome sin. We are too subjective, we are too self-centred. The way to grow is to look at Him, to have faith in Him, to have this knowledge of Him.

I would emphasize the intimate relationship of these to each other – the faith and the knowledge. Faith alone may puff us up; but this knowledge builds us up. There is a kind of knowledge, says Paul, that 'puffeth up'; but 'charity, love edifieth' (1 Cor 8:1). We must spend our time studying the doctrine, we must attain unto 'this unity of the faith of the Son of God'. The revelation is in God's written Word, and the Spirit is given to help us to understand it. I must give myself with diligence to its study; and it is the business of pastors and teachers to inform their people concerning these things and build them up. But we do not stop at that, for it is meant to bring us to this full knowledge of the Son of God – 'That I might know him' – namely this intimate, personal, subjective, experimental knowing of Him, rejoicing in

Him, and receiving Him as our life, and drawing from His fulness, and being filled with His fulness.

We are to go on seeking this 'until we all come in the unity of the faith and the knowledge of the Son of God, unto a perfect man, unto the measure of the stature of the fulness of Christ'. O blessed day! O blessed realization! Then every one of us will be perfect, perfected in Him, and sharing in His eternal blessedness and glory.

18
No More Children

'That we henceforth be no more children, tossed to
and fro, and carried about with every wind of
doctrine, by the sleight of men, and cunning craftiness, whereby they lie in wait to deceive'.

Ephesians 4:14

We have seen that the function of the ministry – apostles, prophets,
evangelists, pastors, teachers – and all that has been appointed by
the Lord, is to bring all the members of the body of Christ to a
'perfect man', to 'the measure of the stature of the fulness of
Christ'. We have also seen that the way in which that end is
achieved is that we all are brought to 'the unity of the faith and of
the knowledge', this full knowledge, 'of the Son of God'. That
is what the future holds for us, that is the goal at which we are
going to arrive. But we have not yet arrived, and much has to
take place before we arrive. The word 'henceforth' in and of
itself suggests this contrast between what we are and what we
shall be. We must always keep our eye on the ultimate goal, but
it is equally important that we should realize what we are at
present and start from that point.

Once more we must comment on the profound wisdom of this
Apostle as a teacher. He does not merely state the goal, nor regard
us as if we had already arrived; he is always practical and realistic
and animated by a profound pastoral care. The first great principle of all good teaching, whatever the subject, is that you deal
with people as they are, not as they should be. The good teacher is
always aware of the knowledge, or lack of knowledge, of his
students and takes trouble to relate his lesson to their condition.
The Apostle does precisely that in this statement and by the word
'henceforth'. As I have indicated earlier he actually interrupts
himself in order to do this.

The Apostle reminds us that there are certain things which we have to realize about ourselves. They are mainly negative, but they are absolutely essential. If we are not aware of these negatives we shall never arrive at the positive and the perfect. Once more I emphasize that it is our failure to realize these negatives that accounts for so much in the present state of the Christian Church; and here we have a perfect portrayal of the Church of today and her problems.

*　　*　　*

The first thing we must understand is that we all start in the Christian life as children. This seems so obvious, and yet we are always forgetting it. 'That we henceforth be no more children', says the Apostle, indicating that we all start as children. It is but another way of reminding us that the Christian life is a new life. It is not a continuation of any other life, it is not an addendum to any other life, it is a new life. The word 'children' draws an absolute line of division between the non-Christian and the Christian. There is no gradual change of movement from being in the world to being in the Church. It is a birth, an entirely new beginning. We are born into an entirely new realm which is in complete contrast with the old realm. And because this new life starts with a birth we therefore start as children. The New Testament constantly emphasizes this vital principle. 'Ye must be born again', says our Lord Himself to Nicodemus (John 3:1-8). This implies at once the whole principle of growth and of development. We start as infants and from that beginning we are to grow and develop and to mature. This is the central principle of the Christian life taught throughout the New Testament.

In his First Epistle John addresses 'little children, young men, fathers' (2:12-13). We all have to go through these stages. Peter deals with the same truth when he writes, 'As newborn babes, desire the sincere milk of the word, that ye may grow thereby' (1 Peter 2:2). Yet in spite of the New Testament emphasis on this foundational truth, there is a curious tendency on our part to forget it and a fatal tendency to assume that once we become Christians we have everything, that we have arrived. Conversion is not an end but a beginning and we must rid ourselves of the idea that becoming Christian is the end of the story and that we are now complete and have only to spend the rest of our lives in activities. Thus we by-pass so much of the teaching of these epistles, and produce the state of confusion which is the main characteristic of the life of the Christian Church at this present time. To illustrate what I mean we have but to read the pastoral epistles to Timothy and Titus, to note that the Apostle writes about novices, and about what novices should not do, and what novices should not be asked to do. Then applying all that to the Church in general as she is today we see how this is almost entirely ignored. Far from teaching that we start as novices and babes the slogan is 'Give the convert something to do'. But the teaching of those pastoral epistles is that the first business of the novice is to grow and to learn and to become fit and qualified to do service for the Lord.

For the sake of emphasis we can state this all-important principle thus. Everyone who becomes a Christian and enters into this Christian life, comes into it as a babe. That he may be a great intellect or that he may be a great man in a profession and have what is described as a strong personality is quite immaterial. Whatever may be true of him when he comes into this Christian life, he, as all others, comes into it as a babe; he is a spiritual babe. He must be regarded as such, and he must regard himself as such. But unfortunately it is assumed that if a man is great in some other realm he starts as a great man in this realm. That this is not so is often found in practice. Failure to remember this has led to the unscriptural practice of placing certain people in positions of leadership immediately, simply because of their prominence in some secular or natural realm.

We must realize that in the realm of the Church we are concerned with something which is altogether different. The Apostle repeats this principle so frequently that it is astounding how we can ever forget it. 'The natural man receiveth not the things of the Spirit of God' (1 Cor 2:14). 'Not many wise men after the flesh, not many mighty, not many noble are called' (1 Cor 1:26). In this realm we are dealing with spiritual truth, truth which must be 'spiritually discerned'. So each one of us starts as a babe, as an infant, and becomes a child. The first test to be applied in the realm of the Church is not natural ability, still less natural position or status or power; what is required here is spiritual understanding, spiritual apprehension, a spiritual knowledge of the truth. We should thank God for this; and realize that this is the peculiar mark of the Christian Church. In the Church all divisions and distinctions are abolished, 'there is neither Greek nor Jew, Barbarian, Scythian, bond nor free' (Col 3:11). But not only so, there is neither great nor small. All these divisions and distinctions become quite irrelevant. We all enter God's kingdom in the same manner and we all start as 'newborn babes'.

*   *   *

The Apostle next goes on to show that children have certain particular characteristics and tendencies. He calls attention to these in the words 'that we henceforth be no more children, tossed to and fro, and carried about with every wind of doctrine, by the sleight of men, and cunning craftiness, wherein they lie in wait to deceive'. Here we have an example of the Apostle's knowledge of what is today described as 'child psychology'. It is a perfect description of children and of the child's outlook and mentality, and it is true of all of us as we begin in the Christian life. There is a parallel passage in chapter 3 of the First Epistle to the Corinthians, where again he analyses this condition, but from a slightly different aspect and standpoint. It is essential to our growth that we should realize these things about ourselves; because if we fail to do so, we shall never learn and we shall remain children. I know of nothing which is more tragic than to see Christian people who remain exactly where and what they always were. They end as children, as they began. They thought that they had everything at the beginning, and so they have never grown and, spiritually, they remain children throughout their lives. They do not seem to have understood that we have to appropriate and grasp what is promised and made possible to every one of us, and that we have to 'grow in grace and in the knowledge' of the Lord.

According to the Apostle there are two main tendencies in children. The first is instability. He uses a most picturesque phrase to describe this: 'tossed to and fro', 'tossed like waves'. It does not mean that we are tossed about by waves but that we are like waves, tossed to and fro and constantly in motion. Indeed, we might translate it by the expression 'pitching about'. The word which the Apostle used, and it is the only instance in which it is found in the New Testament, conveys the sense of violence – 'a violent pitching about of waves'. James has the same idea in the first chapter of his Epistle, where the word used means 'tossed to and fro', or 'agitated'. Nothing is so characteristic of the sea as its restlessness, its constant motion and change. The Apostle's word conveys this idea of the sea tossed to and fro, or the waves of the sea in constant motion, with the suggestion of violence and agitation. And that, says the Apostle, is the characteristic of the childlike state.

But we must analyse it further, as the Apostle clearly intends us to do. The condition reminds us that one of the most prominent characteristics of the child is fickleness and changeableness. How quickly a child can change from smiling to crying! The quick changes can be seen on its face. The child cannot help it, of course, because it is a child. There are many instances of this as it applies to a child-like state in the Scriptures. Take for example what we read in the last chapter of the Acts of the Apostles. Paul had landed, after a shipwreck, on the island of Melita (Malta). The weather was rather cold so they got some sticks together to make a fire to warm themselves. Suddenly out of the fire a viper fixed itself on to the hand of the Apostle. The people concluded immediately that he must be a very bad man and expected him to start swelling up at any moment and to die a violent death. But when they noticed that he did not swell up and die they changed their opinions and said that he was a god. They changed immediately from one extreme to the other. Such conduct is typical of the child, 'tossed to and fro like the waves of the sea'. It is always sad to see that kind of behaviour in Christian people, but we all start as children.

Another thing which characterizes this condition of childhood is a lack of self-control. It is because of this that older people have to control them. Children are creatures of impulses and moods; they know little about self-discipline, and are not able to master and to control themselves and their own spirits. The Book of Proverbs tells us that the man who can control his own spirit is a greater man than he who can capture a city. Self-control is a most difficult task. The child does not control itself; it expresses itself. It wants something, and wants it at once; and shows its temper and displeasure if it is refused. The child manifests an inability to control its reactions and responses to the things that happen to it.

Another characteristic of a child and one which follows from the previous ones is that the child always reacts excessively and violently to things that happen to it. The child acts as a whole, and does so with an element of violence and excessiveness. A child is either very fond of something or else it hates it; there is nothing in between. It goes from one extreme right over to the other. All the child's reactions bring out this element of excess and of violence and of lack of discipline and of control. How disconcerting Scripture can be when it holds this kind of mirror before us! The true and adult Christian is not to react violently and excessively; he is to manifest discipline and control, and an element of temperance. 'God hath not given us the spirit of fear, but of power and of love and of a sound mind', says the Apostle to Timothy, the young man (2 Tim 1:7). 'Sound mind' means discipline and self-control. We must not react excessively and violently to the things that happen to us.

A further characteristic of the child is that it holds its views violently and tends to change them from one extreme to another. We are all familiar with the dogmatism of a child; and what makes it yet more difficult is that when it changes its views completely it holds the new view equally dogmatically. Furthermore you never know when the change is going to take place. The result of all this is that the child is in a state of perpetual turmoil and mental agitation. In much the same way the adult who has just become a Christian tends to show these characteristics both individually and in groups. Look at a little group of children, they appear to be terribly troubled; some trifle has upset them, and they get into a huddle together and all seem to talk at the same time. They are violent in their reactions, agitated, in a state of turmoil. They feel that the end of the world is about to happen, all because some little toy has been broken or because of something equally trivial. They are like the waves of the sea, tossed to and fro. Mental agitation is always indicative of a childish condition unless it is due to actual mental illness.

All this should lead us to ask whether we are manifesting these characteristics of the child, this instability, this constant motion and agitation, this tendency to be violent in these different respects; this lack of discipline and of self-control and especially this inability to control our reactions to the things which happen to us. In other words the child life is a life that is lived on the surface. The child has no reserves on which it can fall back. This is no criticism of the child; it is a description. It is the characteristic of the child. And because it is a child, the child cannot help it. But when you find this condition in one who has been a Christian for some time the first thing needed is to get him to realize that it is very wrong and that he is 'henceforth' not to continue in that state.

*   *   *

The second main fact about the child is his liability to be misled and to be deceived. 'That we henceforth be no more children, tossed to and fro, *and carried about with every wind of doctrine*'. A better translation would perhaps be, 'carried around in all directions'. The wind comes from a certain direction, then suddenly it seems to be turning round to another. The constant turning of a weather vane indicates changing winds. A child in a similar manner turns round and is carried away by every kind of teaching in all conceivable directions. This is simply a graphic and pictorial way of saying that the child is always liable to be imposed upon; because it tends to believe everything it is told. The child, because it is a child, readily falls a prey to any imposter that comes along. The Apostle is particularly concerned about this. That is why he spoke as he did to the elders of this church at Ephesus as recorded in the twentieth chapter of the Book of Acts in one of the most moving passages in the whole of Scripture. He could see what was going to happen to them and consequently he was concerned about them. He could see how liable they were to be imposed upon, because they were still children in the Faith. It is interesting that he should have said all this to the elders of the church at Ephesus to whom he wrote later this very epistle we are now considering.

A most important question to be faced if we are to be delivered out of this state is as to why a child is thus liable to be imposed upon? What is our psychological analysis of its position? Here are some of the answers. This is true of a child because of its ignorance. Ultimately it is indeed due to nothing but lack of knowledge. The child's problems arise because it has not got a standard, and it lacks a standard because it lacks knowledge. Without a standard one cannot test or evaluate anything. And the failure to test it means that you are lacking in judgment. When you are confronted by a number of teachings, how do you tell which is right? There is but one answer; it is knowledge alone that enables us to perform the test, and if we have not got the knowledge we simply will not be in a position to test and to sift and to discriminate. That is the problem with the child; and it becomes tragic when you find it in those who remain children when they should have become adult. It is inevitable in the child because it lacks the knowledge, and it needs to be taught for that reason. But it is inexcusable in those who are adult and who should have gained the knowledge.

It is also true to say of the child, not only that it is ignorant but that it has an innate tendency to dislike being taught and to submit to discipline. We know that this is true when we look back into our own experiences, and also our experience of children at the present time. In particular the child does not like being taught slowly. The child is impatient and always wants to advance quickly. Think of a child who is being given music lessons. He hates having to practise the scales; he wants to play the big classic piece immediately; he dislikes drudgery and regular application. The child who is learning arithmetic does not enjoy learning the Tables, but wants to be solving the problems. The idea that you have to take time and grow from stage to stage is abhorrent to the child. The Apostle knew that the spiritual child shows the same dislike of discipline and of being taught, and always overestimates its own ability and knowledge.

Or, again, there is nothing more characteristic of the child than the way in which it likes novelty and change and something new. The child is not very much concerned about the intrinsic value of anything as long as it is new. The child may be playing with its favourite toys but if you suddenly produce a new one they are forgotten and thrown out of its hand. The childish mind and mentality is fond of change and craves for the novel and the new. We are told of the people at Athens in Acts 17, that they spent their time 'either to tell or to hear some new thing'. That is typical of the child mentality, which is always interested in the latest thing whatever it may be. How typical this is of many

Christians today who betray themselves unconsciously by this liking of change and newness!

Furthermore, the child likes entertainment and excitement. This was true of all of us in childhood. The child tends to have a secret antagonism even to its own parents, if they are parents worthy of the name, because they exercise discipline. The parents are always there, exercising a measure of restraint and enforcing certain principles. How much nicer is a favourite uncle who comes for a week occasionally and who gives us everything we want and refuses nothing! The uncle comforts us when we are chastened and is prepared to play with us and to entertain us and join us in various escapades. He seems to be much better and kinder than father or mother. I distinctly remember the secret joy which I and other boys of my age used to experience when the headmaster under whom I once had to study had his annual attack of lumbago and could not come to school. How exciting it was to be allowed to go through the lesson on our own, and with a teacher who perhaps was also enjoying a little bit of freedom himself!

*   *   *

Unfortunately all this tends to be true of us as Christians. I have sometimes thought that one of the first problems and trials a young pastor has to meet is due to this very thing, that he has to accommodate himself to the fact that so many Christian people display this characteristic of childhood. They like a change; anything as long as it is different; change and novelty and newness, and especially the craving for the element of entertainment and excitement. How much more enjoyable it is to be entertained than to go through the drudgery of a lesson! If you keep your eye on the religious periodicals and their advertisements and apply this teaching of the Apostle you will understand what I mean. The unusual, especially if it has the element of entertainment and excitement, is clearly that which is most popular. That is a clear indication of the child outlook and mentality. The Apostle is concerned to impress this on the minds of the Ephesians, because if they did not realize it and understand it, they would never grow out of it.

The last characteristic of this childlike state and condition which leads to the danger and the susceptibility of being carried about by every wind of doctrine, is that the child is peculiarly susceptible to showmanship. The child instinctively likes a showman. The greater the element of showmanship the more the child will like it. The child has no discrimination, he has no means of assessing these matters. The bigger the show, the bigger the deceit in a sense, the more the child is likely to believe it. Because he lacks knowledge and the ability to discriminate and to understand, he tends to be seduced by the spectacular, the big, the gaudy, anything which is done in a self-confident manner. Showmanship always appeals to children; that is why the child has to be protected, and also why it is so essential that the child should be disciplined and should be taught.

All this is but introductory to that which the Apostle goes on to say. It is important that we should understand this child mentality because of the terrible dangers which surround us. And of all the dangers none is greater than 'the sleight of men', and the 'cunning craftiness wherein they lie in wait to deceive'. But there is no purpose in proceeding to consider these further matters unless we examine ourselves and are aware of the characteristics of the child mentality. Two things are essential. The child must realize that he is a child; and he must also realize that because he is a child he is in an extremely dangerous position. The Apostle places these things in the right order. May God forgive us for being so unstable, so fickle, so ready to be imposed upon, so ready to react violently! May He also forgive us that we are so lacking in discipline, and in that true understanding which leads to a concern for the glory and honour of God and the Lord Jesus Christ, and also the glory of the Church which is His body! We have all entered this life as children, we are 'born of the Spirit', 'born from above', 'born again'. Some of us may have been in the Christian life for a long time. Are we still children 'tossed to and fro, and carried about by every wind of doctrine'? May God have mercy upon us!

19
The Wiles of the Devil

'That we henceforth be no more children, tossed to
and fro, and carried about with every wind of
doctrine, by the sleight of men, and cunning craftiness, whereby they lie in wait to deceive'.

Ephesians 4:14

We must now examine more closely the dangers to which spiritual
childhood and immaturity are exposed. It is quite astonishing to
note the amount of space and of attention which is given in the
Bible to this particular question. There are constant warnings
against this particular danger. Take, for instance, what we read in
Matthew's Gospel: Our Lord warned, 'Beware of false prophets
which come to you in sheep's clothing, but inwardly they are
ravening wolves' (7:15). What a solemn warning! And our Lord
goes on to elaborate it. Again in the 24th chapter of the same
Gospel our Lord says, 'If any man shall say unto you, Lo, here is
Christ, or there; believe it not. For there shall arise false Christs
and false prophets, and shall shew great signs and wonders;
insomuch that, if it were possible, they shall deceive the very elect.
Behold, I have told you before. Wherefore if they shall say unto
you, Behold, he is in the desert; go not forth; behold, he is in the
secret chambers; believe it not' (vv. 23–26). 'I have told you
beforehand' says our Lord; yet how little do we hear about these
warnings today! Indeed, as I hope to show later, many even
resent these warnings at the present time. The Church today does
not seem to be aware of the danger and pays little if any heed to
these endless warnings which are found in the Scriptures.

Consider again the warning of the Apostle Paul to the elders
of this very church at Ephesus, part of which we have already
quoted. He says, 'Take heed, therefore, unto yourselves, and
unto all the flock over the which the Holy Ghost hath made you

overseers, to feed the church of God, which he hath purchased with his own blood. For I know this, that after my departure shall grievous wolves enter in among you, not sparing the flock. Also of your own selves shall men arise, speaking perverse things, to draw away disciples after them. Therefore watch'. In all his epistles these warnings are always in evidence. Hence it is true to say that most of these epistles contain a prominent polemical element. They are full of argument and disputation and reasoning and warning. Think, for instance, of the 11th chapter of the Second Epistle to the Corinthians, where the Apostle warns against false teachers. He says that it is not surprising that these false teachers behave as they do, for the devil is able to transform himself into an angel of light. The Epistle to the Galatians can truly be regarded as but an extended warning against false teachers. In his Epistle to the Philippians Paul writes, 'Beware of dogs, beware of evil workers, beware of the concision' (3:2). In his Epistle to the Colossians we find him warning Christians: 'Beware lest any man spoil you through philosophy and vain deceit, after the tradition of men, after the rudiments of the world, and not after Christ' (2:8). In the Pastoral Epistles he warns against 'oppositions of science [knowledge] falsely so called: which some professing have erred concerning the faith' (1 Tim 6:20–21).

Nothing is more striking perhaps in this respect than what we find in the second chapter of Peter's Second Epistle. He warns his readers that false teachers would arise among them, even as false prophets arose among the children of Israel under the old dispensation; and he proceeds to say terrible things about them. The Epistle of Jude is again entirely devoted to this same kind of solemn warning. In the First Epistle of John much attention is paid to the 'antichrists', the false teachers, that have arisen. In the Book of Revelation the Letters to the seven churches deal specifically with the same problem; indeed the whole Book of Revelation is one great warning to the Church in this respect. Indeed it might almost be said that the New Testament came into being in order to warn Christian people to beware of the terrible ever-present danger of being led astray by false teaching concerning our Lord Himself and His great salvation.

*　　　*　　　*

I would emphasize something of which we are reminded in this verse, namely, the extraordinary language which is used with respect to this danger – the strong language, the almost violent language which is used! This is found even in our Lord's own language. In describing the false prophets He says that they come to us 'in sheep's clothing', looking innocent and attractive and charming. But 'inwardly' He says, 'they are ravening wolves'. In such strong terms He characterizes these false teachers! Again in the 23rd chapter of Matthew's Gospel, when warning His own disciples and followers against the Pharisees, He says that they are 'whited sepulchres'. They are made to look attractive, but within they are full of nothing but bones and rottenness. This is very strong language; it is almost violent; yet it is the Son of God speaking, the incarnation of God's love.

The same is true of the language used by the Apostle Paul in Acts chapter 20, where he describes false teachers as 'grievous wolves'. In his Epistle to the Philippians he terms them 'enemies of the Cross of Christ' (3:18). In his Second Epistle to the Corinthians he warns Christians to beware, 'lest by any means, as the serpent beguiled Eve' these false teachers and apostles may beguile them (11:3). But there is perhaps nothing stronger than what he says in the Second Epistle to the Thessalonians. Paul is warning them against the antichrist in his final form and says, 'Even him, whose coming is after the working of Satan with all power and signs and lying wonders, and with all deceivableness of unrighteousness in them that perish' (2:9–10). He says that there is a danger of our being carried away by 'strong delusion' and that we may 'believe a lie' (v. 11). There is no stronger language in the whole of the Scriptures than the language which is used with regard to this subject. Paul refers to false teachers as 'dogs'. The Apostle John writes about 'the antichrist'; and Peter refers to 'damnable heresies', and 'pernicious ways', and speaks of evil men who 'through covetousness shall with vain words make merchandise' of Christians. All the writers use the term 'lies' with regard to the teaching that is being propagated by such false teachers.

This is not surprising because, according to the Scriptures, all false teaching is the result of the work of the Serpent, and it has the mark and the character of the Serpent upon it. It was through the Serpent that it first came into the life of man. Man was in a state of perfection, in communion with God and enjoying fellowship with God. But the Serpent came in and he 'beguiled' Eve with his subtle insinuations and innuendos and suggestions. Subtlety and deceit, says the Bible, have been characteristic ever since of much of the life of man. But children are not aware of this, and for this reason, says the Apostle, the Lord Jesus Christ has set in the church apostles, prophets, evangelists, and pastors and teachers.

*   *   *

I have painted in the background in order that we may realize that it is not something peculiar to Paul. The so-called 'Higher Criticism' school has ever been ready to argue that this is peculiar to Paul who, they assert, was a legalist and intolerant in his narrowness, and annoyed that anyone should disagree with what he said. Unbelievers are ready to accept such teaching and young and ignorant Christians have been deceived by it. I have quoted the Lord Jesus Christ to show that this is not true and that He spoke of 'ravening wolves', 'blind guides', 'whited sepulchres', and so on. I am emphasizing this matter for the reason that I cannot imagine, and I defy anyone to produce, a more perfect description of the situation of the modern Christian than that which we have in the 14th verse of Ephesians 4. The modern Christian is surrounded by cults and false teachings, so as we study the terms which the Apostle uses, we must apply them to the many false teachings and errors which are offering themselves to the children in the faith at the present time.

The first term we must examine is 'every wind of doctrine'. Paul's words, 'that we henceforth be no more children, tossed to and fro, and carried about with every wind of doctrine' suggest a multiplicity; they suggest that false teachings may suddenly come from the north, or from the south, or east, or west. We are literally surrounded by errors and false teachings and heresies. This was the case in the early Church and it is so still. Even in the days that immediately followed the life and death and resurrection of our Lord, and in the days of the apostles themselves, these winds of false doctrine began to blow.

[234]

The next expression reads: 'by the sleight of men, and cunning craftiness, whereby they lie in wait to deceive'. The real meaning of *deceive* here is *error*. It means a straying from orthodoxy or piety; it means something which is false, untrue, and a lie. The object of all false teachings, Paul says, is to persuade us into the way and the grip of error, and we must not be surprised that he uses strong language with respect to them.

Let us observe next the manner in which he tells us that these errors are taught and propagated. 'Every wind of doctrine', he says, which is liable to mislead us and to entrap us, is manipulated 'by the sleight of men'. 'Sleight' is a very interesting word. Incidentally, let us take note of the fact that two words are used in this one verse which are not used elsewhere in Scripture, and a third which is only used here and again in this same Epistle in chapter 6 verse 11. These words are 'hapax legomina', a technical term which is employed to describe words used once only in the Scriptures. Another such word was 'tossed to and fro', which we have already considered.

The word 'sleight' is only used here in Scripture; we must therefore pay attention to it. The actual word used by the Apostle is the word which we know as 'dice'. It refers to playing with a dice, a game of chance which is played and determined by the throwing of a dice. The impression he conveys is that in connection with such games there is an opening always for the element of deceit and of trickery, of cheating and chicanery. While you are not watching carefully, the man who is about to throw the dice manipulates it somehow so that he gets the particular figure he desires. Dice playing and chance give an opportunity to the man who by the quickness of the hand can deceive the eye. The Apostle is describing false teachers who come with great plausibility to the young Christian. He says that they are like men who are experts at the games which depend upon the throwing of the dice and the element of chance. They know how to manipulate, they are quick and subtle, and while in your innocence you are not watching carefully, they deceive you and mislead you.

The Apostle is not content to leave it at that; he goes on to say that they do this 'according to their cunning craftiness'. This refers to the craft or cunning which they employ. This again calls attention to the sophistry, or trickery, the cleverness, the subtlety of their teaching and methods. They know what they are doing, and are full of cunning and of craftiness.

We now come to another word, the one which is only used here and in chapter 6 verse 11. Paul says, 'whereby they lie in wait'. 'Lie in wait' is one word which originally means 'to follow someone and to track him as a wild animal tracks and follows its prey'. Think of a weasel on the track of a rabbit; once the weasel starts upon the scent he goes on and on and on. The rabbit runs and periodically stops and listens. It thinks that it is safe and goes on, but the weasel follows slowly and relentlessly until it captures its prey. Or think of any one of these predatory beasts of prey waiting for and then pouncing upon its victim. From that original meaning the word developed this sense in which the Apostle uses it. It conveys the idea of the method of a well-laid plan, indeed the whole notion of deliberate planning and system. It is translated 'wiles' in the sixth chapter, in the verse 'Put on the whole armour of God, that ye may be able to stand against the *wiles* of the devil'. The Apostle uses this particular word in order to emphasize that we are confronted by something which is very methodical, and which is planned almost to perfection. It works as that beast does which by its instinct begins to track its victim; and the word therefore brings out both the subtle cunning of the false teachers and the pathetic weakness of the victims. We may explain the phrase, therefore, by saying that the Apostle teaches that the sleight of men operates 'according to the cunning or craft which is used by those who wish to entrap or to capture', or 'cunning according to the craft which error uses'. This, says the Apostle, is the danger with which spiritual children are confronted.

*   *   *

Certain questions must be asked at this point. Are we aware that this is our position at the present time? Our Lord says, 'I have told you beforehand', and the Apostle Paul makes the same statement in addressing the elders of the church at Ephesus; so I repeat my question, Do we realize that this is our position? But let me sub-divide the question into a series of questions. Do we realize as we should, that error is not merely negative, but that it can be very active and very positive? Error is not merely the absence of full truth or of full teaching; it is positive evil. I speak thus because there is a teaching which has gained a good deal of currency, to the effect that sin should never be regarded as positive, that sin is merely negative, merely an absence of good qualities. According to the popular sentimental teaching we should not say that a man is really bad; what we should say is that he is not good. It does not believe that there is such a thing as positive evil. In the same way it contends that there is no such thing as positively evil teaching. But that is to deny the teaching of the entire Bible, which, as we have seen, emphasizes the positively evil character of false teaching.

The second fact we have to realize concerning false teaching is that it is planned and organized; that it does not happen accidentally. If we are at all aware of what is happening today we must be familiar with the planning and the method and the organizing of the false teachers. Foreign missionaries tell us that they have more trouble with false teachings and errors, and with false religions, than they have with unbelief as such. Furthermore we find that errors and cults and false teachings very rarely get direct converts of their own from the world, they win them among young Christians. After the missionary has done his work and there are converts, they begin to seek their prey, and like beasts of prey they pounce upon them. This is not confined to the foreign field; it is equally true of the British Isles. Young converts are attacked by those who create doubts in their minds as to the authority of the Bible, the Person of our Lord, the substitutionary atonement, and various other essential aspects of the Christian faith, and in their ignorance they may be led astray temporarily.

We must also emphasize that these teachers 'lie in wait', that they are methodical, and know exactly what they are doing. False teaching is always well-organized, and is also characterized by extraordinary zeal. When false teachings are compared in this respect with orthodox teaching, they often put the latter to shame. This is often seen in the financial resources which they command and the sacrificial contributions made by their followers. It is seen also in their literature, their meetings, and the readiness of their people to work. Our Lord once said that 'the children of this world are wiser in their generation than the children of light', and it is certainly true in this particular respect. The false teachers 'lie in wait'; they have planned their campaign and execute it with remarkable skill and astuteness and zeal and energy. This is not surprising when we remember that it all emanates from the Devil himself. He is 'a liar from the beginning', says our Lord, he is 'the father of lies', and he can transform himself into 'an angel of light'. The most brilliant plan that has ever been executed in this world of time was that of the Devil in respect to Adam and Eve in the Garden of Eden. What a perfect plot! what a perfect scheme! how well the Devil knew how to approach them! and how plausible and insinuating was his method! Such has been the great characteristic of his followers ever since.

The next characteristic of the false is its subtlety. This is seen in the words 'cunning', 'craft', 'sleight' and 'deceive'. They describe the attractiveness of the false. It is because it appears to be so attractive that people are ready to accept it, and especially those who are but children in the faith. It always seems to be so simple and so direct. The false teaching tells us that we need not spend so much time in studying this Epistle to the Ephesians and struggling to understand doctrine; the truth is all so simple. You simply believe and you have everything. It offers 'short cuts'; it is always simple and direct and immediate, and it is always so 'gloriously simple'. It is here we see the subtlety of it all. This is the secret of conjuring, as it was the secret of men who in former days used to go round the Fairs throwing things into a bag, and apparently offering a great bargain for a small amount of money, but which the foolish and innocent who fell victims to the plausible tongue found to be valueless.

*   *   *

This can be illustrated very easily in the spiritual realm by mentioning certain particular teachings. We are invited to join a section of the Church which offers to do everything for us. We simply confess our sins to the priest and leave our soul in the keeping of the Church. How subtle, how plausible, how attractive it seems to be! That is why it succeeds, and why every error and false teaching has succeeded from the beginning. It shows the subtlety of the serpent. 'As the serpent beguiled Eve' so his emissaries and agents still continue to deceive and beguile the innocent and unsuspecting.

[238]

When we come to consider how all this trickery is to be recognized, there is one invariable characteristic of the false teaching, which is, that it always takes from and detracts from the glory of the Lord Jesus Christ. It is not surprising that the Apostle wrote of 'the sleight of men', because in every one of these false teachings man is given prominence in some shape or form. It is not that they deny the Lord Jesus Christ altogether; of course not, they are much too clever to do so. But they deny Him and detract from His glory. They emphasize the priest or the Virgin Mary or the Church, or the Pope, or dead saints, or some woman who claims to have had a vision. There is generally some person who is given prominence and is at the centre, and in a very subtle manner the Lord Jesus Christ is not the 'all in all'. This is because the Devil hates the Son of God above everything else, and in subtle ways he takes from His central glory, and exalts man or a collection of men or an institution, or some organization. It is no longer Christ and Christ alone, and Christ exclusively.

It is good and wise to test every teaching by this criterion. The Apostle John in his First Epistle, after warning us not to believe every spirit, and assuring us that many false prophets have gone out into the world, and that there are many antichrists, tells us that the test which we must apply to all teachings is, 'Every spirit that confesseth that Jesus Christ is come in the flesh is of God; and every spirit that confesseth not that Jesus Christ is come in the flesh is not of God', but is antichrist (4:2–3). Everything is to be tested by the position given to the Lord Jesus Christ. If He is not essential, if He is not central, if He is not unique and above and beyond all, and dwarfing everyone and everything, then the teaching is false.

Finally we are taught here, as elsewhere, that all false teaching is to be hated and opposed. We are told in the New Testament that it was hated by our Lord and all the apostles, and that they opposed it and warned the people against it. But I ask again; is that being done today? What about your personal attitude towards this? Are you one of those people who says that there is no need for those negatives, and that we should be content with a positive presentation of the truth? Do we subscribe to the prevailing teaching which dislikes warnings and the criticizing of false teachings? Do you agree with those who say that a spirit of love is incompatible with the negative and critical denunciation of blatant error, and that we must always be positive. The simple answer to such an attitude is that the Lord Jesus Christ denounced evil and denounced false teachers. I repeat that He denounced them as 'ravening wolves' and 'whited sepulchres', and as 'blind guides'. The Apostle Paul said of some of them, 'whose god is their belly, and whose glory is in their shame'. That is the language of the Scriptures. There can be little doubt but that the Church is as she is today because we do not follow New Testament teaching and its exhortations, and confine ourselves to the positive and the so-called 'simple Gospel', and fail to stress the negatives and the criticisms. The result is that people do not recognize error when they meet it. They accept what appears to be nice, and are impressed by those who come to their doors speaking about the Bible and offering books about the Bible and prophecy and so on. In their ignorant child-like condition they often help to propagate the false teaching because they see nothing wrong in it. Moreover they do not realize that error is to be hated and to be denounced. Imagining themselves to be full of a spirit of love, they are beguiled by Satan, the predatory beast who was on their track, and who has suddenly caught them and pounced upon them in his cleverness and subtlety.

It is not pleasant to be negative; it is not enjoyable to have to denounce and to expose error. But any pastor who feels in a little measure, and with humility, the responsibility which the Apostle Paul knew in an infinitely greater degree, for the souls and the wellbeing spiritually of his people is compelled to utter these warnings. It is not liked and appreciated in this modern flabby generation, but if it is not done the people will be beguiled by false teachers 'as the serpent beguiled Eve'. We are not any longer to be 'children, tossed to and fro, and carried about by every wind of doctrine, by the sleight of men, and cunning craftiness whereby they lie in wait to deceive'. May God open our eyes and have mercy upon us, and give us spiritual understanding and discrimination, so that we may be able to resist all the wiles of the Devil in our day and generation, and thus bring honour and glory to our blessed Lord and Saviour, the Head of the body the Church, of which we have the priceless honour of being members!

20

Speaking the Truth in Love

'But speaking the truth in love, may grow up into him in all things'.

Ephesians 4:15

This phrase is, of course, part of a larger statement. It introduces the positive aspect of the Apostle's teaching with regard to the function of the ministry in the Christian Church. The object of the ministry is to bring us all to 'a perfect man, unto the measure of the stature of the fulness of Christ'. But as we have seen, in order to attain to that objective, we must start where we are: and the first thing we have to do is to realize that we are children and subject to some of the characteristics of children; children, that is, in a spiritual sense. So having warned us that we must not henceforth continue as children, the Apostle exhorts us to 'speak the truth in love' and to 'grow up into him in all things, which is the head, even Christ'.

Firstly, we must seek out the meaning of the word translated 'speaking'. While in a sense it is correct it does not convey the full meaning of the word used by the Apostle. The word he used is not normally translated 'speaking'. Or, to state the matter from the opposite angle, the words which are generally translated 'speaking' are not the word the Apostle used here. The Greek word means 'professing', so we may translate the phrase, 'professing the truth in love'. Many have urged that a very literal translation, though it is not a pleasant one, is 'truthing' – 'but truthing in love'. What the expression conveys is that we are 'in the truth' and that we are 'walking in the truth'. Perhaps the best translation of all would be 'having or holding the truth in love'. That, of course, includes speaking it, and discussing it together, and teaching it. But it is not merely speaking; it covers the whole of our deportment. We are to be true and to walk in the truth

[241]

and in love. So what the Apostle says is that we must no more be children, tossed to and fro, and so on, but rather, holding the truth in love, we must grow up into Christ in all things.

I am tempted to assert that at the present time there is no single statement in the whole of the Bible which is so much abused and misquoted as this particular statement. This phrase, together with the phrase in the 21st verse of the seventeenth chapter of John's Gospel, 'That they all may be one', are the two favourite texts of the participants in the œcumenical movement and of those who advocate a great 'World Church'. Together they have virtually become a slogan. It is therefore most important that we should examine and consider this phrase very carefully.

It has become the favourite text of so many because it has been wrested out of its context. It is always extremely dangerous to take a phrase out of its context and turn it into a slogan. Every statement in the Scripture should always be taken in its context. It is to violate Scripture to treat it in any other way. We shall see the importance of this principle as we proceed with our exposition. As we do so we must be careful to bear in mind the Apostle's fundamental concern in this entire section. When he says 'speaking the truth in love' he does not mean merely being nice and loving. I am compelled to start with that negative because the text is commonly interpreted today in this fashion. This has become the controlling idea at the present time in discussions concerning church unity. Fellowship is put into the first position. We are told that nothing is as important as fellowship; unity in and of itself is the supreme thing. We are told that the lack of this unity is the main if not the insuperable hindrance to evangelism. We are also told that we have no right to expect revival in the absence of this unity. The explanation of the state of the Church and of the fact that the masses are outside the Church is that there is so much division in the Church. Indeed we are told that nothing today is more important than that we should all be one in one great Church and that at all costs we must put fellowship and unity in the supreme position. To that end we are told that we must tolerate almost anything and everything; that as long as a man is nice and loving, and shows a friendly spirit and does good works, especially if he makes a sacrifice in order to do so, then what he believes or does not believe is comparatively unimportant.

What matters, we are told, is that a man should have 'the spirit of Christ' and that he should desire to imitate Christ's example. That makes him a Christian! Doctrinal correctness, they maintain, has been over-emphasized in the past. A man may be shaky on the very Person of Christ, may not believe in the doctrine of the Atonement, or in the Virgin birth, or in the literal physical resurrection of our Lord, but if he has an open mind, and is tolerant of other opinions, and is kind and friendly and 'gracious' and concerned about others, and especially about suffering and need and anxious to right all wrongs, political and social, he is a true Christian. What a man is, and does, we are told, is of much greater importance than his doctrinal views. Moreover, it is argued, nothing but a demonstration of this so-called 'Christian spirit' will have any effect upon those outside the Church who have no interest whatsoever in doctrine. Indeed, to hold doctrinal views strongly and to criticize other views is virtually regarded as sinful and is frequently described as being 'sub-Christian'. This is how the phrase 'speaking the truth in love' is being commonly interpreted.

It would be very easy to give some remarkable and almost astonishing illustrations of what I am saying. For instance, it is quite amusing to notice how a well-known reviewer of religious books, when he comes across any criticism of other views in the book he is reviewing, immediately criticizes the spirit of the author. That seems to be his one test of scholarship! 'Scholarship' has come to mean that you find all views very interesting, and that there is something to be said for all points of view. If you want to be regarded as scholarly you must not say that one view is right and the other wrong; you must not criticize, for to criticize is to deny the spirit of Christ, and to be entirely devoid of love. 'Speaking the truth in love' has come to mean that you more or less praise everything, but above all, that you never criticize any view strongly, because, after all, there is a certain amount of right and truth in everything.

*   *   *

We must therefore ask the question, Is this a right and a true interpretation of Paul's statement? Is this what is meant by 'speaking the truth in love'? I answer immediately that it cannot

[243]

be, for the reason that the Apostle does not simply tell us here to speak lovingly. What he says is 'speaking the truth' or 'holding the truth'. We are not told by the Apostle to cultivate a vague, loving spirit, but to hold 'the truth' in love. The very word *truth*, in and of itself, makes the modern popular exposition of the statement obviously and patently wrong. Furthermore – and this is where the context is so important – if the phrase merely denotes a loving spirit, how is it connected with what the Apostle has said in verse 14? If 'speaking the truth in love', 'holding the truth in love', means that we are to smile upon all views and doctrinal standpoints, and never criticize and condemn and reject any views at all, how do we avoid being 'children, tossed to and fro and carried about by every wind of doctrine'? This supposed 'loving spirit' makes it impossible to use terms such as 'sleight of men' and 'cunning craftiness' and 'lying in wait to deceive'. The very text itself, and especially the context, make that interpretation completely impossible; indeed it is a denial of the Apostle's statement. We must not hesitate to say so plainly. To put life, or 'spirit', or niceness, or anything else, before truth is to deny essential New Testament teaching; and in addition is to contradict directly the Apostle's solemn warning in verse 14. It is to set up ourselves, and the modern mind, and 20th-century man, as the authority rather than the 'called apostle' Paul and all others whom the Lord has set in the Church to warn us against, and to save us from, this attitude which dislikes discrimination and judgment. Never was it more important to assert that friendliness or niceness or some sentimental notions of brotherliness do not constitute Christianity. You can have all such qualities without and apart from Christianity, and even in men who deny it, but you cannot have Christianity without 'truth'. So that, whatever else it may mean, 'holding the truth in love' does not mean a vague, flabby, sentimental notion of niceness and fellowship and brotherhood.

Looking at it positively, note that the Apostle says 'but holding the truth'. The fact that he introduces this with the word *but* tells us that the verse is to be interpreted in a manner that emphasizes the contrast with verse 14. We are not to be 'children, tossed to and fro, and carried about with every wind of doctrine' but the opposite of that. Instead of being like weather-vanes, turning round in every direction and believing everything, we are to 'hold to' something particular and definite, even the truth. Instead of believing one thing one day, and then something different another day, we must be stable, and hold on to and walk in the truth as it is made known in the Scriptures. Holding the truth is the antithesis of being carried about by every wind of doctrine. How important it is to observe the context! Many problems and difficulties vanish the moment you allow the Scripture to speak for itself instead of wresting statements out of their context and using them as slogans.

*   *   *

We come now to the question as to *how* we are to hold on to the truth in love. What does it mean in actual practice? I cannot hold on to the air, I cannot grasp a mist in my hands and hold on to it. But I am told to 'hold on' to something. Now it is but a matter of simple, elementary thinking to say that before I can hold on to anything I must know what it is. It must be something that can be held on to, something definite which can be described. And the Apostle says that it is some such thing, namely, truth. Obviously, therefore, this truth to which he is referring is capable of being defined. This, surely, follows of necessity. How can I judge these various 'winds of doctrine' that blow round and about me if I have not got a standard? How may I know whether these winds of doctrine are true or false? How do I detect this 'sleight of men' and their 'cunning craftiness', or realize that they are 'lying in wait to deceive' me and to lead me into error, without having some standard? In business we believe in having a gold standard, and a yard measure; we have standards in 'weights and measures'. We do so of necessity, for without them we would never know whether we were being dealt with fairly or being robbed; we would have no check on one another and business would be impossible. It is precisely the same in the spiritual realm and in the Church. You cannot avoid being carried about by every wind of doctrine unless you have a standard of judgment. You cannot hold on to something which is amorphous; you cannot lay hold on something which is as nebulous and vague and indefinite as the wind which blows in all directions.

By definition, the very term used, and the contrast with verse 14, insist upon our saying that 'the truth' is something which can be defined and analysed and stated in propositions. And yet, saying so, I am running entirely counter to what is being said at the present time, in spite of the fact that what I am asserting and arguing is based upon elementary logic and thinking, and upon honest dealing with the Word of God. But this, we are told, is fatal to brotherhood and fellowship and friendliness and unity, and by saying such things we are causing division. In the present century there is a marked dislike of creeds and confessions and precise definitions. Christianity has become a vague, indefinite spirit of good-will and philanthropy. This is stated quite openly in books and sermons, and the pronouncements of congresses and conferences. It is time we faced this issue and examined it in the light of Scripture. How can this modern attitude be reconciled with that which the Apostle is saying here? In the light of Paul's teaching how can such things as congresses of Christians and Jews, and congresses of world faiths, be justified on the grounds that we are out on the same quest, and that there are many different routes for reaching the summit of a mountain?

This modern idea, moreover, is not only a denial of Scripture, but also a denial of the entire history of the Christian Church. There are sections of the Church in which in every service the worshippers recite together the Apostles' Creed, the Athanasian Creed, or part of the Nicene Creed. All the large Churches have Confessions of Faith; the Church of England has the Thirty-nine Articles, the Presbyterian Churches recognize the Westminster Confession of Faith, the Lutheran Church on the Continent has its Augsburg Confession, and many Churches use the Heidelberg Confession and Catechism, and subscribe to the Belgic·Confession. In the light of this great fact of history, and without any desire to be critical, I am constrained to say that this modern attitude is arrogant. It is arrogant in that it dismisses virtually the whole of Church history and condemns all Creeds and Confessions.

Why and how did these Creeds and Confessions ever come into being? Although we know that the Apostles' Creed was not drawn up by the Apostles themselves, it was drawn up by the early Church in order that believers might have a succinct statement of what the Apostles preached and taught. But why did the early Church believe that that was necessary? Why were the Athanasian Creed and the Nicene Creed ever drawn up? These are very pertinent questions. Are they to be dealt with by saying that life was leisurely in those days, and that philosophers and theologians enjoyed discussion and argumentation and the systematizing of thought? Was it the case that legalistic and argumentative men turned the delightfully 'simple' Gospel of Jesus into something that was almost the exact opposite? Church history reveals very clearly that such was not the case and that every one of these Creeds and Confessions was drawn up to save the life of the Church and to safeguard the truth concerning our Lord and His great salvation. False teachings and errors had crept in, as the Scriptures had prophesied would be the case, and as the Apostles had warned. The result was confusion in the Church. In the providence of God there were leaders in the Church filled with the Holy Spirit who saw quite clearly that if this kind of teaching continued the Church would be destroyed. So they met together in great œcumenical councils, which simply meant that Christian leaders came from different parts of the world to deal with the situation.

Unlike the modern œcumenical idea, they did not come together to say that they were all one and that differing views were of little consequence; they came together in order to state clearly what must be believed, and to state that those who refused to subscribe to such truth must be denounced as heretics and ex-communicated. They felt that the whole life of the Church and the whole future of the Church was at stake and that there must be an end to the uncertainty and the confusion concerning vital doctrines. So they drew up their Creeds in which they defined what must be believed, and they drew a sharp distinction between right and wrong, and truth and error. History records the heresies and errors that came in about the Person of the Lord Jesus Christ, the Arian heresy and others, but Athanasius and eventually others, stood against it, and condemned it. But all that is dismissed with a wave of the hand today. It is, I repeat, not only a denial of the teaching of the Scripture but also a denial of the most glorious periods in the history of the Christian Church.

You cannot 'hold on' to the truth unless you know what the truth is. There are certain doctrines which are absolutely essential to the Christian faith. One is the authority of the Bible. Without the absolute authority of the Word of God in matters of faith and of conduct, how can one discriminate between truth and error? If this is not acknowledged as the sole authority, then 'every wind of doctrine' is permissible; but if that were so, then there is no Christianity and therefore no salvation. Likewise there must be no argument about the Person of the Lord Jesus Christ. He is Son of God and Son of man; fully God and fully man. As we have seen, the early Church saw the crucial importance of this doctrine. The New Testament teaching is based entirely upon it. The great Epistle to the Hebrews was written to assert this and to show His pre-eminence and to maintain that 'God hath spoken in these last days by His Son'. It was because certain Hebrew Christians had become doubtful about this truth that the author wrote his great Epistle to them. There must be no discussion concerning the fact that the Lord Jesus Christ, the Son of God, is the only Mediator between God and men. The Church is not to argue about Him, His person, His miraculous birth, His sacrificial atonement, and His literal physical resurrection. If His bodily resurrection is not true and factual, says Paul to the Corinthians, 'our preaching is vain, and your faith is also vain, you are yet in your sins'. It is as vital as that! Likewise with respect to the doctrine of the Atonement. Paul tells the Corinthians that the message which he was called and commissioned as an ambassador to preach was that 'God hath made him to be sin for us, who knew no sin, that we might be made the righteousness of God in him' (2 Cor 5:21).

Also, as we have had occasion to emphasize already, there is the crucial doctrine of justification by faith. Paul tells the Galatians that if they deny this by introducing any works as contributory to salvation, they have 'fallen from grace' (5:4). Let us remember that the false teachers who were troubling the Galatians were not actually denying the Person of our Lord, or His sacrificial atonement, but they were teaching that Gentiles must be circumcised in addition to believing in Christ. So specific is the truth that Paul cannot tolerate this false teaching and 'withstood Peter to the face' for ever having appeared to countenance it. Paul did not regard this question as to whether a Christian should be circumcised as a matter of indifference, and say that as long as one had any kind of vague belief in Christ all was well. He would make no concession at this point because to do so would be 'to preach another gospel which is not another'. Indeed, what we have already considered in verses 4–6 is absolutely essential.

*   *   *

The Christian Church is as she is today because the doctrine of revelation and the truths of revelation are being denied. The truth revealed in the Scriptures, 'the truth once delivered to the saints', has been replaced by philosophy and modern thought, especially in the form of science. Instead of exposition of Scripture we have philosophical attempts to try to find God and to define the being of God. That is why there is virtually no biblical teaching any longer. It has been replaced by ethical addresses and sentimental appeals, talks about courage and doing your duty, and political addresses. But this is not the biblical teaching, it is not performing what the Apostle tells us the apostles and prophets and evangelists and pastors and teachers have been called and ordained to do. Instead of clear doctrine there is vague teaching about God and of brotherliness and Christ-likeness and of doing good and of being loving. This happens because, obviously, there can be no sound teaching unless the teacher knows what the truth is. The business of the Church is not to speculate about God and about the Person of Christ; it is to teach the revealed truths concerning them, to communicate the principles revealed in Scripture, and to build herself up on her most holy faith.

Obviously we must know exactly what the truth is. We are not to spend the whole of our time arguing about preliminaries, and presuppositions; we are to start with the revealed truth and expound it. Every one of us is to understand, to believe, and to 'hold the truth', not to speculate philosophically about life and its meaning and its problems. It is not for any preacher to stand in a pulpit and say, 'I think this', or 'I have come to this conclusion', but rather 'Thus saith the Lord'. We are to repeat what Paul said in writing to the Romans, 'But God be thanked, that ye were the servants of sin, but ye have obeyed from the heart that form of doctrine (sound teaching) which was delivered you' (6:17); or what he said to Timothy, 'Hold fast the form of sound words which thou hast heard of me' (2 Tim 1:13). Paul had taught Timothy 'a form of sound words'; and he does not write to Timothy merely to tell him to imitate his spirit, the spirit which he had seen in him, but he says to him, 'Hold fast the form of sound words'. Paul wrote similarly to the Galatians, not because what he preached was his idea, but as he says, 'I certify you, brethren, that the gospel which was preached of me is not after man. For I neither received it of man, neither was I taught it, but by the revelation of Jesus Christ' (1:11–12). To Timothy he says, 'And the things that thou hast heard of me among many witnesses, the same commit thou to faithful men, who shall be able to teach others also' (2 Timothy 2:2). The Christian message is precise truth, consisting of propositions about God, and the Lord Jesus Christ, His Person and His work, about the Holy Ghost and His work, the only way of salvation, the Church, and all necessary truth about life. I have had to emphasize all this at length, because there is no purpose in going on to the next statement if we are not clear about this matter. 'We hold the truth'.

But we must be equally careful to 'hold the truth in love'. Once more I emphasize that this addition, like the entire statement, must be interpreted in the light of verse 14. In interpreting that verse I laid great stress upon the strength and almost the violence of the language used by the Apostle. Yet here he is exhorting us to 'speak the truth in love'. Is there a contradiction between the strong language of verse 14 and 'speaking the truth in love' in verse 15? Obviously there is no such thing, but it helps us to interpret this phrase about love. Clearly, in the light of verse 14, it cannot only mean being nice and kind. The Apostle Paul was not a 'nice' man in the commonly accepted sense. A man who is filled with the love of Christ is not merely 'a nice man' in a natural sense, which is mainly due to one's physical constitution and entirely accidental. That is not the love of which Paul is speaking. What the Apostle is arguing is that while we 'hold the truth' we are to watch our spirits. False teachers are liable to disturb us and to annoy us, and we have to oppose them, and to do so strongly. But we must not do so in a wrong or bitter spirit.

*   *   *

But in particular the Apostle is dealing with the way in which we speak to one another as believers in the Church, and correct errors that may appear among us. The severity applies mainly to false teachers, to those whom Jude describes as 'having crept in unawares', but among ourselves we are to speak the truth and hold the truth in love. The Apostle means that while we must emphasize the absolute necessity of definitions and creeds, we must never be hard and rigid, we must never be legalistic or self-righteous. We must never behave in such a manner as to give the impression that our one concern is to prove that we are right and everyone else wrong. We must never do so merely to win an argument or a dispute. Many of us may have to plead guilty to this.

Similarly 'party spirit' is always wrong; labels are always wrong; a censorious spirit is always wrong. There are people who are controlled and animated by a party-spirit and by labels; and if you do not subscribe to their particular shibboleth you are condemned. I recall how a good friend once told me that he was somewhat disappointed, because in my exposition of the second chapter of this Epistle to the Ephesians I had not once mentioned Calvinism as I worked through the chapter. My simple reply to him was, The text does not mention that term. My friend was so much in the grip of a party-spirit that he was becoming doubtful of my position! A party-spirit is generally the result of approaching truth in a purely intellectual manner, and also being governed by prejudice which is often the result of one's upbringing.

The truth of which the Apostle writes must never be approached with the intellect only. If my heart is not moved by the truth, if I do not feel it and its power, my spirit is wrong. Truth must produce passion, and in a truly Christian profession there is emotion and feeling. A truth which is only held in the intellect becomes hard, and arid and dry; and a man of whom this is true can never speak the truth in love. We are to state the truth strongly only in order to make it clear, in order to help others, in order to win men. We should do so because we are sorry for those who are misguided and led astray: not in order to show that they are wrong and we are right, but in order to bring them to the truth. We should do so therefore with humility, and recognize our own fallibility, that we all make mistakes, and that we all may fall into error. We are always to speak with humility, and to be careful that we do not wrest the Scriptures or in any way misinterpret them. We must 'rightly divide the word of truth' (2 Tim 2:15).

In other words, we must never start by denouncing; we must

start by explaining and expounding. If I believe another man's view is wrong I must not attack him immediately; first of all I must put the truth to him, and try to do so in as persuasive a manner as possible. I must try to win him to it. Indeed I must go further and say that I must have sympathy with the man. I must recognize that perhaps he is only a babe in Christ and that he holds the wrong views because he is a babe and has not been taught; I should have a sense of compassion towards him. We are told that, as our Lord looked upon the people, He saw them 'as sheep without a shepherd and had compassion on them'; such is the manner in which we should look on those who are young in the faith. We should bear with them and exercise great patience with respect to them.

Recall what the Apostle says in 1 Corinthians concerning the question of meats offered to idols. He was quite clear about the matter himself, but he says that although he had a right to eat such meats, and that there was nothing wrong in doing so, nevertheless if it proved to be a hindrance to a weaker and less-enlightened brother he would exercise his right not to eat: 'Wherefore, if meat make my brother to offend, I will eat no flesh while the world standeth, lest I make my brother to offend' (8:13). Still more clearly is this stated in 1 Corinthians 13, verse 1, and vital in the entire chapter: 'Though I speak with the tongues of men and of angels, and have not charity, I am become as sounding brass, or a tinkling cymbal'.

But all this does not mean that we compromise the truth: we are to hold the truth at all costs. But we must hold it in this way of love in order to persuade people and to win them and to try to enlighten them. It is the very antithesis of saying that truth does not count, and that Christians may believe what they like as long as they are living a good life and are showing a Christian spirit. Error must be exposed; verse 14 comes before verse 15.

Above all we must realize that love is not sentimental and weak; love is strong, love is true, love is pure. To love a person truly is to desire the very best possible for that person. Love sometimes has to hurt; occasionally we have 'to be cruel to be kind'. The parent who never corrects the child is a very unsatisfactory parent. 'Whom the Lord loveth he chasteneth; and scourgeth every son whom he receiveth' (Heb 12:6). If we are really animated by a spirit of love we shall be anxious for our beloved fellow Christians to be delivered from error and to cease to be children. To that end we may have to speak very severely to them at times, and chastise them, and rebuke them, and show them the error of their position with all the strength that we have. Love does not mean that we smile at everything and show ourselves indulgent, saying that nothing matters as long as we are all one. Love is one of the most virile, strong, magnificent qualities in existence. And love is so powerful that it is prepared to hurt its object in order to win it and to save it and to safeguard it from a dreadful fate. 'Love is strong as death'.

'Speaking the truth in love' is illustrated perfectly in the fourth chapter of Paul's Epistle to the Galatians. Having written very strongly to them, and having reprimanded them severely, he suddenly says, 'Am I therefore become your enemy because I tell you the truth?' The childish Galatians, because he told them the truth, might feel that he had become their enemy, and that he was a hateful person who hated them. He assures them that he had nothing but love for them, and writes in verse 19: 'My little children, of whom I travail in birth again until Christ be formed in you'. He loved them as a mother loves her children; and it was because he loved them, and valued their souls so highly, that he wrote so strongly against the particular heresy that had troubled and ensnared them. He hates the error, but he loves them. Because they cannot see the error he has to write very strongly, just as, for the sake of truth, he had once to withstand to the face the Apostle Peter. It was all for the sake of the truth; but he does it in love, as a mother loves her children, and so he won Peter and the Galatians back to it.

The principle which should govern us in all this is the well-known principle enunciated early in the history of the Christian Church – 'In things essential, unity; in things indifferent [things which are not essential, and concerning which there is no absolute certainty] liberty; in all things charity.'

21
Growing Up

'But speaking the truth in love, may grow up into him
in all things, which is the head, even Christ: from
whom the whole body fitly joined together and
compacted by that which every joint supplieth,
according to the effectual working in the measure of
every part, maketh increase of the body unto the
edifying of itself in love'.

Ephesians 4:15–16

In these verses we come to the end, the climax, of the Apostle's
statement concerning unity in the Church which began in the
first verse of the chapter. We must be careful therefore as we
come to examine them to bear in mind the entire context. The
Apostle is not interested in unity in general among Christians, but
in particular in the unity that should be evident among Christians
as members of the body of Christ, the Church. This has led him,
and especially from verse 7 onwards, to deal with the nature and
constitution of the Church herself. His primary object is not to
write on the doctrine of the Church; but he shows that a true
understanding of the nature of the Christian Church makes the
principle of unity quite inevitable. The doctrine of the Church has
been implicit throughout, but now it becomes explicit in the
words, 'may grow up into him in all things, which is the head,
even Christ', in verse 15, and still more so in verse 16. We are not
to be children, but we are to 'grow up', and not only to grow up
individually, but to grow up together in the Church so that the
entire body may become more mature and eventually attain 'unto
the measure of the stature of the fulness of Christ'. The Apostle
emphasizes that we are to 'grow up into him in all things'.

The Scriptures constantly emphasize the importance of balance
in the Christian life. To grow in some respects and not in others
leads to a monstrosity; for some parts to be over-developed and

others under-developed produces a lack of symmetry and form which is ugly. The Christian is to grow symmetrically 'in all things', in every respect. We are to grow up and develop, not only in our minds and understandings, but also in our hearts and feelings and our sensibility. We must therefore test ourselves along those lines and also in respect of our conduct and behaviour. Are we growing intellectually? Have we more knowledge of the truth than we had a year ago? Do we understand the Scriptures better? Are we less frequently in trouble and perplexity about spiritual matters?

Let us take an obvious illustration. A student who takes up a subject for study finds himself plunged into the midst of lectures. At first he understands practically nothing and feels somewhat confused. He may even feel like giving up; but he is advised to go on, and he does so, and sits and listens, still not apprehending very much. But suddenly, after a few months, he begins to feel that he is beginning to get hold of the subject and that it is beginning to make sense to him. From then on the subject becomes clearer to him, and he feels that he is mastering it.

It is much the same in the Christian life. People have often told me that when they first began to attend Christian services they had very little idea as to what was being said. They were aware of some general spirit in the meeting which laid hold of them, but they could not really follow and understand the messages. However, they continued to attend and gradually they began to understand the teaching. That is a sign of growth and development; and it would go on increasing progressively. As year follows year our knowledge and comprehension of the truth should become greater and greater.

The same is true with respect to feeling and emotion. Does the glorious truth of the Gospel grip us more than ever? Does it move us more than ever? or have we become what has been described as 'gospel-hardened'? We are in a sad and seriously defective condition if the Gospel does not move us more and more and fill us with an increasing sense of wonder and amazement and astonishment. There are far too many Christians whose feelings were only engaged in their Christian life when they were converted. They look back to that, but they do not seem to have experienced anything similar since then. But we should feel what

[255]

we believe more and more as we continue in this life; and if our emotions are not kindled more and more it really means that our understanding is not growing either. To understand Christian truth is of necessity to be moved by it. The one follows the other as the night the day. The more we know the Lord Jesus Christ, the more we must love Him. The more we know any truth about Him, the more it must move us in a very deep and vital sense. In the same manner we must show development in the matter of our conduct and behaviour. We are to 'grow up into Him in all things'.

Let me confirm this teaching by quoting what the Apostle says elsewhere. In his First Epistle to the Corinthians he writes, 'Brethren, be not children in understanding: howbeit in malice be ye children, but in understanding be men' (14:20). Malice is to become less and less evident in our lives, but in understanding we are to be 'men'; we are to grow up and develop. Again, in his Epistle to the Romans we find, 'Your obedience is come abroad unto all men. I am glad therefore on your behalf: but yet I would have you wise unto that which is good, and simple concerning evil' (16:19). We ought to remain children as regards evil, and even die altogether with respect to it; but with regard to that which is good, we are to be wise, to grow and to develop.

We must no longer remain as children, but grow up in everything and in every respect. But we are to grow and to develop 'into him who is the head, even Christ', a doctrine that we have already expounded in verse 13. It means that, as individual members and parts of the body, we should all grow up into a conformity to Christ the Head. In other words, Paul is saying that every part of the body ought to be worthy of the Head, ought to correspond to the Head. The head is the pattern and standard, and the Head is 'even Christ'. Every part of the body, even the smallest parts, however small or apparently insignificant, should be in conformity to, should be worthy of the Head. There should be no clash or defect. We are all familiar with a lack of proportion and symmetry in nature. You may see a very beautiful face but ugly hands, or a beautiful body but ugly legs. The Apostle says that there should be no such clash or lack of correspondence, but that the entire body in every part should be perfectly proportioned and balanced, with nothing standing out as a kind of oddity or eccentricity. Everything should fit together perfectly and in due proportion. This should be the result of our speaking the truth in love as we deal with one another. We should all be growing up together, at the same rate if possible, with the same kind of maturity, so that the body shows a delightful proportion and beauty, and perfection of form; and we should especially seek that there should be no clash between the head and the various other parts of the body.

There is also another aspect of this truth which is important, namely, that every part of the body should be so developed as to be always ready to respond to the Lord. We are not only to be conformed to Him, but to be at His disposal and at His service; so that when He, the Head, desires something, there will be no hindrance, no restraint, no failure to respond in any part of the body. This becomes yet clearer in verse 16 where the apostle, having reminded us that the Head is Christ, proceeds to add, 'from whom the whole body fitly joined together and compacted by that which every joint supplieth, according to the effectual working in the measure of every part, maketh increase of the body unto the edifying of itself in love'.

*   *   *

This is undoubtedly one of the most complicated statements the Apostle Paul ever wrote. It is interesting to note that some of the commentators of the past, indeed some of the Fathers in the early church, had the temerity to suggest that Paul became somewhat muddled for once, and that his heart or his imagination ran away with him as he piled phrase upon phrase until he forgot what he had written at the beginning of the sentence. It certainly is an extremely difficult verse to read; and difficult to understand, unless we employ the key which the Apostle himself has already provided for us in his previous statements. For myself I feel confident that the Apostle was now bringing to a conclusion and grand climax the theme of the unity of Christians as members of the body of Christ, and he was so anxious that no part should be missing that he made so many additions as to produce a somewhat involved statement.

What we have here, of course, is another picture of the Church as the body of Christ. We have had occasion to remark already that this was undoubtedly his favourite metaphor when he comes to describe the Church. But even this is inadequate as we shall discover as we look at this particular picture. For there are senses in which he himself goes beyond his picture, because the picture, however good, can never convey the full truth. This is the difficulty with every illustration, and that is why several are needed to convey the truth. The Apostle compares the Church to a body, to a building, to a bride, to a great commonwealth. He does so because no one illustration can say everything; and this particular picture of the body, though it is the most adequate of them all, still leaves us with certain difficulties.

We shall look first at the particular terms used, and then at the whole. The first statement is that the Head is Christ. As with a body, we must always start in any consideration of the Church with the Head. The Apostle has already done so in the first chapter where he says that 'God hath put all things under his feet, and gave him to be head over all things to the church, which is his body, the fulness of him that filleth all in all'. He is repeating that statement, for we must always start with the fact that Christ is the Head of the Church. He is the source of all her life, her energy, and her growth; apart from Him there is no Church and could not be.

With regard to our position as Christian believers he makes two statements. The first is that we are being 'fitly joined together', and the second that we are 'compacted'. With regard to the phrase 'fitly joined together', fortunately for us Paul has already provided us with the key to understanding it in the second chapter of this Epistle: 'In whom all the building *fitly framed together* groweth unto an holy temple in the Lord' (v. 21). In that statement as we have already noted the Apostle was mixing his metaphors; having started with a building he ends with a body. The expression means 'parts fitted closely to each other' in a kind of harmony. The word the Apostle actually uses means 'several parts bound together', fitting into one another. Speaking then of us as members of the Church, he says that the Head of the body is Christ and that we are members in particular; and as members we are articulated and fit into one another. Everything should be in the right position, ball and socket are to be articulated, fitly joined together. All these terms carry exactly the same meaning. The idea is of a number of parts not simply bound together, anyhow, somehow, but bound together as the various parts of our bodies are joined together.

At this point a certain amount of knowledge of anatomy is helpful. In the case of a joint in the body there is a kind of cup on one bone and into that cup there fits a kind of ball at the end of another bone. The surfaces of both are smooth so that there is no friction, and everything works easily and harmoniously and in an effective manner. According to the Apostle's teaching this should be true of the members of the Church. It is the way in which they are to grow up into Him in all things. The ideal condition of the Christian Church is that in which every member is what he is meant to be, fitting in with every other member and so preserving 'the unity of the Spirit in the bond of peace'. There is to be no creaking, as it were, in the joints, no angularities; everything is to be 'fitly joined together'.

But the Apostle is not even content with that; he adds another term, 'compacted', which means 'closely knit', in order to drive home his point. It means 'brought and held together'. It is a term which is often used in a figurative sense to suggest a kind of mental unity, sympathy of understanding, concord. In other words the Apostle is changing his emphasis slightly from the purely mechanical which we have in 'fitly joined together', to the notion of minds fitting in together, compacted, closely knit. This is essential, of course, for a true organic unity, and for proper functioning. Christ is the Head, and we as parts of the body are to be fitly joined together, and compacted.

*   *   *

We come now to ask how all this is brought into being and how it is maintained. The answer is found in one of the most difficult of the Apostle's phrases, namely, 'by that which every joint supplieth'. The difficulty arises in the word 'joint', because we instinctively think of the word *joint* in the way in which I have already been using it, as a ball and socket fitting together to form a joint. But this new term has a somewhat different meaning and could well be translated 'band' or 'connecting link'. In other words Paul is saying that these bands not merely unite us together. They do so, but they do something much more important; it is through these bands or connecting links that the supplies of life and energy pass to every part of the body. Actually it is misleading to read 'which every joint supplieth' because this phrase gives the impression that it is the 'joint' which does the supplying. But that is not so. The supply does not come through the joint but through the 'band'. Some commentators therefore translate the phrase thus: 'through every joint for supply', or 'through every joint which serves for supply'. In other words, the bands to which Paul refers are the channels through which the supply of life and nutriment and energy passes to all the various parts of the body. This vital supply is communicated through every band. So we may read thus, 'from whom the whole body, fitly joined together and compacted through the supply communicated by [or through] every band'.

We come next to the term *supply*, which is most important. The word the Apostle used carries the meaning of an 'abundant supply', a 'superabundance'; not merely a sufficiency, but an abundant supply. It is the same idea as that which the Apostle John expresses in the prologue to his Gospel in the words, 'of his fulness have all we received, and grace upon grace' (1:16). Paul has already conveyed the idea in this Epistle in the words 'the exceeding riches of His grace' (2:7), 'the love of Christ which passeth knowledge . . . filled with all the fulness of God' (3:19). The supply is an 'abundant supply'. It comes to the various members of the body through these bands of communication, these channels of supply along which it passes. This is the meaning therefore of 'fitly joined together and compacted by that which every joint supplieth'.

Yet the Apostle adds something even to that: 'according to the effectual working in the measure of every part'. 'Effectual working' means 'operative energy', energy that does something. 'The measure of every part' means 'the capacity of each part'. This operative energy, this effectual power – of which Paul says there is an abundant supply – passes through the bands of communication to every part; and then he adds that the amount of this energy which is given to every part is 'according to the measure of its capacity'. Each part in the body does not receive exactly the same amount, but each part receives all that it needs according to the measure of its capacity.

Summing up the various phrases we can state the teaching thus.

The Head of the body is the Lord Jesus Christ. We as individual members should function as the Head desires us to do. We are all fitly joined together, compacted and held together and energized through bands of supply by an endless superabundant supply that comes to us from Him. Every single part, whether great or small, is absolutely full; it gets all it needs and no more. Each part is not identical; we are not all absolutely the same. We differ tremendously; each one of us has his particular capacity, and every one of us should be filled according to his capacity. In other words, the Apostle is summing up here, and repeating, what he has said in verse 7, 'Unto every one of us is given grace according to the measure of the gift of Christ'. There are differences in administrations, there are diversities of gifts, some members of the body are more important than others, some more comely than others, as we are told in 1 Corinthians chapter 12.

The eye and the hand and the foot, the nose and the tongue, are not equal in importance, but they are all members of the body, and they are all essential to the working of the body. And every part is given a full and an abundant supply of life and energy to enable it to carry out its particular function in a perfect manner.

What is the object of all this? Why is the Church so constituted? Why is the body thus constructed? The Apostle says that the object is that it all makes for 'the increased growth of the body'. He has actually introduced a parenthesis after 'from whom the whole body', namely, 'fitly joined together and compacted by that which every joint supplieth, according to the effectual working in the measure of every part'. Then he completes the statement with, 'maketh increase of the body unto the edifying of itself in love'. In other words, the Church has been designed and constituted in this marvellous manner in order that it may grow. That is why there are the joints fitting in together, why there are bands of communication, and why there is this abundant supply of life and energy. It is that the whole body may grow. Note that Paul says, 'from whom the *whole* body fitly joined together . . .' The purpose is to promote growth, or to state it in another way, in order that the body may be 'built up', as has previously been stated in verse 12: 'for the perfecting of the saints, for the work of the ministry, for the edifying (the building up) of the body of Christ'.

Then, lest we forget what he had said at the very beginning, the

Apostle adds, 'to the edifying of itself in love'. Love is the final perfection, the acme. 'Now abideth faith, hope and love, but the greatest of these is love'. In this matter of unity nothing is more important than love. If the Head is love, the body must be love. We are to conform to the Head, He is love everlasting, eternal love. He became incarnate love; and the body is to correspond to Him; so we build up ourselves and we grow together 'in love'.

*   *   *

We can now suggest another translation of the entire statement: 'From whom all the body – being closely bound together, and constantly being knit together, by means of the bands through which the abundant supply of the vital energy passes which is put forth to supply the capacity of each part – works together for the increased growth of the body, resulting in the building up of itself in love'. This description of the Christian Church corresponds closely to what we know of the human body. The Apostle, writing over 1900 years ago, seems to have anticipated modern physiology sufficiently to use this particular illustration. In the human body the head contains the brain; and the whole nervous system of the body comes originally from the brain and is connected to it. The smallest nerve or nerve tendril in the tip of your finger can be traced right back to the brain. It goes back first into the spinal cord, which in turn is connected by strands of nerves to the brain, the highest centre of all, which contains everything. Our bodies are indeed 'fearfully and wonderfully made'. They are full of the articulations of which we have been speaking. Joint fits into joint, forearm fits into arm, arm fits into the trunk, and all the rest. But, over and above all this, there are bands of communication; the nervous system links the whole body together and keeps it together, and makes of it an organic unity in a manner which ligaments and joints cannot do.

The same thing, of course, can be said of the blood system, the vascular system. This again combines everything together, centering everything in the heart. The result is that the smallest venule in your fingertip can be traced right back to the heart, and the blood which courses through it goes everywhere. The nervous system and the vascular system correspond to these bands of supply of which the Apostle writes. What is remarkable is that the energy, the nervous energy, with which I move my little finger really comes originally from my brain. By thinking and willing I initiate that movement in my brain which then sends out energy that passes through my nervous system, and I am thus enabled to move my finger. That is the kind of idea which the Apostle has here; and his picture is a perfect one. What he is saying is that the supply, the origin of the life and energy and power and sustenance and all we need as Christians, is in the Head, which is Christ Himself. It passes from Him to every part of the body.

* * *

There is a kind of paradox here. The Apostle sounds at first as if he is contradicting himself; yet that is not so. He says on the one hand that everything comes from the head; but he has also said that every part of the body has its supply according to its capacity, in order that the whole may grow up and develop and edify itself in love. There is no contradiction because the growth of the whole depends in a sense upon the condition of every part. Ultimately we are all entirely dependent upon the Head. He alone is the source of supply. Yet at the same time it is true to say that if there is any defect in any part, the development of the whole is interrupted and rendered imperfect. This results from the wonderful inter-relationship, the organic unity, that obtains between the various parts of the body.

Let us take a single illustration. You may say that what alone matters is the condition of the brain, the seat of vital nervous energy and power, the seat of my thinking and my ultimate ability. And you may say that, in comparison, my little finger is of no significance. But that is not so; and the little finger may become highly important. If you should suddenly develop an acute infection in the tip of your little finger as the result of a slight prick from a blackthorn or a rose-bush, you soon find that it begins to throb and to give terrible pain; but not only so, you yourself become ill; you develop a severe headache and may become delirious and incapable of using your brain. The disease in the little finger produces poisoning and a paralysis, as it were, of the head and the entire body.

Now that is an illustration of the importance of the individual parts; but we must not press it too far. But it does help us to understand what the Apostle is saying. For the purposes of the Church Christ is the Head. He is all-powerful and in one sense He is not bound by the Church. Yet there is a sense in which a limit is placed upon Him by the failure of the Church. Thank God this is not true in an ultimate sense; but it is true in a temporary sense. The Apostle teaches that, if the whole body is to grow and to develop and to build itself up in love, then it is very important that every particular part should be filled up to its capacity with this vital life and energy, and be functioning as it is designed to do. So we see that every single member of the Church is of most vital importance. It is not surprising that the Apostle piled term upon term. He was concerned to show the glory of the Church and the glory of our position as individual members of the Church. What a privilege to be in such a body! To belong to such a Head and to receive this supply of life and energy from Him! Have you received up to your capacity? Are you fulfilling your function? Is this vital energy of Christ the Head in you, whatever you are, whatever your place in the Church? Such is our privilege.

But think also of your responsibility as a member of the body. Are you causing pain and trouble in other parts of the body by being diseased, by being sinful, or by being lethargic? These are the questions that inevitably arise. The Apostle's great appeal is that we be no longer children, no longer remain undeveloped, but that we all grow up in everything into Him who is the Head, even Christ, from whom the whole body fitly joined together and compacted by that which every joint supplieth, according to the effectual working in the measure of every part, maketh increase of the body unto the edifying of itself in love'. There is no value in intellectual knowledge unless it finally leads to love. There is no value in any emotion unless it leads to love. Our works are useless if they do not produce this love; ' . . . though I give my body to be burned and have not charity it profiteth me nothing'. So let us build up ourselves in love.

22

Activities and Life

'But speaking the truth in love, may grow up into him
in all things, which is the head, even Christ: from
whom the whole body fitly joined together and
compacted by that which every joint supplieth,
according to the effectual working in the measure of
every part, maketh increase of the body unto the
edifying of itself in love'.

Ephesians 4:15–16

As we conclude our study of this section of the Epistle to the
Ephesians I shall pick out certain important principles which have
emerged as we have been working our way through it. They
relate to matters of intense practical importance and relevance at
the present time. There is a sense in which this portion of Scripture, taken in connection with the seventeenth chapter of John's
Gospel, is one of the most urgently relevant sections of the Holy
Scriptures at this present time. This is so because of the great
interest in the Church and the question of unity. As Christian
people we should have an intelligent understanding of the Scripture, lest we be carried away by specious arguments and vague
generalities and a sentimental interest in unity, for these may well
lead us into a position which is actually contradictory to biblical
teaching.

A further subsidiary reason for emphasizing these principles is
that we can only understand what has been happening in the
Church in the first half of this century if we understand the
teaching of this section. It is because Christians have not understood the biblical doctrine of unity that things are as they are. We
shall therefore, of necessity, be dealing with matters which are
highly controversial; but to avoid controversial matters in a spirit
of fear is to deny the Scriptures. 'God hath not given us the spirit

of fear, but of power, and of love, and of a sound mind' (discipline) says Paul to Timothy. We must face difficulties and examine them in the light of the Scriptures. So I propose to select certain outstanding principles which are of the most urgent importance.

*   *   *

Let us start where the Apostle himself starts with the principle of unity: 'Endeavouring to keep the unity of the spirit in the bond of peace'. The Apostle starts by saying that this whole matter of unity is of supreme importance, and that we must never lose sight of it. There is a tendency in some to ignore the principle of unity because, reacting against the false notions of unity, they tend to go to the other extreme of saying that unity is of no consequence. But if the Church is the body of Christ, unity is essential and vital. The New Testament leaves us in no doubt about this. To be guilty of schism and of wrong division is sinful, as the Apostle makes clear in 1 Corinthians chapter 12, and in other places. Our Lord in His high-priestly prayer prays that 'they [believers] might be one' (John 17:21). So there is no need to argue this matter. But in addition to such clear statements, the importance of unity should be obvious to all who have ever considered the doctrine of the Church in terms of the analogy of the human body. That analogy likewise makes any argument as to the centrality of the doctrine of unity quite otiose. Organic unity in the body is what makes it a body.

Nothing is therefore more important than that we should understand the true nature of unity. There can be false ideas with respect to unity. Unity is essential; indeed there is a unity in the body of Christ whether we are aware of it or not, a unity of the Spirit; but this is meant to manifest itself; therefore we must be clear as to the character, the nature of this unity. What is it that brings the unity into being? What is it that hinders unity? The Apostle makes certain things very plain in terms of his analogy of the body. The first is that we must never think of unity in the Church in a merely external or mechanical or organizational manner. The illustration of the body makes that quite wrong; yet many are thinking of unity in such terms at the present time. They start by looking at the big denominations as they are, and simply raise the question as to how these can be brought together.

[266]

But that is to approach the problem mechanically. Now if the analogy of the body is correct they have already gone astray, because a body is not simply a collection of parts, and unity is never a matter of addition, adding this to that, and that to another. Such thinking must inevitably lead to false conclusions.

To state the matter in a different form, according to this analogy we must never think of unity merely in terms of the removal of divisions. This, again, is very prevalent at the present time. Starting with the proposition that a divided Church is the greatest tragedy in the world today, the one question considered is how we can get rid of these divisions? It is a negative approach which imagines that, by removing divisions, you produce unity. But according to the analogy of the body, that is false reasoning. It is based upon the fatal error of starting with things as they are – with the organizations and the sects and the denominations and so on – and trying to do something about them. Instead, we must think in a more fundamental manner and realize that our first business is to understand the nature of the Church before we can realize the nature of the unity of the Church.

In other words the principle of unity must never be placed first, for unity is not something in and of itself; it is always the result of something else. We are not to start with unity, but with the nature of the Church, and then see that the unity is inevitable. The body itself is of primary importance, and unity – essential as it is – is but one of the characteristics of the body.

These principles are absolutely fundamental with regard to this whole matter of unity, and I suggest that it is because all this is forgotten, that we find ourselves in this modern confusion. In other words I am bold enough to make the assertion that the way to face the present situation is not simply to look at the position as it is and ask: 'What can we do about it?' We have to be much more radical and to say to ourselves: Let these big denominations and groupings be what they like and do what they like, our business is to discover the real nature of the Christian Church. Are we not more or less in the same position as Martin Luther in the sixteenth century, when he saw that he had to go right back to fundamental truth and to the origin of the church. We shall have to return to that same position. If we allow our thinking to be determined by the existing situation we shall be so bound by it that our whole conception of the Church will be wrong. Like others, we will begin to think in mechanical terms and try to lower barriers, and try to improve the situation a little here and there, instead of realizing that the entire situation is wrong. The vital question to be faced is, What is it that determines unity?

* * *

The first essential, as the Apostle's teaching has clearly shown, is true belief in the Lord Jesus Christ. He has reminded us of this in the words, 'One body, one Spirit, even as ye are called in one hope of your calling; one Lord, one faith, one baptism, one God and Father of all, who is above all, and through all, and in you all' (vv. 4-6). Surely this should be self-evident to anyone who has studied this Epistle to the Ephesians. The Apostle does not begin to talk about endeavouring to keep the unity of the Spirit in the bond of peace in chapter one, but in chapter four! Having already laid down the great fundamental doctrines of the faith, he says 'Therefore', and introduces his teaching concerning the unity of the Spirit in the bond of peace. But the 20th-century Church places unity in chapter one; it starts with it, and men are preaching unity instead of preaching Christ. They are preaching the Church instead of preaching salvation. All the talk is about unity, and men and women are not being saved, and the true Church is not being built up.

This is the case because they do not realize that unity results from something else and is the consequence, the corollary of something else. This principle is seen also in the phrase 'speaking the truth in love' (v. 15). We must not put love before truth; we are to speak the truth in love. We are not merely to speak lovingly, or simply to be nice and friendly; we are to speak the *truth* in love. Truth must always come first. The result is that it is quite impossible to discuss unity with a man who denies the deity of Christ. Although he may call himself a Christian I have nothing in common with him. If he does not acknowledge this one Lord, born of the Virgin, who worked His miracles, and died an atoning death, and rose literally from the grave in the body, I cannot discuss the unity of the Church with him. There is no basis for the discussion of unity. It is a sheer waste of time and a travesty of Scripture teaching to do so. We must both be rooted and grounded in the truth, and believe in all the doctrine taught in chapters 1, 2 and 3 – the sovereignty of God, who has called us and chosen us before the foundation of the world; the unique deity of Christ and the shedding of His blood for us and our sins on Calvary's Cross; the truth concerning ourselves as 'dead in trespasses and sins' and walking according to the course of this world, the creatures of lust and passion and vices, children of wrath even as others – before any discussion on unity is possible. I have no fellowship with a man who says that being born in this country makes us Christians. I cannot have fellowship with a man who tells me that because I was christened as a baby I am therefore a Christian. These things are absolutely vital and central, and the same applies to the doctrine of the Holy Spirit and the doctrine of the nature of the Christian Church.

Such is the truth which we are to speak in love. To talk about maintaining the unity of the Spirit in the bond of peace is nonsense and a waste of time, if we disagree about the very vitals and fundamentals of the faith. I have no union with a man who denies the unique deity of Christ, the Virgin Birth, the miracles, the atoning sacrificial death, and the resurrection of our Lord and the Person of the Holy Spirit. I cannot pray with such a person because we are not praying in the same manner. Paul teaches us in chapter two that we can only pray acceptably as 'We both [Jews and Gentiles] have access through Him [Christ] by one Spirit unto the Father' – and this is the only way. So we must not waste our time and our energy in talking of unity or praying together, before we have spoken about these doctrines, about this truth.

The next principle is our right relationship to the Lord, and our union with Him. We are not to have any 'fellowship with the unfruitful works of darkness'. And, as the Apostle John says in his Second Epistle, we are not to have any fellowship with, or to bid God speed to a man who does not preach and hold this truth. At the same time we are to understand this doctrine of our relationship to the Lord Jesus Christ. Union is not a matter of organisations, it is rather a question of being a branch in the vine, or being a limb, a member of a body. The whole question of unity has to be looked at in this manner. The doctrine of the Church as the body of Christ makes that quite inevitable. The question is not, Can I have fellowship with this person or that? but Am I 'in

[269]

Christ' and is he 'in Christ'? That is the point at which we start – Am I a branch in the true Vine? For if I am, I cannot have fellowship with those who are not branches in the Vine; and vice versa.

*　　*　　*

With such general thoughts on the question of unity in our minds, let us now look at another great principle, namely, the whole question of spiritual life. Life must come before unity because, after all, unity is a result of life. That which produces and maintains the organic unity of the body is the life that is in the body. So we must place this question of life in the forefront. The Apostle tells us that the Lord Jesus Christ is the life of the Church, and is the source of all energy and vitality and power in the Church. He expresses this in the words, 'But speaking the truth in love, may grow up into him in all things, which is the head, even Christ: from whom the whole body fitly joined together and compacted . . .' Apart from the Lord Jesus Christ there is no life in the Church. Our Lord Himself made this quite plain in His parable of the vine and the branches, as recorded in chapter 15 of John's Gospel. The life is in the vine; and it flows into the branches. Christ is the life, and without this union, this organic vital relationship, the Church is lifeless and useless. This is obvious in theory, but it is something we can so easily forget. And as I have suggested, the real explanation of the state of the Christian Church today, and during much of the 20th century, is that she has not understood this.

The Church has become confused over the difference between activity and life. This is a vital difference. It is the difference between what is done by a machine and what a man does, or the difference between a machine and a plant or a flower. The Apostle Paul, in Galatians chapter 5, emphasizes the difference by contrasting the 'works of the flesh' and the 'fruit of the Spirit'. The flesh 'works', it produces works as a machine does; but the Spirit produces fruit as a tree does. Everything which is spiritual is the result of life and of growth. This distinction between activity and life was brought home forcibly to me once by a lady who told me of a visit she had made to a certain church while staying with some relatives. She told me that the church in question was 'full of life'. I enquired as to the manifestations of this life, and she replied by saying that there was some kind of activity in the church almost every night of the week. I enquired further as to the nature of these activities, and found that they consisted of dramatic productions and concerts and clubs and sports, and entertainments of various kinds. The lady was obviously confusing activities with the manifestation of spiritual life. A church with such activities was not a live church; a dead church can be full of works and activities.

This essential difference can be illustrated by something which happened in the early 1920s. At that time we read in the newspapers of two men, Mr Howard Carter and Lord Carnarvon, who had been working in Egypt and digging and searching in old tombs for months. At length they discovered a kind of coffin which seemed to be almost perfectly preserved, and they soon realized that it was that of an early Egyptian King called Tutankhamen. They opened it, and to their amazement they found the body of that King, who had been dead thousands of years, perfectly preserved. Although he had been dead for so long the body showed no sign of decomposition whatsoever. The explanation of this phenomenon was that the Egyptians employed a system of embalming whereby, when a person died, they treated the body with various chemicals. This, together with the nature of the atmosphere in Egypt, ensured that you could preserve a body almost indefinitely without any signs of decay or decomposition. They found the body of Tutankhamen perfectly preserved; but it was also perfectly dead! There were no obvious signs of decay or decomposition, but if you had asked that dead man a question he could not have answered. His body was quite unable to manifest life and power and activity, though perfectly preserved.

I have a feeling that the Christian Church in general has simply been preserving an institution for the past fifty years. The emphasis has been on external appearances and on finance. I find that the debts on churches and chapels are lower than they have ever been; but what of the spiritual condition? The finances are sounder in spite of the fact that the number of people attending is smaller. The entire approach has been wrong. Since about the middle of last century the churches' thinking has been dominated by the institutional idea. The controlling idea has been to find means of holding the young people who do not like sermons but

[271]

like drama and entertainment and games. So the institutional church came in: and for a while it seemed to work; but only for a very short period. All this because of failure to understand the doctrine of the Christian Church! You cannot maintain the Church, the body of Christ by such means and methods. Christ is the life of the Church, and if there is no vital relationship to Him there will be no life, and the Church will be dead.

It is essential that we should be clear about the crucial importance of spiritual life. But the Church is not talking about life, she is interested in numbers, and is convinced that if we could but get rid of denominational barriers and divisions and become one, the world would then listen to us and marvellous things would happen. But that is not spiritual thinking. To believe that numbers, or the size of the Church, is what counts is a contradiction of the whole teaching of the Bible. In the Old Testament we find one doctrine which seems to run through from beginning to end – the doctrine of the remnant. God works repeatedly through a remnant, sometimes through one man. How worldly we have become in our thinking, how mechanical! The Lord Jesus Christ left the Church in the hands of twelve men, a mere handful of nobodies. We seem to have forgotten that! And as we read the history of the Church since the end of the New Testament canon we find precisely the same thing. One thinks of 'Athanasius contra mundum' – how that one man stood against the whole world for vital doctrine and prevailed! The explanation is that the power of Christ was in him; he was linked and joined to the Head. Martin Luther also stood alone after all the centuries of deadness, and of Catholicism, and in spite of all the material power of the Roman Church he prevailed because the power of the Head was in him.

What matters in the Church is not numbers, but our relationship to Him, and the purity of our doctrine, and the purity of our life and living. What matters is that the sap should be flowing into the branches from the Vine. So we must not be concerned primarily about the size of a particular denomination, or about what can be done to turn all the denominations into one Church, and then expect great things to happen. That is to face the problem in an utterly unbiblical manner. The first question should be: Are we filled with the life of the Vine? Until this becomes true of us, anything we do will lead to nothing. Our Lord said, 'Without me ye can do nothing' (John 15:5). When will the churches realize the truth? When will they realize that apart from His activity all our activities lead to nothing. Life is the one thing that matters; and the life is in Him. Our first concern, therefore, should be to know that we are vitally connected to Him, and that the channels, the bands of supply, are open, and that His power, strength, life and sustenance are flowing into us.

*   *   *

That, in turn, leads us to another principle, which follows with simple, direct logic. It is that it is the Head who acts. The body does not act; it is the Head that acts. The Head acts, of course, through the body, but it is nevertheless the Head who acts. It is He who decides and determines when to act and how to act. Our concern should be to be usable at His behest. He is the originator, His is the action, and we are but the vehicles or the channels through which His activity passes. As I look at the history of the Church during the past fifty or hundred years, what I see standing out boldly is a complete failure to remember this principle. I see much feverish activity; but it has been the activity of the members, not the activity of the Head.

The fallacy involved in this can be shown by an illustration. What my body is to me, the Church is to the risen Lord. What do I ask of my body? What do I expect my hands and my fingers to do? What is the function of all the members of my body? Is it to act instead of me? Is it to act on their own and independently? Of course not! The business of my body is simply to be at my disposal. I decide to do something, I initiate a movement, and I act through the body, through its members. It is not for the members of my body to do things apart from me or instead of me. As a matter of fact, if the members or the parts or the limbs of a man's body begin to act independently of him, it is because he is in a diseased condition, he is suffering from convulsions. In that condition a man's arms move wildly, and perhaps his legs and his head also; but he does not want them to do so. They are acting on their own, apart from him. The actions are not voluntary but involuntary. The amount of energy expended by the poor sufferer is tremendous; but there is no point in it, it serves no purpose and is a sheer waste of energy. A man suffering an attack of convulsions is tremendously active, the output of energy is amazing; but it is of no value; it is disease, it is utterly useless.

Now the Church is the body of Christ; so the questions we must ask are, What is the nature and the character of our activities? What is their spiritual value? Do they lead to spiritual results? The fact that a church is very active does not of necessity prove that what she does is right; it may be all wrong. A church may be living on her own energy, doing things on her own initiative, and deliberately ignoring the Head, and refusing to be subservient to Him. Is it not time that we began to ask these questions? I suppose there is a sense in which the Christian Church has never been so active as she has been during the past hundred years. I am quite convinced that if the Protestant Fathers and the Puritans could return and look at the modern Church they would think for a week or so that they themselves had done nothing at all. They did not have brotherhoods and sisterhoods, and divisions according to ages, and organizations and clubs and leagues and badges. They had got none of this; and so they might very well think at first that they had done nothing. It all depends on how you estimate activities. The correct manner of doing so is not to measure the mere output of energy; but rather to judge by the results to which it leads, the product. Are we not misleading ourselves with our organizations and activities? What has happened to the Church? That is the vital question.

It is at this point that the question arises as to the difference between an evangelistic campaign and a revival. The thinking which leads to an evangelistic campaign works in the following manner. Men begin to realize that the Church is in a lifeless condition and that but little has been happening. So they meet to consider the situation, and they decide together to have an evangelistic campaign. So they decide on an evangelist (or sometimes decide to accept the offer of an evangelist's services) and begin to organize an evangelistic campaign. They put up big posters outside the churches, advertise in the Press, and use other media, and perhaps get the local mayor to attend the opening meeting. The motive is quite pure and is to call the attention of the world to the church, and to 'bring the people in'. They decide to do this in order to deal with the state of the local church.

But there is another way of approaching the problem. It is that the church should meet together to consider the position, and to ask the vital question, Why are we in this position? The first question should never be, What shall we do? but, Why are things as they are? Why are the churches empty; why does the Church not count in this country? Why is the position so different from what it once was? These are the first questions that should be asked; and they lead to an entirely different approach. They lead to certain other vital questions, for example: Has our doctrine been right? I do not doubt that the churches are empty very largely because so many pulpits during the last hundred years have been denying the Christian faith. A new approach to the Bible called 'Higher Criticism' began to undermine its authority, and led to a teaching which said that Christ was only a man, and which emphasized 'the Jesus of History', not the Christ of faith. At the same time it denied the Person of the Holy Spirit, the substitutionary character of the Atonement, and the supernatural and miraculous elements in Christianity. This led to a lack of prayer and to the turning to morality and ethics and political and social emphases. Learning and scholarship took the place of revelation. Contact with the Head was lost, the channels of spiritual life became blocked. This entirely different approach makes us realize that the Church, as she is, is not in a fit condition to be advertised to the world. Our first task is to examine ourselves; our first business is to make sure that the life of the Head is flowing through us. This will cause us to fall on our knees and repent and confess our sins, and acknowledge with shame our transgressions, and then cry for mercy and compassion. Then we shall plead with the Lord to send His Spirit upon us in mighty reviving power.

The latter way was the one adopted by the true Church throughout the centuries. By and large, the history of the Church in her most glorious periods, until the middle of last century, is the history of revivals. But since about the middle of the last century this has not been the case; and the story has been one of evangelistic campaigns. This is just a sheer fact of history. How often do you hear of revival? How often do you pray for revival? Instead of praying and waiting upon God and pleading for blessing, we set up our committees, and have lunches, and then draw up our plans of action. Having done so, we then ask God to

[275]

bless our proposals and efforts. A horrible term called 'prayer backing' has appeared, as if prayer is something which 'backs' what we decide. Instead of starting with prayer, and discovering God's will, and putting ourselves at His disposal and waiting upon Him we decide and act. But it is the Head who decides and acts.

It is time that we examined the results of the two different methods. Those who trust to evangelistic campaigns will obtain individual conversions, but what is the over-all picture? In spite of all the evangelistic campaigns and the individual conversions, the Church as a whole has continued to decline; whereas, as is seen clearly in the story of the great revivals in the Church throughout the centuries, in a revival more can happen in one day than generally happens in fifty years of our activities and efforts. The whole Church is revived and a new period of success and progress is ushered in. That is our need today. Revival means being firmly bound to the Head, receiving from Him His activity, and placing ourselves happily at His disposal.

*   *   *

We come now to a final principle, which is, that the call of the New Testament to us primarily, is not to do anything but to be something. The one thing absolutely necessary is that we should be usable. The main hindrance to His working is that we are not usable as we should be. The lives of all the men who have been used of God in the most mighty and signal manner all reveal the same striking truth. Their first intense struggle was always the struggle with themselves, and with their own abilities and powers. A point came when they were driven to their knees, realizing their impotence. They then submitted themselves utterly to their Lord, and were filled with the power of His Holy Spirit. You will find this in the life of Whitefield, in the life of the Wesley brothers, in Jonathan Edwards, Howell Harris and Daniel Rowland in Wales, and many others in many lands and in many centuries. They all realized their utter and absolute dependence upon the Lord Jesus Christ and the truth of His words, 'Apart from me ye can do nothing'. Then, they were 'baptized with the Spirit and power', they went out as men transformed, and did amazing and mighty things. What they were enabled to do was not temporary but permanent. Their works have left their mark upon the history of the Church because they were used to revive the whole Church and to build up the people of God. Primarily, it is for God to act, not for us. The first question must not be, What can I do next? but, rather, What am I? Am I being filled according to the measure of my capacity with this divine energy that comes from the Head, the Lord Jesus Christ, through the Holy Spirit? Every one of us should ask that question personally and ask to be filled with this energy divine; and let us not only ask it for ourselves, let us pray this for the whole Church.

I exhort you in the name of God to pray for revival. Do not simply pray that God will bless some enterprise in which you are engaged; do not pray only for the missionaries who work in other lands; pray also for revival in this country. Let us pray for revival in the Church everywhere throughout the world. Let us pray that the whole Church may be connected vitally with Him, the Head, so that His life and His power may come upon us and into us, and may work through us so that the Church may be revived and that many sinners who are outside may be converted. Christ is the Head. He said 'I am the vine, you are the branches'. Let us make sure that we are 'growing up into him in all things, which is the head, even Christ'.